REFLECTIONS OF A WARRIOR

Franklin Miller
with
Elwood J. C. Kureth

PRESIDIO

Published by Presidio Press
31 Pamaron Way, Novato, CA 94949

Library of Congress Cataloging-in-Publication Data

Miller, Franklin, 1945-
    Reflections of a warrior / Franklin Miller and Elwood J. C. Kureth.
        p.   cm.
    ISBN 0-89141-387-1
    1. Vietnamese conflict, 1961-1975—Personal narratives, American.
2. Miller, Franklin, 1945-   .   I. Kureth, Elwood J. C., 1957-   .
II. Title.
DS559.5.M54   1991
959.704'38—dc20   90-19247
                                                                            CIP

Typography by ProImage

Printed in the United States of America

Contents

Preface

I was into the fifth day of a one-year tour in Seoul, South Korea, when I met the man my sponsor had spoken of in reverent tones. The words that entered my gray matter days before suddenly stepped forward, front and center, ready for inspection.

Medal of Honor.

He came strolling into our office that day, a big grin on his face as if he'd just heard a joke. His manner was easy and his mood was light. Physically, he didn't measure up to the Hollywood version of a Medal of Honor recipient. That is to say, he didn't resemble Sylvester (*Rambo*) Stallone or Clint (*Heartbreak Ridge*) Eastwood. So I immediately consulted the Hollywood Medal of Honor Recipient Checklist:

Square, iron jaw? No.

Piercing, steely eyes? Not quite.

Ramrod-straight posture? Maybe in his younger days.

Broad-shouldered, tight-waisted, barrel-chested physique? Ahhh . . .no.

Only one item left.

"Hello, Captain Kureth. Welcome to DLOG."

I mentally checked the block in the "negative" column beside *Deep, raspy, gravel voice*. So much for stereotypes.

He extended his hand and I took it. Hmmmmm. Average handshake. No viselike grip or shoulder-wrenching arm pumping. And I noticed that he didn't exude an air of intensity or violence; in fact, he generated a very relaxed atmosphere.

He sat down, still smiling. I glanced at my watch, and when I looked up—what's this?—where a second before had sat Sergeant Major Frank Miller now sat a laughing, wildly gesturing and articulating kid! A rather profane kid to be sure, who alternately laughed and swore as he recalled some of his experiences in the land sixteen hundred miles to the southwest of us. Everyone in the office halted their activities and went along for the ride as his boyish enthusiasm and adept story-telling skills placed us next to him in the dense, incredibly green vegetation of Vietnam.

His monologue lasted for about twenty minutes. He'd get up from his seat occasionally to emphasize a point with a particular body stance. No one interrupted him as he paused to collect his thoughts, ensuring an accurate, detailed, and living account of each situation. At the conclusion of the journey, our tour guide strolled out of the office as easily as he had come in.

That short interlude, combined with the stories my sponsor told me about Sergeant Major Miller, spawned a thousand burning questions that raced through my information-starved mind. When I finally collected and collated my thoughts, two questions stood above the rest.

My opening query was the one most people would probably ask first: What did he do to deserve the Medal of Honor? The next question, however, was perhaps far more intriguing than the previous one: What made him want to stay in Vietnam for six consecutive years (that's right, six years!) when most soldiers, from the moment they set foot in-country, lived for the day they took the "freedom bird" out of there? Why did he continue to extend year after year?

When you read *Reflections of a Warrior* you will discover that the answer to my Medal of Honor inquiry was simple, straightforward, and quite spectacular. The second question required a series of much more complex and thoughtful responses. Responses that might surprise you. Sergeant Major Miller explains throughout the book why he never wanted to leave Vietnam.

I was impressed by two facts, the first being Sergeant Major Miller's ability to command an audience. His communication skills and personality allow him to interface effortlessly with people. Secondly, not all his stories were about conflicts, or "asskicks." Several accounts painted pictures of a beautiful land and truly interesting people. Some stories illustrated that humor can be found in the most unlikely places.

It didn't take long for me to realize this was one very interesting individual. His stories, I was positive, would be as fascinating to the general public as they were to the soldiers in the office that day. His background in the Special Forces, his six consecutive years in Vietnam, and his Medal of Honor meant that he spoke with the voice of authority. He was the genuine article, the real McCoy. Exactly what the public wants.

I approached him a few days later with the idea for this book. He readily embraced it. As it turned out, he had been wanting to pen his experiences for quite some time. He was told on numerous occasions that his story had tremendous market value. So my book idea was nothing new, except now I was there to assist him in this venture.

Right up front we had to make a decision. What was going to be the purpose of this book? Were we going to "set the record straight" about "how it really was" in Vietnam? Or would this book serve as a document to show how screwed up things were at the time? Horrors of war? Man's inhumanity toward his fellow man?

Fortunately, we were of the same mind regarding its contents and intent. We wanted this book to entertain the reader. Pure and simple. There was no "record" to "set straight" because each participant in the war had his or her own perspective and perception of the conflict. It's not possible to conclude that one person's version of the war is valid and another's is not, simply because each version is the way it was for the person who lived it. Isn't that valid enough?

There would be no preaching. One person's virtues are another person's vices. We wouldn't draw profound conclusions or get into philosophical discussions. We'd leave those activities for the readers. We'd simply present bits and pieces of the Vietnam experience as one man saw it.

One point Sergeant Major Miller wanted to make clear was that even though this book may give the impression his life in Vietnam was constantly filled with excitement and danger, that was not the case. There were months on end when his unit walked around the country without seeing any sign of the enemy. In fact, there were long periods of time during his six years in Vietnam that were downright boring. However, he did have more than his share of "fun" as you will learn from reading this book. And when he did encounter exciting and dangerous situations they were, in a word, intense.

Perhaps you'll also notice that the book skips around frequently. It begins in chronological order but soon starts jumping back and forth through the years. I could have organized the book into a straight chronological sequence, but I preferred to put Sergeant Major Miller's experiences down on paper in the order he recalled them. By doing so I felt the book would take on a real "storytelling" quality. I believe we've accomplished that goal. And please remember that *Reflections of a Warrior* is written from Sergeant Major Miller's point of view, so the "I"s in the following text refer to him.

Finally, we've kept the names of people, places, and units to a bare minimum. In many cases we couldn't give such information. It's just as well, because in *Reflections of a Warrior* the play's the thing.

Over the next several months we talked about everything from Kool-Aid and orange soda to major confrontations with Mr. Victor Charles. From the seemingly trivial to the incredibly significant. It's all here, and it's quite a slice of life.

Let Sergeant Major Miller guide you through a world that few ever know. The world according to the Special Forces. I believe you'll be entertained.

Capt. Elwood J. C. Kureth

PART ONE

My Birth

THE DELIVERY

I arrived on a Saturday. I can't recall the date, but I know it was a Saturday because I kept thinking, man, what a fucked-up way to start a weekend. I was twenty years old. I should've been out messing around with my buddies or chasing chicks. But no, I was there.

I would spend many weekends there.

Vietnam.

March, 1966.

It was a long trip from the land of freedom. I can't sleep on planes, so I stayed awake the entire flight. I played cards and shot the breeze with those around me who weren't trying to sleep. The whole time I kept thinking that soon an announcement would come over the speakers stating that this was just a test to see how I would respond to pressure. It still hadn't hit me that I was on my way to a war zone. I wasn't issued a weapon when I boarded the plane, so how could I be going to a place where I was expected to shoot people?

Our plane reached the coast of Vietnam early in the morning. I stared out the window at the dark earth thousands of feet below us. I couldn't see anything, but I continued searching the ground, looking for a sign. A sign that it was there.

A sign of war.

Occasionally the field of black was interrupted by tiny orange flashes of light. I was told it was artillery fire. Those words had no effect on me as I watched from my lofty perch. I was too ignorant to grasp the significance of what I was seeing. I actually wanted to see more. Soon, however, I would witness artillery fire up close and personal. As all sane men do, I would come to fear it.

We landed at Tan Son Nhut Air Base, in Saigon, during nautical twilight, around five-thirty. My body certainly wasn't ready for the blast of heat that rammed through the door as it was thrown open. Remember in *Close Encounters of the Third Kind* when Richard Dreyfuss's truck stalled at the railroad track and that light engulfed his vehicle? Remember the sound? That *wwwhhhooommmm*? An incredible wave of heat filled with pulsating, rumbling, vibrating power. That was my first memory of Vietnam.

I stepped out of the plane. Helicopters were flying everywhere. Fast movers (jet planes) were taking off from the runways, moaning deeply under their heavy loads of bombs. People were running around doing this and that. It was like a giant ant farm. An explosion of activity.

I still wasn't aware of my situation. Combat was so far removed from my mind that even this scene wasn't having any effect on me. I didn't have a weapon or any equipment. And it seemed like the picture in front of me was being projected on a screen. It just didn't feel real.

An NCO (non-commissioned officer) loaded us onto a bus bound for Camp Alpha, where we would be assigned to our various units. I studied the bus closely as it rolled to a stop in front of us. A faint alarm went off inside my head.

This was no ordinary bus. Heavy-duty mesh screen covered every window. The wheel wells were completely encased in steel, all the way to the ground. Steel plates were welded over various areas of the body.

I felt a slight twinge in the pit of my stomach.

It was a short, uneventful trip to Camp Alpha. Once there I was issued two new uniforms. Then I waited as my group was quickly sliced up and passed out to numerous units.

"PFC Miller, step forward."

I did so quickly. The activity in my stomach jumped a notch in intensity.

"You now belong to Headquarters and Headquarters Company, 1st Cavalry Division. Move over to that table." The staff sergeant motioned toward a rickety picnic table against the far wall. I went to it and sat down. No one followed me. I was all that unit was getting that day.

A sergeant from my unit appeared almost instantly. He introduced himself, welcomed me aboard, and, not missing a beat, led me to our chopper. Our destination was a base camp known as An Khe, 150 miles north of Saigon.

Reality was setting in.

Even though the trip to An Khe was lacking in excitement (I should've been thankful), it did illustrate a difference between what you were taught in training and what went on in the real world. It was the first of many contradictions I would experience that first day.

In a training environment you are strapped into your seat and the chopper doors are closed anytime you fly, regardless of the flight duration. I realize these are safety measures, but they are drilled into your brain to the extent that you can't imagine doing it any other way.

So there I was, strapped in my seat, looking across at my escort. He was sprawled out across two seats. He was definitely not strapped in, and he was lazily looking through the door openings, which were definitely not closed.

His casual attitude led me to believe he'd spent more than a few hours in a chopper. In fact, "casual" was the word of the day.

Casual? In a combat zone?

We arrived at An Khe around two o'clock in the afternoon. At the onset of our flight we passed over open terrain composed mainly of rice paddies and elephant grass fields. Approximately twenty-five to thirty miles from the camp the open terrain metamorphosed into jungle.

Very dense jungle.

So dense that it resembled a green shag carpet.

It looked very tranquil.

My aerial impression of the base camp was this: a brown sore on the green jungle. An Khe occupied roughly two square miles of terrain. At one point in time the camp's terrain color mirrored that of its intensely green surroundings. But thousands of boots and hundreds of vehicles quickly killed the vegetation, leaving either brittle, brown grass or bare, baked earth.

A small, waist-deep stream cut through the center of the base camp. Wire obstacles fifty feet deep surrounded the camp's perimeter. Just inside the wire was a ring of deeply entrenched security bunkers.

It was Tent City. Dusty tents of all shapes and sizes covered well over half of the camp. An Khe was composed of many units, with the 1st Cavalry Division headquarters as the primary tenant. Combat, combat support, and combat service support units were represented, contributing to the extensive maze of canvas.

Toward the back of the camp was a short, rolling runway dubbed "the Golf Course." It was so short that the pilots of C-130 aircraft had to throw their engines into reverse immediately after touchdown or they would run through the bunkers and wire at the end of the strip. No time for a leisurely landing here.

We landed on a small chopper pad near our company area. So much dust kicked up when we landed that I thought I would suffocate. I gathered up my stuff and, closing my eyes and holding my breath, fought my way through the sandstorm. The sergeant and I walked about fifty meters to the company area, then straight into the orderly room.

We were greeted by the first sergeant. He was a lean, wiry guy from Kentucky who wore his hair in a crew-cut. He welcomed me to the company and in the same breath informed me I was now a member of the Reconnaissance Platoon.

There was nothing going on at that moment, so the first sergeant called over the company clerk, who was instructed to take me to my quarters. I gave a specialist my medical records, and we departed the orderly room.

The very first thing I noticed about the company clerk was the large cast he wore on his left leg. It was beat-up and rather dirty, with a big bloodstain soaking through at midthigh. I was naturally curious about his injury, but since I was a new guy I didn't feel it was my place to ask about it.

We arrived at my tent and went inside.

Hot damn!

Literally. Hot, musty air did a full frontal assault on my person when I stepped inside. The combination of blazing sun, Army canvas, and stagnant air had created a potent steam bath.

I wondered how in the world I was going to sleep in there. I was sure (I hoped) it got cooler at night.

As it turned out, I would never spend a night in that tent.

I was told to take an unoccupied cot. Since things were quiet, I was told to just take it easy and get settled in. Recon Platoon was in the field, and I would link up with them in a few days. I was to relax for now.

I found a cot and started to empty my duffel bag. Hot as it was in there, I was ready to sleep. It had been quite some time since I racked out, and I was starting to feel it.

I was almost finished unpacking when the clerk came back.

"Hey, Miller. The first sergeant wants you to go to the supply room and pick up your gear. In about thirty minutes a chopper is taking some supplies out to Recon Platoon, and he wants you to be on it."

Oh, man! In ten minutes I went from taking it easy to gearing up for the field.

The company clerk took me to the supply tent and told the supply clerk my situation. I started drawing my equipment.

I couldn't help but notice that the supply clerk was in the same boat as the company clerk. He, too, had an injury. His left shoulder and arm were encased in plaster.

The sight of these injuries set my mind in motion. I began to realize that maybe there was some activity going on that was harmful to my health. And that I was headed for it.

As I drew my field gear, I worked up the nerve to ask him what happened. Turned out he was shot in the shoulder. He also let me know that if you get wounded in the field and you're not bad enough to evacuate to a hospital, you get a good job working in the rear, away from the shit. Just like him.

Great. Now I had something to look forward to.

He helped me correctly rig my equipment, showing me little tricks of the trade, indicating that he had spent some time in the field. After I was squared away, it was time to draw my weapon.

He went behind the counter and pulled an unsecured M-16 from the metal rack and handed it to me. The fact that it wasn't locked up blew my mind. The weapons room at my last unit was like Fort Knox. You had to sign your life away before you were issued a weapon. In this unit the weapons were just . . . there, and I don't even remember signing for the one he handed to me!

"Here, this one's yours. I'll just write down here that you got it."

He next directed my attention to a footlocker behind me.

"There's ammo in that footlocker. Take as much as you want, but I recommend at least five hundred rounds in magazines."

Blow my mind again! Take as much as you want? No careful, meticulous counting of each and every round for accountability and safety, like in basic training?

I opened the locker lid. There were 5.56mm rounds everywhere. I took the recommended amount.

"In the other footlocker you'll find hand grenades. Take as many as you like."

This was too much. Inside the locker were what seemed to be hundreds of grenades. They weren't neatly stacked or arrayed. They were just in there like someone had thrown them in with a shovel. In training they hand you a grenade with the reverence accorded a nuclear bomb. Here, it's simply reach in and grab a handful.

I took six.

I was now ready to go. The supply clerk told me to wait out in the open area behind the supply tent. He said the chopper would be along shortly. He wished me good luck.

I went outside and waited with the supplies. Soon I heard the distinctive *whop-whop-whop* beat of my ride. I turned away as it landed (the damn dust again), and when the dust settled somewhat I helped the door gunner load the supplies. Inside the chopper another guy positioned and secured them for flight.

As we got the last of the supplies on board, the door gunner turned to me and shouted above the prop noise, "Are you the replacement for those guys that got greased last night?"

I felt my skin crawl. "Say what?"

"Are you the replacement for those guys that got greased last night?"

"Yeah . . . I guess so."

"OK. Get on."

I was a long way from home.

The flight to Recon Platoon's patrol base seemed like the longest I'd experienced in any military aircraft. It was also the most tense.

Because, man, we were over Indian country.

We flew nap of the earth the entire distance, and all I saw were treetops. I imagined that any second a rocket or fire storm of bullets would come screaming up at us from a thoroughly hidden enemy. I pictured the chopper exploding in a tremendous fireball, leaving a dark, smoky trail all the way to the ground as we smashed through the trees.

I thought about death for the first time since I joined the Army.

And I finally realized: Holy shit—this is no joke.

We were about halfway to the patrol base when straight outta the blue, as they say, a couple of fast movers appeared off in the distance. They were flying higher above the treetops than we were, just cruising along. I watched them with mild interest.

Suddenly, one fast mover dipped toward the treetops and let loose a large bomb. As he pulled up I could see tracer rounds ripping wildly upward from the vegetation. A massive explosion rocked the jungle, throwing plumes of charcoal gray and brown dust high into the air.

Son of a bitch! An air strike!

The tracer barrage was the first indication to me that the enemy actually WAS down there. For real.

My pucker factor skyrocketed.

Step on it, James!

*   *   *

Recon Platoon was in the heart of some bad bush. As the chopper approached the camp, I strained to see where we were going to set down. Try as I might, I couldn't detect an opening through the trees, much less the position of the platoon.

Soon I spotted an area ahead of us that looked less dense than what we were flying over. As we got closer to the area, I could see that it was a clearing, although I couldn't see the ground. Moments later, we were descending to the grassy floor.

We set down in a clearing that was almost wide enough for two choppers side by side. While our chopper hovered a couple of feet above the ground, the door gunner and I hopped out as the swirling air violently beat down the waist-high grass. We quickly unloaded the ammunition, food, and water. When we were finished, the door gunner jumped back into the chopper, plugged in his mike, mouthed a few words to the pilot, and they were gone. I just stood watching as the chopper rose above the treetops and vanished. At that moment I felt totally isolated from the world.

I didn't know how right I was.

Several members of the platoon came out to retrieve the supplies. One of the soldiers looked at me, and our eyes locked. Suddenly I realized that I knew many of these guys! We had attended basic training and jump school together, and now, thousands of miles from our homes, we were together again.

We quickly exchanged bear hugs, handshakes, and crude comments. Man, I can't begin to tell you what seeing familiar faces in the middle of that ominous place did for my mental well-being. It juiced me up. I felt more at ease.

But after the initial burst of joy, I throttled back to a state of edginess. Two facts immediately grabbed my attention as I surveyed my new home.

Fact number one. The trees surrounding me were huge. They were easily over one hundred and fifty feet tall, and must have had diameters of over thirty feet. Their roots were like gigantic, ancient serpents snaking into the earth. I had never seen trees like these. I was amazed.

Fact number two. As bad as the heat was in Saigon and An Khe, it was far worse here. Until we landed I hadn't noticed how cool it was in the chopper, with the doors open and the air rushing through. On the ground, in the middle of the jungle, the air conditioner was off. There was no breeze to circulate the air. It simply hung there, humid beyond belief. And it wasn't even the hottest part of the day. Wonderful.

As we walked out of the clearing with the supplies, I noticed several tiny, well-concealed tents just outside the boundaries of the clearing, in among the trees. The presence of those tents, just the way they looked, gave me a chill. Somehow they certified that this was a serious place.

As we entered the trees, a sergeant came up to me and said, "Let me take you over to meet the Bummer." He said it in a very businesslike, serious tone. It was almost as if he'd said, "I'd like to introduce you to Genghis Khan."

The company clerk had told me about my platoon sergeant, Staff Sergeant Bumstaten, when I was at An Khe. He had used a very reverent tone when he invoked his name, whispering to me that the sergeant was going to be my salvation. He was, simply put, the best.

Almost everyone in 'Nam—especially guys with unusual looks or names—was given nicknames that supposedly fit their physical characteristics, personalities, or simply made their names easier to handle. Somewhere along the line Staff Sergeant Bumstaten was tagged the Bummer. I never knew the origin of his alias, although I assumed it was just a natural contraction of Bumstaten. But unlike many nicknames, his was always spoken with the utmost respect.

An ironic aspect of Staff Sergeant Bumstaten's nickname was the fact that the phrase "What a bummer" enjoyed great popularity back in the States while I was in 'Nam. I left before the phrase entered the American vocabulary; consequently, I had never heard it, nor had anyone else in my platoon.

Anyway, after a firefight, everyone got together and talked about who did what and who shot who. Most of the time none of us had shot anybody, yet there'd be two or three dead enemy troops at the scene. Each one had caught one or more rounds straight through the heart or square in the head. We'd look at each other, point at a body, and say, "That's a Bummer!", because the calculated, precise nature of the kill indicated Bumstaten had put him down.

As new guys rotated in from the States, the phrase took on a dual meaning, such as "What a bummer for that dude, man, because that's a Bummer!"

When I finally met the Bummer he wasn't exactly what I expected. From everything I'd been told, I was looking for some supermacho individual. A Sergeant Rock type.

What I saw instead was a small, wiry guy, about forty-five years old, with an extremely short haircut. His voice smacked of the country, and he had a ready, pleasant smile.

When we came upon him he was squatting over a burning block of C-4 explosive, heating a cup of coffee. The sergeant introduced me, and the Bummer told me to sit down.

He asked me where I was from. I told him I was born in North Carolina, but I was raised in New Mexico. That was an instant hit with him because he, too, was from North Carolina.

We talked for just a few minutes, in short bursts of conversation. After all the hype I had received, I was just awed at the fact that I was around this individual. Although he didn't act the part, you could tell he was a bad motherfucker. He had some of the things on him that indicated he was bad.

He had on enemy equipment.

I learned later it's an unwritten rule among grunts that you don't eat anything or wear anything of the enemy's unless YOU took it, YOU captured it. If it's your kill, it's your shit. And the Bummer had on some shit. A few of the enemy items he had in his possession were a field mess kit, a bayonet, and a rucksack.

Anyway, at the end of our conversation, he said very nonchalantly, "By the way, there's an enemy village on the other side of this ridgeline here. We got in a fight with them yesterday, and we're going over there in about thirty minutes to kick their ass. Would you like to go?"

His statement really floored me. He uttered it so casually, so calmly, it was like he'd just said, "Hey, let's go down to the Burger King and get something to eat." There was no alarm in his voice, no tenseness.

So what do you say to something like that? You're a new guy. Naturally you want to cooperate with everything. So I said, "Yeah, OK."

Before we moved out the Bummer quickly went over his plan of attack with the platoon. It seemed like a simple plan, and there were no questions from the assembled soldiers. Minutes later we were underway.

When we started moving, the Bummer came alongside me and whispered, "I don't want you to do a thing. Just take it easy. If you have a chance to fire your weapon, go ahead and fire it. It'll just add to the confusion, and that'll be good for us. Just make sure there are no friendly people in front of you. Be careful and don't worry about it. Just stay with us." I was with him, his radio telephone operator (RTO), and a couple of other dudes that were traveling in his section.

About forty minutes later I found myself chest-deep in a stream we were crossing on our way to the enemy village. I was thinking, Man, what did I get myself into?

We were moving en masse, and everybody was being quiet. Very quiet. Downstream I could see other guys wading across, M-16s poised barely above the water. Some guys were already on the stream bank and moving swiftly toward the treeline. I saw machine guns rapidly moving into position. I could tell we were close to the target.

Once out of the stream, the various groups came on-line quickly. I was in about the center of mass of the formation as we slipped into a deeply wooded area.

All of a sudden I heard a *pop* on the right flank. Not a *crack*, just a *pop*. A pause, then two more *pops*. Then three, four, five, and suddenly the place was a beehive of activity! Rounds were flying everywhere!

The Bummer had maneuvered the outside elements of the platoon in toward the flanks of the target, so the platoon was formed like a semicircle. We were laying down some heavy fire on whatever was in front of us.

I didn't see any enemy soldiers during the exchange of hostilities. The only things I saw were the very tops of several small hooches about thirty to forty meters ahead of me and a few thin wisps of smoke rising through the vegetation. The hooches were well camouflaged, and I could see their peaks only because I was so close.

The Bummer was on the radio almost immediately after we engaged the enemy. He was talking to our headquarters and our support, while calling out to the teams at the same time to check their statuses and situations. I didn't understand exactly what was going on, so I simply concealed myself as best I could and tried to stay out of the way.

Since I really didn't have anything to do, I decided I'd fire my weapon. I spotted a knothole in a tree about twenty-five meters in front of me. I made sure none of the people in my platoon were in the vicinity, and I fired at it. I had the M-16 on semiautomatic, and I squeezed off a few rounds. I was actually checking the sighting on my rifle, since I hadn't had a chance to zero it.

Luckily, the sights were almost dead-on. I made a few adjustments and fired several more rounds at the defenseless tree. Let me tell you, man, I was blasting the shit out of that knothole. I shot a total of about twelve rounds.

Can you believe it? There I was, in the middle of a fucking shoot-out, and I was trying to blow away some Vietnam vegetation!

The encounter was over in a matter of minutes. The enemy knew, because of their previous encounter with Recon Platoon, that we would be coming up there, so they had withdrawn. They left five or six of their people behind to slow us down. We killed two of them, wounded another, and the rest took off for tall timber because they didn't want to mess around with us anymore.

Fortunately, nobody on our side got hurt, except for one guy who got slightly wounded in the shoulder. He was patched up quickly as we moved into the village.

So there we were, in the middle of all these hooches. It felt really neat, like being a kid and playing king of the hill. Because all of a sudden you were in the enemy's village. You had just taken it away. YOU took it from him. YOU were now king of the hill.

What a feeling!

We did a quick search of the area as we secured it. They'd suffered some casualties from the previous meeting, because there were bloody bandages all over the place.

Everything around us was handmade. The hooches were sturdily constructed and cleverly designed. The fireplaces were dug down into the ground, and there were big vats of rice that they'd cooked but had to abandon because we were coming. We captured a few weapons, maybe six rifles, and a whole bunch of medical supplies. We discovered a couple of radios and other operations support equipment.

We also captured a cow, some chickens, and a few pigs. I hate to say it, but we destroyed them all. We had no use for the livestock, and we weren't going to leave them for the enemy. If we'd been in a better location we might have evacuated the animals to another area, instead of slaughtering them in place. We did what was necessary. It had to be done.

After shooting the animals, we torched the village. We carried as much of the captured stuff as we could. What couldn't be transported was destroyed. We then quickly departed the AO (area of operations).

As soon as we returned to the patrol base, we established our security, and everybody got ready to RON (remain over night). In the morning we would move the entire operation to a new location. Such was the lot of the Recon Platoon. Here today, gone tomorrow.

My first priority when we got back was to set up my sleeping space. Recon elements generally use ponchos as tents. It was these poncho tents that I saw when the chopper dropped me off. Now I would get some firsthand experience in the art of poncho tent construction.

I found you could either pair up with someone and construct a two-man hooch or go it alone. Since everyone else was already set up, I did the latter. One of my amigos lent his expertise, I provided the labor, and soon I was in business.

One note about this fine craft. If it rains early on in your hooch-building career, you will get wet. That is a fact of life. However, as you become more experienced you begin building shelters that will withstand anything and keep you dry. I don't care if it's a light mist or a driving rainstorm, a properly set up poncho will keep the elements off your body. I came to appreciate this skill.

I was still excited about our little adventure. The two guys who killed the enemy soldiers displayed their AK-47s and other spoils of war. My buddies and I shot the shit for a while, swapping outrageous lies about our manhood.

As we settled in for the evening, I had a chance to reflect on where I was now and where I was going. At that point in time my life hadn't been seriously threatened, even though some bullets had come in my general direction. I couldn't help but think how the whole thing reminded me of a camping trip. Honestly. It was just me and the boys going on a long camping trip. Only problem was, this camping trip would end prematurely for many of my closest friends.

Thus ended my first day in Vietnam. It wouldn't be the dullest day I experienced there, and it certainly wouldn't be the most exciting.

I got very little sleep the first week. Excitement and nervousness created a volatile mix that ran through my veins, allowing me two or three hours of restless sleep a night.

As the weeks rolled by, I found it increasingly easier to rest. Sure, I was getting more comfortable with my surroundings and becoming less nervous. But I was racking out with less effort primarily due to exhaustion. We walked all day long, constantly on the move. The jungle terrain we traversed didn't allow for an easy, shuffling gait. We rarely walked on paths (too dangerous), so we were constantly stepping over and through the dense, matted vegetation.

BUSTED CHERRY

I was on Vietnamese soil for approximately four months before I killed anyone. Prior to that I'd really never had a chance. It was always another team that engaged the enemy, which I truthfully didn't mind. But I knew my time was coming.

When my day finally arrived, the kill was very fast, very quick. There was no thought process involved. It was basically a "scare" kill: you see somebody and you shoot immediately.

We got into a small skirmish with about seven people who had split up and were doing their thing when they realized we were much bigger than they were. Our platoon numbered twenty-eight, giving us four-to-one odds. We began hosing them down big-time, so they decided discretion was the better part of valor and tried to disengage.

Two of them ran across my front, going from right to left. They were about twenty-five meters away, dodging between trees. The Bummer had once said to me, "Don't try to shoot *at* them. Just pick a point in front of them and fire on automatic. They'll run into the rounds."

And that's all I did. I didn't even think about it. I saw them run, and before I was even aware of it I was raising my M-16 to my shoulder and it was going off. I was getting the weapon under control when I saw the guy fall.

Right after he fell everything got real quiet. Everybody tensed, wondering what was going to happen next. Nothing happened. Turned out the enemy had fled and we were alone.

We walked up to the body. A couple of guys in my element saw me shoot this dude. I didn't know what I was going to think as we approached the still figure. Was I going to say, "Oh, my God, I've just killed another human being"? Was I going to feel terrible remorse and guilt?

The first thing that happened when we got there was that the NCO in charge of the element slapped me on the back. "You got that motherfucker! All right!" he said gleefully. Several other members of the element came up to me and offered congratulations.

It was a strange, almost exhilarating feeling standing over the lifeless form. Perhaps the exhilaration came from the fact that I was alive and he wasn't. I did it to him before he did it to me. Therefore, I didn't feel guilt or remorse. I couldn't afford those feelings. You begin to feel that way and you get dead real fast.

It was my kill, therefore everything he had on him was mine. I simply reached down and took his bayonet. Nothing more. I'm not sure why I didn't take anything else. I didn't go through his pockets or gear, though the "law of the jungle" gave me that "right."

I left the rest for anyone who wanted it. It was like a lion taking down an antelope, eating his fill, then letting the scavengers have what's left. After I walked away, several guys moved in to pick over the body.

I was one of the bad motherfuckers now.

DEATH HITS HOME

Most of my experiences for the first six months were rather lightweight. We'd run across two or three dudes here and there. Rounds would be thrown back and forth, and many times I wouldn't be anywhere near the action. Occasionally we'd grease one of the bad guys, but surprisingly none of the good guys bit the bullet. Occasionally there'd be a wound or two, but nothing serious on our side.

I'd cut my killing teeth within four months; during that time I also experienced the death of a member of the platoon. He was the first of many friends to perish during my 'Nam years.

I really don't remember very much about that day. I recall we stopped about midday to grab a quick bite and rest. We were in some fairly dense jungle vegetation. We established perimeter security, as always. I was in my position, and once I looked my sector over I reached for my usual lunch, a C ration pound cake. I was in the process of opening it when one of my buddies, Private First Class Kelly, came up behind me and asked if I had something. I don't remember what he wanted, but I didn't have whatever it was. So he left me and went over to the next guy in the perimeter, about ten meters away. I saw the guy shake his head, and Kelly continued his quest.

About ten or fifteen minutes passed when I heard a short, muffled blast. It didn't sound like a gunshot; it sounded more like a weak grenade. I tensed up and looked around the perimeter. Everyone was looking at each other, but nobody was moving. We sat still and poised, listening for what seemed like hours, waiting for something else to happen. But there were no further disturbances. We relaxed slightly and went about our business.

A little while later another friend of mine walked up to my position. I watched him as he approached. He appeared to be moving very carefully, very deliberately. When he reached me, he said, very softly, "Did you hear what just happened to Kelly? He's dead."

I just looked at him. "Get the fuck out of here," I growled.

He stared at me with glazed eyes, as if I hadn't said a word. "Yeah, just stepped on a mine," he continued. "Blew his legs clean off. He's dead." After delivering the message he slowly turned and retreated, being careful to use the same route he took coming out to me.

I was stunned! At first I refused to believe it. I just talked to him a few minutes before. "He can't be dead," I said aloud, to myself. Although I repeated this several times, I knew it was true. Kelly was dead, and all my denials couldn't alter that fact.

I remember Kelly most for the times we spent playing cards. You name the card game, and we played it. We were both avid card players, and even though our card games were strictly for fun, we were both highly competitive and hated to lose. The winner always took great delight in the loser's whining, excuses, and accusations of cheating. Good-natured miniscuffles broke out on occasion.

My most vivid memories were of the times we played cards by moonlight. The moon appeared so much larger by the equator, and the absence of air pollution out in the bush allowed the moonlight to bathe us unfiltered. There we sat, playing game after game inside the platoon's perimeter when we weren't pulling guard or on patrol. At night we played without the usual theatrics, in silence, whispering only to name the game or utter a put-down. The stillness of the jungle and the glossy blackness of the night sky combined with the moon's frozen brilliance to create an eerie, haunting setting. The worn, creased cards that Kelly always carried were never idle for long under those conditions.

Now they'd be idle forever.

Death was now close to home.

And suddenly, as though I was struck by a bolt of lightning, another thought jolted me. A mine! Where the fuck did he step on a mine? Holy shit, are there *mines* in this area? Maybe the enemy was out there, covering their booby traps, ready to open up on us any second! How close had I come to stepping on one of their little surprises?

I felt a slight surge of panic, but quickly suppressed it. Panic was the destroyer of judgment, the eliminator of thought process. To panic now might mean *my* death. I remained calm.

I looked over at my flank and saw that I was being waved in. After taking a final look at my sector, I began slowly picking my way back to the center of our perimeter, taking great care to follow my original path. I watched the ground closely, looking for signs of disturbed earth. After an eternity I was back with the main body of the platoon. We were leaving the area.

We radioed for a medevac chopper to transport what was left of Kelly. I never saw the body, nor did I want to see it. His image was still in my mind, and I didn't want it to dissolve. I would remember him as he was.

After the chopper left with Kelly's earthly remains, we saddled up and quickly, but very cautiously, moved out.

We had a job to do.

PART TWO

Recon Platoon

GETTING INTO IT

The first thing you did in the morning when you woke up, and I mean
the *very* first thing, was to jack a round out of your weapon's chamber
and slide a new one in. Overnight, moisture would accumulate in the
barrel and chamber, and that tiny bit of water could eventually ruin
your whole day.

As soon as every member of the element was awake, we'd take
turns cleaning, oiling, and pulling normal maintenance on our weapons.
We'd clean our weapons in shifts because obviously we didn't want
to have every weapon apart should the enemy visit us. Weapons were
top priority. You didn't eat, shit, or do anything until your weapon was
good to go. It was part of your business, and heaven help you if your
business card didn't work.

LUXURIES (OR THE LACK THEREOF)

One of the many lessons I learned early on was that you didn't carry
what you didn't need. Unnecessary weight was, quite literally, a drag.
And sometimes the extra things you carried created bizarre situations.
A case in point.

One day we spotted an air mattress on a chopper that was dropping
off supplies. Nobody wanted the air mattress because they said, "Man,
humping all that extra weight with all the walking we do? Hell, no."
I thought, an air mattress, that's great! Up off the ground, nice and
comfy. So I took it.

Well, I used it for the first two nights. It definitely added to my
burden, make no mistake about it. But when I slept it made for a
comfortable resting place.

During the third day we stopped in a secluded spot to eat and rest.
I pulled out the old air mattress, huffed and puffed, and sat down on
it with a sigh of relief. The extra weight was burning up some extra

calories, so every chance I got I pulled out the son of a bitch and damn well used it.

So I sat there, eating and resting, when I noticed that the mattress was sagging so that my ass was bumping the ground. That shouldn't have been the case, because I blew the thing up very firmly, specifically so my ass *wouldn't* touch the ground.

I rolled off the mattress, checked the air valve, and finding no leak, blew it up again to full firmness. I then assumed my earlier position.

A minute later my ass resumed its meeting with the ground.

I was highly annoyed, to say the least. I grabbed the deflating mattress and turned it over to inspect the bottom.

Surprise!

Hundreds of carpenter ants had set up shop on the underside of my rubber bed. Apparently they became angry when I moved around on the mattress, perhaps crushing some of their kin. Whatever the reason, they proceeded to chew up my little luxury to the extent that it was impossible for me to repair their handiwork. I buried the now-defunct accessory, thanked the ants for showing me the error of my ways, and never again thought about carrying an air mattress.

It came down to basically this: you carried your "fightin' gear," consisting of web belt and suspenders, ammo pouches, water, hand grenades, first-aid pouch, and weapon. You also carried your food and poncho. That's it. Occasionally you'd see a guy in the unit who'd carry a camera, and a couple of dudes might carry decks of cards, but beyond that, nothing. You just led a very Spartan life-style, because the luxury tax you paid was additional fatigue, the last thing you need in combat.

HEARING FROM HOME

Mail is such a critical thing to soldiers in the field because of their Spartan way of living. Mail can make or break any situation. When you get a letter, man, your morale shoots sky-high. Especially when it smells just like your girlfriend. That perfume smell, you know? There you are, sitting in the middle of nowhere, and the next thing you know someone comes along, says "Here you go, man," and flips you a letter. A letter that he's probably sniffed most of the perfume out of before it gets to you.

They don't have mail call out in the field like you'd think. If we all gathered round the sarge to receive our mail we'd probably be attacked. It would be an ideal time to do so, with all of us clustered together in one big, easy target. So one or more guys distributed the goodies.

Just as receiving mail will boost your spirits, absence of mail will, over a long period of time, dramatically lower your morale. This is particularly true if you're expecting something. You start getting jealous of guys who get mail, especially if they are receiving it on a constant basis. I've seen two guys exchange heated words because one was extremely happy about hearing from his girl, while the other hadn't heard from home in weeks. Enough said.

YOU ARE WHAT YOU EAT (?)

After about six months of humping the bush, I was in the best shape of my life. I didn't have any junk food to eat. There were no commissaries or Burger Kings in the bush. Therefore, I ate only what the Army wanted me to eat. And what the Army wanted me to eat was C rations, which became pretty boring after a while. So I eventually cut way down on consumption of food.

My diet wound up being something like this: a can of fruit in the morning, a pound cake in the afternoon, and some kind of meat in the evening. So basically I was eating one meal a day. My body got accustomed to that routine, and it worked out fine for me. Now I knew guys who had to have three full meals a day. They'd eat all the C rations they had. That's how their bodies operated at peak performance. It was really just an individual thing, of course.

SNAKES

I rarely saw any snakes in the jungle during all my years of humping in the bush. They may have been there, but I just never saw them. Lots of people said they saw snakes all the time. Many claimed they killed cobras and other dangerous reptiles on a routine basis. Not me. But even though my snake sightings were few and far between, some of the most memorable moments during my six-year tour involved these legless creatures.

My first memorable encounter with a snake occurred during my early days with Recon Platoon. We'd spent the morning vainly searching the brush for signs of enemy activity. As I was sitting on the ground during a leisurely rest halt I noticed, out of the corner of my eye, some faint movement in a bush about a meter away from where I was sitting. I directed my attention to the bush and saw a rather small green snake crawling from one branch to another. He was only about ten or eleven inches long, and he was moving at a snail's pace.

I'd seen plenty of snakes in my young life back in the States. I'd catch them and play with them like most kids, so I didn't have any fears about snakes. At least no fears about relatively small snakes. This one fell into that category. I was good to go.

Without getting up I leaned over, stretched out my arm, and gently grasped the little thing. I was expecting it to make a mad dash for freedom as my hand approached, but it didn't alter its slow pace. And when I grabbed it I expected a flurry of activity as it tried to break away. It merely twisted its head slightly, eyeing me as if to say, "Now what?" Indeed, now what?

I examined it for a minute, then thought I'd let it crawl around on me for a while, like I used to do with garter snakes. So I set it on my shoulder and let it explore my web gear. It slowly made its way around to my other shoulder, never appearing to want to drop to the ground and take off. I thought it would make a neat little pet.

When the time came to resume our business I picked it up and put it in my pocket. It slid in without protest. It was more docile than any snake I'd ever seen.

Once more we pounded the bush. As the sun dropped low on the horizon we still hadn't seen any sign of the enemy, so we took a dinner break.

I was just about to eat a C ration when I remembered about my passenger. I took it out of my pocket. It appeared none the worse for wear and was still acting in a very mild manner. I got up and walked over to my platoon sergeant to show him our new mascot.

He looked up at me as I approached, and his gaze fell to the object in my hand. I was just about to say something when he jumped up as if somebody had lanced his rear end with a needle.

He took a couple of quick steps backward. "Get that fucking thing out of my face!" he said with a hint of horror in his voice.

I was confused. "What's wrong?" I innocently asked. Was my tough-guy platoon sergeant afraid of snakes?

His eyes never left the snake. "That's a bamboo viper, you moron! If it bites you, you'll be dead inside of ten seconds! Throw that fucker away *now*!"

His words got my attention immediately. Only one problem. I was now paralyzed with fear. Every nerve in my body was frozen. There was green death in my hand, and I couldn't drop it.

After a few seconds had elapsed, I slowly moved my other hand over toward the viper's head. The viper was still just lying there, seemingly not too concerned that my other hand was slowly descending upon it. My fingers closed around the area directly behind its head.

I squeezed and squeezed and squeezed. After what seemed like an eternity I realized that the viper was dead. Its body lay limp in my hand. At that point all my nerves thawed and I hurled the lifeless reptile as far as I could. I vowed I would never pick up a snake again.

MORE SNAKES

One time some friends and I took R and R (rest and recreation) and went to Bangkok to screw around. There were four of us, and when we arrived in the city, one of the guys said, "Hey, let's go to this snake farm they have just outside the city limits." We all voted for it, and we found a guy named Adul with a Mercedes who agreed to take us to the place. So the four of us piled into the guy's vehicle and we cruised on out.

The snake farm was about ten miles away from the city. It was incredible. Not only did they have snakes, but they were also raising crocodiles. Big crocodiles. But the biggest of them all was this sea crocodile they had just captured. It apparently had eaten someone, and they had all kinds of photographs showing the capture. They placed it in a concrete pool which was elevated above the ground, so that you had to walk up some stairs to peer down into the pool. So we climbed up for a look.

We got up there and stared down at this prehistoric monster confined between the concrete walls. The length of the pool was a good sixteen to eighteen feet, yet this creature's snout tip touched one end and his tail flattened up against the other wall at a right angle and ran about three feet farther. Its head and belly were massive beyond belief, and it was easy to picture this thing swallowing a medium-sized human being. Wild.

We spent the day wandering around this place, and I mean to tell you they had an example of every poisonous and nonpoisonous snake in Southeast Asia, which is definitely more than a couple. You'd walk along this trail which snaked (pun intended) through some deep vegetation. There were huge glass cages everywhere that contained the snakes. You'd turn a corner and suddenly you were face to face with a large, agitated king cobra. It was behind glass, of course, but it was a bit startling nonetheless. Next to the cage would be a sign, printed in several languages, that provided information on that particular species. Really sharp.

We finished up the trail tour next to the main house. Right beside the house was a large banyan tree, umbrella-shaped and hanging low to the ground, almost to the top of my head. We walked over to the tree because we noticed a glass cage underneath it, about four feet long by three feet high by three feet wide. In the cage was a piece of wood running from one bottom corner to the opposite side top corner, and on it was a huge knot of bamboo vipers, some of the most poisonous snakes in the world.

So we looked and bullshitted for a while, and then we decided to have a beer and a little something to eat. We bought the necessary supplies and were kicked back when in rolled this bus load of Japanese tourists. Thailand is a popular vacation place for Japanese. Anyway, in chugged this bus crammed with sightseers.

Everyone piled off the bus and did the sight-seeing bit. After a while I noticed a dude standing under the giant banyan tree next to the main house. He was just standing there, looking up. I couldn't see what he was staring at, so I wandered on over beside him. I looked up but couldn't see anything. So finally I looked over at him. He looked at me and realized I was kind of saying, "Hey, what are you looking at?"

He smiled and pointed. There, hanging down from a branch, was a green snake, a tiny green snake not much bigger than a pencil. Its head bobbed from side to side as it barely hung there, with most of its body in space. It was really just a tiny thing.

I recognized right away what it was, so I tapped this guy on the shoulder. His head swiveled in my direction, with a look that said, "What's wrong?" I motioned for him to follow me. I led him over to the bamboo viper cage on the other side of the tree and pointed at the snakes inside the cage. He leaned really close to the glass, carefully examining the knot of reptiles on the branch. He then read the accompanying sign describing the vipers.

Suddenly, his eyes got really big and he gave me a look of panic. He turned around and ran out from under the tree like a madman. He saw some of his fellow tourists and shouted something in a panic-stricken voice. He must have said something akin to, "The snakes are out of their cages!" because the next thing I knew, the Japanese were killing each other trying to get back onto their bus. It was so comical, like it was straight out of a movie. They were running over one another as they scrambled for the aisles. A couple of guys were pushing the bus driver on the shoulders, like they were telling him, "Get it on, man! Let's get the fuck out of here!" And the bus departed in a cloud of dust. My buddies and I laughed our asses off.

The owner came out of the main house when he heard all the commotion. I walked him over to the tree and he gave a short, startled shout when he saw the unrestrained viper. He ran back into the house to get a device to handle the very lethal baby. Minutes later he had the snake captured and whisked off to a presumably safe location. What fun!

STEAM BATH

There were times when I'd get scared shitless in the most unusual places. I'm not talking about terrifying times in the bush, although I've experienced plenty of near-heart-stopping occasions out there. I'm referring to places where you wouldn't ordinarily think you'd be in danger, yet there you were, and suddenly you believed your life was about to end. A steam bath in Qui Nhon was one such place.

We'd been out in the field for about four months straight, getting into periodic skirmishes with the VC. We really hadn't had any major confrontations, and the ones we did have usually ended up with many rounds exchanged and a few casualties on both sides. Every once in a while during combat we'd see the enemy up close. So close, in fact, that we'd see detailed features of our opponents. During that four-month period we did some close-in work, and some of the enemy got away even though we were close enough to make eye contact. That's how it goes sometimes.

After we came out of the bush, my companions and I got a little vacation. I had a tooth that was messed up and needed attention, so my unit sent me to the hospital down in the coastal city of Qui Nhon to have it fixed. My buddies joined me so we could party it up after my business was concluded.

I got the necessary dental treatment right away. A couple of days later we were still screwing around when we decided to go to a steam bath downtown.

We arrived at the place and were waited on immediately. We removed our clothes, wrapped towels around our waists, and prepared to enter this big steam room. I casually noted that the door to this room was thick and massive, with a small window in it that had a chunk of glass about six inches thick. Very sturdy.

Everyone filed in. I was the last to enter. Just as I got inside I turned around to close the door when I saw a dude already doing it. As the door swung shut he looked me in the eyes. He looked exactly like one of the VC we'd encountered in a firefight!

I yelled, "Hey! That's one of the motherfuckers we saw in the . . . " *Fflloomm*. The door was closed.

I was near panic. I turned to the guys, who were now looking at me. I shouted, "That guy looked like one of the fucking VC we ran into out in the field!" Man, when I said that their eyes opened really wide. I pushed against the door. It wouldn't move!

Now I was really scared, and so was everyone else. Two other guys ran up to the door and we all pushed. No good. Holy shit, I thought, they're going to turn up the heat and roast us!

We all got a little insane at that point.

We started pounding on the door. We threw our shoulders against it repeatedly, adrenaline fueling our force. After several blows the door burst open, nearly flying off its hinges.

When I got outside I saw that there was a board lying on the ground, close to the door. I figured that's what he'd used to barricade our exit. I rushed over to a corner of the steam bath where I'd taken my weapons (wrapped in plastic) snatched one, and wheeled about. I was highly excited, to say the least.

The owner and a few others, including the target of my ravings, came rushing into the room to see what in the hell was going on. They saw us standing there, looking mighty upset. I screamed at him, "That dude is a VC! I saw him in the field!" I was pointing my weapon at the dude. He sort of put his hands up and took a step backward. He appeared as scared as I was.

Meanwhile, the owner was trying to calm me down, assuring me that the man I had my weapon trained on was not a VC. He told me I was mistaken, that the man had worked for him for many years. He repeated this several times.

I told him about the board, how he'd jammed the door so we couldn't get out. "He was about to cook us," I stated. The owner said the board was used to hold the door closed because there was no catch on the door. He asked me to go see for myself. I walked over to the wide-open door, and pushed it closed. It slowly opened up about two feet. Perhaps he was telling the truth.

I lowered my weapon, and after a few more minutes of debate I was convinced that I was in error. By now the owner was visibly pissed off that we'd raised so much hell, but still he insisted that we sit down and have a beer on the house.

We drank his beer. Afterward the guys wanted to go back into the steam bath. There was no problem now, they said. So they went. I didn't. There'd be no steam bath for this kid that day.

PAPER ANNIVERSARY

It came—slowly at first, then finally with a rush.

But I was ready for it.

I would meet it head-on and deal with it quickly, without hesitation or mental reservation.

The end was in sight, and I didn't like it one damn bit.

My one-year tour of duty was practically over—the time was rapidly approaching when I could (thank you very much) rejoin "the

World" I'd left almost a dozen months ago. But by now the World for me had become the small Southeast Asian country I was living in, and I'd decided months earlier I wasn't going to leave.

Not if I had anything to say about it.

I realize it may seem strange—even slightly deranged—that at a time when most soldiers were anxiously plotting their "escape" from 'Nam, I was actually thinking just the opposite. Now before you label me a lunatic, let me explain why I desperately wanted to stay in a place most people considered "the fuckin' asshole of the world."

The way I see it, most guys wanted to leave 'Nam so badly because of the very real possibility of personal maiming or death. Can you blame them? You really don't have to think too deeply to realize those are pretty damn good reasons to want to get the fuck outta Dodge. But once you conquered, or at least tightly controlled, those fears (most never did) you saw your surroundings in a much different, less hostile light. You looked to extract the maximum satisfaction from each situation instead of simply worrying about surviving.

As the days grew into months and my combat skills became sharper, I gradually lost my fear of being maimed or killed—lost it to the point that I felt I simply would not die in 'Nam, no matter how much time I spent there. Notice I say "would not" instead of "could not"; I was still very mindful of the fact that I was mortal like everyone else, and if I didn't watch my step I could quickly end up as worm fodder. I felt that only my carelessness would do me in, and I vowed never to be careless. Therefore, as my tailor-made logic indicated, I was good to go. Obviously my ego and elevated sense of worth caused me to oversimplify my situation tremendously, but what the hell—at least my mind was carrying one less burden, which allowed me to perform more efficiently.

Another factor that contributed to my loss of fear was the very presence of my buddies, my fellow soldiers. Now I suppose it's generally true that there's safety in numbers, but the mere fact that they were still there—alive and well after almost a year—gave me a great feeling of security. My unit had suffered very few casualties in my first year, so the trauma associated with the deaths of close friends was very limited. Each day that I looked around and saw the same, familiar faces simply reinforced my belief that we were destined to survive it all and achieve great things.

So once I cleared that major mental hurdle, I began to take stock of what I was getting out of my 'Nam experience. For one thing, I was completely satisfied with what I was doing. I finally felt I was doing something worthwhile with my life. And I was good at what I did. Now I wasn't the smartest guy or even the best shot. But the one quality that I possessed that set me above most of the guys in my platoon was my ability to keep very cool when the shit started flying. The Bummer always preached to us how it was absolutely essential to remain cool under fire and to keep a clear head. Easier said than done, believe me.

But I made it a point to practice what he preached. And surprisingly enough to me, I was able to follow his advice with a level head under adverse circumstances. That was one of the reasons I was put in charge of a squad early in my career. And let me tell you, leading other guys in critical and dangerous situations was pretty heady stuff for a private first class.

I loved it. I couldn't get enough.

Question: Would a private first class back in the World have the kind of responsibility I had in 'Nam?

Answer: Fuck no!

As my leadership skills grew, I became more and more respected. Guys came to me for advice and assistance. I was looked upon as someone to be emulated, someone you could count on in tight spots.

My self-esteem skyrocketed.

Next question: How much respect do you think a private first class received back in the World?

Answer: Zero.

And then there was the freedom. We were our own masters, the captains of our own ships. We received general guidance regarding a mission and executed the basic plan any way we saw fit. The bottom line was that nobody fucked with us when we were on a mission (except maybe the enemy every once in a while), and nobody fucked with us when the day was done. Nobody fucked with us period. We were left to do as we damn well pleased.

Last question: How often do you get fucked with back in the World?

Answer: All the time.

So I added it up: Job Satisfaction plus Responsibility plus Respect plus Freedom equals A Pretty Outstanding Deal.

So why in the hell would I want to leave?

As my departure time drew nearer, I started asking about extending my tour. The Bummer told me all I had to do was sign some papers back at base camp. I still had a month to go, but I wanted to get the formalities over with. I planned on taking a resupply chopper into camp the next time one came our way.

As luck would have it, a week later our company clerk came out to the field. On the spur of the moment he'd decided to jump on one of the choppers that was shuttling supplies from our base camp to our AO. I guess he was bored and wanted to see what Recon Platoon looked like out in the boonies.

When the chopper set down I saw him straddling one of the ration crates. He had this wide-eyed stare that said, Hey, wait a minute . . . I'm out here where the shit really happens!

I ambled over to the chopper, put one foot up on the deck, leaned on my knee, and yelled above the engine whine, "Hey, Kurko! What's up, man?"

"Not much, man," he said in a less-than-steady voice. He appeared more than a bit nervous. His head swiveled from side to side as his eyes scanned the wood line. He licked his lips constantly. A couple of guys came to remove the crate he was sitting on, and he quickly moved toward the center of the Huey. It was clear he wasn't going to set foot outside the chopper. At least not until it returned to base camp.

"Say, listen," I shouted. "I want you to fill out all the paperwork I need to stay in-country, and then sign my name to it. OK?"

He finally tore his eyes away from the woods and looked at me. His entire body was rigid. When he noticed I was smiling, he tried to relax his posture so he wouldn't look too tense. But it was no use. He couldn't conceal his anxiety. "What'd you say?" he asked, with all the casualness he could muster.

I was starting to get a kick out of his behavior. "I said I want you to fix up the paperwork so I can extend. I won't be able to get in to sign it, so you sign my name for me. Got it?"

He nodded his head as he began to fidget. "Hey, sure. No sweat, Mill. No problem. I'll do it as soon as I get back."

By now the supplies had been unloaded and the pilots motioned to me that they were getting ready to pull out. As the turbine's whine grew louder, Kurko became more relaxed and even managed to smile. He was finally heading out of the badlands.

I laughed out loud as I moved away from the chopper, yelling, "Hey, why don't you stay with us tonight? We'll get you out of here on another chopper in a few days. You'll dig it here with us!"

A panicky look quickly spread across his face. "Hey, some other time, man! I gotta get on your paperwork right away . . . ." He was still talking as the chopper left the ground.

The World for me would remain Vietnam.

At least for a while.

STARVING (ALMOST) TO DEATH

Have you ever gone without food for an extended period of time? I can recall many instances of not having anything to eat for one or two days as we finished up a mission that took longer than we expected. One or two days is no big deal. But there was a point in my 'Nam career where my buddies and I had to endure severe hunger while operating under stressful and hazardous conditions. The incident occurred right after I'd marked my one-year anniversary in 'Nam.

I'd since been promoted to E-4 and was in charge of a recon element within Recon Platoon. One day the entire platoon received a mission to check out some dense, hilly jungle areas that bordered a large valley of rice paddies. The plan was to airlift us into the valley and extract us five days later.

We had a slight problem with the insertion. We drew some hostile fire from one or two comedians who happened to be hanging around the LZ. They made things difficult for a few moments, causing us to shoot up a bunch of ammo and go through some wild gyrations with the choppers. They withdrew after harassing us for several minutes. The kind of impact just one or two concealed people can have on an entire operation is truly amazing.

When we finally got on the ground each recon team headed for its mission sector to gather whatever intelligence there was to be found. My team was assigned a sector to the northeast of our patrol base, so we made our way in that direction.

We walked for about a day and a half, and everything seemed cool. We didn't encounter any opposition or have any troubles. We found several villages that had been knocked out by aircraft a long time ago. Vegetation had grown over the rubble. It had easily been a year since the villages had been leveled, judging from the size of the jungle growth around the demolished hooches. We even found a couple of choppers that had been shot down. It had definitely been a hot area at one time, and probably was once again even as we walked through it. It didn't appear that anyone had set foot into the bombed-out villages since their destruction. But it was a sure bet that the enemy had moved back into the surrounding bush. He'd had about 365 days to do so since the time of the air strikes. Yes, he was out there, all right. But where?

We continued to do our thing as the days went by. Normally our missions lasted for five days from the day of insertion to the day of extraction. On Day Four the platoon received a change in its mission. All the recon teams, with the exceptions of mine and one other, were extracted and placed in another area about fifteen kilometers away. Apparently our folks had gotten word of some enemy activity and wanted it investigated. They still wanted two teams to continue sweeping the original target area. By this time I'd reported signs of recent enemy activity. My superiors wanted us to stay on the trail. We drove on.

It was still raining. It had started raining lightly almost as soon as we were inserted four days earlier, and it hadn't let up yet. In fact, the weather got progressively worse as the day wore on. We were soaked to the bone. Thick, black clouds rolled in, the wind picked up, and the temperature dropped sharply. Now we were not only wet but cold as well.

The choppers managed to get the other recon teams to their new sites before the weather turned nasty. Now conditions were such that there was no way the choppers back at the base camp could get off the ground, which was bad news because they couldn't get any chow to us. Since we had anticipated a five-day mission, we carried only enough food for those five days. Any additional food would have been unnecessary weight.

Unnecessary, that is, until your people are unable to pull you out within the allotted number of days.

As bad as the weather was, I managed to make clear contact with our support people at the base camp. I knew we had no choice but to carry on with the mission. We were too far away to walk back to the camp. Besides, we were on the scent of the enemy. All we could do was hope for a break in the weather so the choppers could resupply us or extract us when we needed it.

We used up what little food we had left on Day Five. The weather was still shitty. No choppers would be coming our way that day.

Ditto Day Six.

During the evening of Day Seven we were sitting on a ridgeline when we noticed traces of smoke coming up through the trees covering a mountain on the opposite side of the valley. We observed the area for a while but didn't see anybody. We continued our sweep pattern. Two days now without chow. And counting.

The downpour continued. It was a heavy, cold rain that showed no signs of letting up anytime soon. The dark clouds seemed like they were right on top of the trees. As long as the visibility remained poor, the choppers wouldn't fly. That meant we'd go another day without something in our stomachs. Three days had passed since we last ate, and we were feeling the dreadful pangs of hunger. It was extremely difficult to concentrate on the job at hand.

Day Nine found us really hurting for food. I kept calling the base camp, but they kept explaining that the weather was still a no go for chopper support. They realized that we were in an emergency situation, but there was nothing they could do.

We found another bombed-out village on the tenth day of our extended patrol. Five days had elapsed since we consumed the last of our C rations. By now everybody in the patrol was sick. I had a throbbing headache that wouldn't quit. We were in dire straits. If the enemy had attacked us at that point, we'd have offered little resistance.

We halted in the village. We were stopping frequently then, as our strength was ebbing quickly. I sat down and started rummaging through my rucksack. I don't recall what I was looking for, but what I found was pure heaven.

There in the bottom of my ruck was a bag of sugar! It was a small bag of sugar like you use for coffee. Amazingly enough, it was also somewhat dry.

I couldn't believe my good fortune. *Food*! It wasn't much, but it was food. My first reaction was to rip the top off of the bag and throw the sugar down my throat. I wanted it all to myself.

After minutes of indecision I finally decided to share it with the other five members of my patrol. When I showed that bag of sugar to the other guys they went wild. Imagine, six adults sitting around going ape-shit over a bag of sugar. We had reached that level.

I got an agreement out of everybody that each would wet his index finger up to the first knuckle and dip it in the bag. The sugar that stuck to their moistened digit would be their ration, and I would consume the remainder.

I carefully tore the top off of the bag and held it as everyone took his turn. When the last man had "dipped," I wetted my finger and ran it around the inside of the small bag. You can imagine that there wouldn't be much sugar left after five grown men had coated their fingers, but there was enough remaining to almost cover my finger. We all sat there relishing the little "feast" we'd just had. Although we really hadn't taken in any nourishment, we felt a little better. Those tiny grains of sugar satisfied us mentally, and for the moment it was a tremendous help.

Of course the good feelings quickly wore off and we returned to the situation at hand. It was still raining like a son of a bitch. We took the thatch from a destroyed hooch and made a tactical lean-to so we could at least dry out somewhat. We established perimeter security where two guys set up on the most likely avenues of approach to our "home" and would provide early warning. We changed the guard every hour. It probably would have been useless even if we had spotted enemy closing in on us. It wouldn't have been any kind of fight. We didn't have the energy.

Day Ten turned into Day Eleven. We didn't move. We no longer made an effort to do anything requiring more than mild physical activity. The changing of the guard was our most energetic move. We all prayed for the rain to go away. Our prayers weren't answered.

The morning of Day Twelve came and went. The rain continued. Our base camp was still unable to send a chopper to us. I was really surprised that I had communications with the camp. They weren't crystal clear, but we could understand each other. Usually in bad weather like we were experiencing, the radio wouldn't function, especially over a long distance. But all too clearly I heard them say no go.

Seven days without food and no end in sight.

Time for bold action.

Remember, we were deep in Indian country. Days earlier we'd spotted signs of enemy activity. We were being as quiet as possible so we wouldn't draw any unwanted attention, which in our case would have been deadly. But our situation had reached the crisis stage. I decided to act.

I grabbed my most energetic man and told him we were going hunting. There was some game in the area, but we'd refrained from shooting anything for fear of bringing the enemy down on our heads, an enemy we couldn't handle in our condition. Time was now the critical factor, and there was no more time to worry about a possible confrontation.

Before we left I told the other guys to prepare to move as quickly as possible in case we got into some shit. I was almost positive that our shots would signal the enemy and bring him after us. However, we checked our weapons and headed out of the ville.

We hadn't walked much more than fifty meters when we saw two small wild pigs! They were walking along a trail headed straight for us. I couldn't believe our luck! Without even thinking I raised my weapon to my shoulder and squeezed off a round. I hit one of the pigs square in the neck, killing it instantly. The other pig took off into the bush. We let it go because all we needed was one.

I was really startled by the noise from that one round. The shock wave echoed loudly through the surrounding mountains. It was impossible for the enemy not to hear it, regardless of how far away he was located. I was sure that shot signaled the beginning of the end for us.

We grabbed the pig and headed back. As I expected, the guys were a little edgy after hearing the shot. They were a little nervous, too, and rightly so, because of the significant amount of noise I'd made. We had to act fast.

I had them make a superhot fire. It's possible to make a fire in the rain, especially with slivers of bamboo. Due to our time constraints, I did none of the things they tell you to do when butchering a pig. I didn't bleed it or do any of the other stuff. I just skinned it and chopped the meat from the bone as best I could. I cut it into little pieces that we skewered with sticks and thrust straight into the fire to cook as fast as possible. The outside of the meat was burnt black, but at least the inside was cooked, which is critical with pork.

The whole time we were roasting the kill, we expected to come under attack. Two guys hastily cooked the meat while the rest of us formed a perimeter, weapons at the ready. Collectively, we were acting like a dog guarding his bone. In a way, that's how I felt at the time.

When we got it all cooked we stuffed it in our clothes and equipment and got the hell out of the area. We traveled as far as we could, and then we stopped to eat. We ate like cavemen, ripping and tearing the meat and gorging ourselves. What relief! I can't tell you how good it felt to have a full stomach again. After the feast some guys slept. Before that it was nearly impossible to sleep. Hunger kept us awake.

Our pork supply lasted two more days. Day Fifteen dawned bright and clear. The choppers were able to get to us and let me tell you, it was like Christmas. They dropped off only one case of C rations and some water, but no presents ever looked as good. We tore into the case and ate our fill. We divided the remainder of the case and the water among ourselves and moved out. We still had work to do and spent another seven days in the field. We didn't find the enemy, but we did discover some weapons and medical supply caches. After the last cache discovery we were extracted.

From that day forth I had the fear in the back of my mind that bad weather would somehow contribute to my death, as it nearly did on that patrol.

KOOL-AID

Kool-Aid was a big thing for me during my first year in 'Nam. Water was dirty and rank where I was then, especially in the field. Water purification tablets did nothing to improve the water's taste. In order to kill the stale taste, many of my fellow soldiers and I used Kool-Aid.

Whenever we wrote home, we instructed our families and girl-friends to send a packet of presweetened Kool-Aid with the letter. As you can imagine, Kool-Aid improved the water's taste a thousandfold, so it became a valuable commodity. Almost every letter that came our way contained a packet of the sweet substance, and we guarded them closely. Some guys carried around plastic bags holding twenty to thirty packets. For guys willing to part with their goodies from home they became excellent trade material. Other troops wouldn't trade them under any circumstances. I fell into the latter category.

It's written somewhere that good things come in small packages. Kool-Aid was, at least for me, an example of that axiom.

FOOLISH BEHAVIOR

A person's inexperience and lack of common sense can be fatal in a shoot-first, ask-no-questions-later environment. One of the rules of survival is to anticipate the actions of people under certain situations.

Failure to do so results in a one-way ticket to oblivion. Sometimes.

Once when I was with Recon Platoon we hooked up with a regular grunt unit that was near our AO. We decided to RON with the unit. They told us if we stayed with them for the night we had to take a sector of the perimeter. No sweat.

Our position was on a small hill surrounded by tall elephant grass. Like any squared-away unit we cut fields of fire for our sector. One of our fields of fire cut across the front of a grunt's interfacing defensive position. My friend and I were in position and had a clear view down this seventy- to eighty-meter lane of cut-down grass. There was a very bright moon that evening, so we'd easily spot anybody trying to sneak up on or assault our position. We were good to go for the night.

We had just settled in when I caught a glimpse of someone crossing through the lane, moving *away* from the perimeter! I turned to my buddy and whispered excitedly, "Did you see that?!"

He said, "Holy shit, yeah!" as he stared down the lane. I said, "Motherfucker, that son of a bitch must be good! He's already been up to the perimeter and is going back out!"

We both got a little tense. Keeping my eyes glued on the opening through the grass, I said, "If we get lucky and see that son of a bitch again, you toss a frag and I'll open up on him."

Sure enough, a couple of minutes later we saw someone step into our field of fire. We couldn't make out any details because he was way down the lane and it was dark. But we could clearly make out his silhouette, thanks to the strong moonlight. He hesitated for a moment and started across the five-meter span.

We opened up on him as planned. My partner threw a grenade and I started shooting. The solitary figure turned out to be farther down the lane than we'd initially thought, and the frag exploded harmlessly between him and us. I started shooting but missed him on the initial burst, and he quickly dropped to the ground. I lost sight of him in the short elephant grass and was just preparing to fire up his general vicinity when I heard somebody screaming, "Don't shoot! Don't shoot! It's Lieutenant Jackson! He's outside the wire! Don't shoot!"

We held our fire but closely watched as the prone individual emerged from the grass and scrambled inside the perimeter. A minute later Lieutenant Jackson came over to our sector and started jumping dead in our shit.

"You stupid assholes! What the fuck do you think you're doing?

You tryin' to kill me? I was outside of our perimeter checkin' to see how we looked, and you ignor—"

The Bummer arrived on the scene and abruptly cut him off. "Sir," he said, fighting hard to maintain control of himself, "Sir, I've got people here that are doing the job. You go outside the wire without informing everyone and you're asking for it. You were very lucky this time."

That's all the Bummer said. He wasn't disrespectful, although it was obvious to me that he wanted to call the lieutenant every name in the book.

But that's what I mean by lack of common sense. What the hell did that lieutenant expect us to do when we saw what we thought was an enemy troop? Invite him into our camp with open arms? Common sense dictates that if you go outside of the wire—for whatever reason— you inform everyone on the perimeter so they don't try and shoot your ass off when you return. Do you have to be an old combat veteran to think of such a thing? Certainly not.

THE SCREAM

Recon Platoon was patrolling a very mountainous area in central 'Nam near Bhon Blek when we discovered a cow in a crude pen situated in the middle of nowhere. We'd been working the higher elevation areas for several days before we descended into a heavily vegetated valley that stretched for miles. It was in the valley that we found the cow. Up to that point we'd seen no signs of the enemy.

Right away the Bummer said, "Let's ambush it." It was late in the day, around six o'clock, and we were getting ready to RON anyway. So the Bummer left eight of us there as the ambush element and took the remaining sixteen guys elsewhere to establish a patrol base for the evening.

Whenever you found food like that, especially a cow in a pen, you knew somebody was going to come and get it eventually. This time was no exception.

We went about setting up our Claymore mines and completing all the little details required of a well-planned, deliberate ambush. When we finished we settled in and waited, eager to spring the trap.

About three hours later company came calling on the cow. Through our starlight scopes we saw seven people in patrol formation moving into our ambush site. There must have been something else hidden in the area, because just before they stepped into our kill zone they stopped and began poking around in the surrounding bush. After a few minutes they apparently found what they were looking for, and they cautiously moved toward the cow. One of them removed a thick branch that acted as the pen's gate while someone else untied the cow. Just as they were getting ready to leave, we sprung the ambush.

Claymores went off, 40mm rounds went out, and flashes of light filled the night as tracers hurled through the darkness. All this activity echoed monstrously through the mountains surrounding us. Our assault was so sudden and devastating that we received no return fire.

Less than a minute later it was dead silent in the valley, except for the static crackle of our radio. The Bummer wanted to know what we took down. We weren't sure, so we went down for a closer look.

We found six bodies and several weapons. A quick search of the area yielded nothing. The seventh member of the patrol was nowhere to be found. Apparently he had escaped. That upset us slightly but we didn't dwell on it.

After we searched the bodies and took their weapons we headed back to the Bummer's location. He wanted us to link up with the main body of the platoon in case the guys we'd just greased had been part of a larger force in the area. He wasn't far away and we moved out immediately.

When we got to the patrol base we showed the Bummer the weapons we'd captured and everything we'd found on the bodies. He was pleased with our work. We were all kind of excited because we'd just kicked some ass, so we sat around talking about the ambush and other things.

The Bummer had established our patrol base on the side of one of the mountains surrounding the valley. Like it did in the valley, the jungle smothered our mountainside position. We couldn't see the stars because of the overgrowth. I couldn't see my hand in front of my face. We were engulfed by the proverbial pitch-black darkness. And the temperature was dropping rapidly.

About two o'clock in the morning we heard it.

The scream.

It was a single, gut-wrenching scream that crashed through the valley and bounced off the mountains. It was a scream of utter pain and agony that could only have come from a person who was severely or mortally wounded.

That scream sliced right through me. I couldn't see any other members of the platoon, but I know they were wide awake and rigid with attentiveness.

I'm sure it was the missing enemy soldier from our ambush. He was probably trying to make his way back to his unit and could no longer endure his agony or had hurt himself further while moving at night. Whatever the reason, he just couldn't keep the pain inside himself any longer.

The new guys in the platoon were probably spooked by that scream in the dead of night. It chilled me, and I'm sure many of the vets, myself included, sat there thinking, "It could just as easily be me out there." I didn't hear anybody say, "Yeah, serves the motherfucker right!" The guys in my platoon were somewhat reverent about it. For at that moment he wasn't an enemy soldier; he was a guy somewhere out there badly hurt.

I stayed awake long after that scream, straining to hear any further sounds. None were forthcoming. I was sure that the man, like the scream, had died in the night.

THE BONG SON

During the latter part of 1966 I was a private first class in charge of a patrol in Recon Platoon. Some people would think it was unusual for a private first class to be leading a patrol, but the simple fact of the matter was that individuals in the rank of sergeant and above were constantly getting killed, wounded, or rotated back to the States after completing a one-year tour of duty. The demand for NCOs was surpassing what the supply system could produce, so someone had to step in and fill the void. As a result, it was fairly common to find E-3s and E-4s leading the way.

One memorable mission took us into an area known as the Bong Son. This area was in the south central part of 'Nam near the coast. The Bong Son was one of the more beautiful parts of the country. It was a large rice-producing area that stretched for miles on end. High mountains bordered the Bong Son to the west, and the geography of the land was such that it created a lowland, bowl-shaped region.

Within the bowl were many rice farms, and three-quarters of the entire area was covered with water. Everywhere you looked you saw crisscrossing earthen dikes that originated from tiny islands in the middle of the rice paddies. On each island were a few coconut trees and several small hooches where the farmer and his family lived. There were scattered patches of jungle that disrupted the continuity of the scene, but for the most part the rice farms dominated the area.

Recon Platoon entered the Bong Son region late in the month of November 1966. Once we arrived, the platoon split into its established patrol elements. I was in charge of a six-man team. Sector assignments were made and each team went on its way.

As luck would have it, there was a typhoon a few miles off the coast, and rain lashed us continuously during our first week in the area. There was almost no relief from the driving, pelting rain, as the sparse wooded areas offered little shelter from the storm. Powerful, gusting winds frequently whipped the rain nearly horizontal. Each day seemed worse than the previous one.

One evening we came upon a rather large haystack on one of the farmers' islands located near the edge of the Bong Son basin. It was still raining, although not as hard as it had been earlier in the week. But by then we'd had all we could take of the bad weather. I turned to my folks and said, "I know how we can get the hell out of this rain and dry out."

We started pulling hay out of the side of the stack. Soon we had a hole big enough for a person to crawl inside. I got in the opening and continued to remove hay until I had tunneled my way into the center of the haystack. I then went about the business of hollowing out the interior of the stack to accommodate all six of us. In no time we were all inside and out of the elements.

It was warm and dry inside all that hay, which was exactly what we needed at that point. We had walked around soaked to the bone for days on end. It was a great feeling to finally not have any rain pelting my face.

We really shouldn't have been in that haystack. I had put us into an indefensible position, but I was aware of the possible consequences as we started tunneling into it. If the enemy had discovered our location he would have greased us with little effort. But after being wet and cold for a week I was willing to take the risk.

We were very tired to begin with, and now that we were more comfortable we all wanted to go to sleep. But first I set up a watch rotation. The sentry would lie in the haystack's entrance tunnel and hopefully give us early warning of enemy activity. After establishing the order and length of each person's watch we racked out. I curled up and fell asleep almost instantly.

It seemed like I'd been asleep only a few minutes when I felt someone nudging my shoulder. I woke up immediately. The sentry got really close to me and said, "I think I hear somebody outside moaning."

It took me a few seconds, but soon I also heard the moaning. I had no idea what was going on, so I whispered to him, "We're goin' to check it out by ourselves. We don't need to wake the others."

We grabbed our weapons and cautiously crawled out of the haystack. It was still raining lightly, and the temperature had dropped significantly since we'd entered the mound of hay. Once outside we crouched low as we attempted to pinpoint the source of the sound. We quickly determined it was coming from one of the farmers' hooches about twenty meters away.

When we had crawled into the haystack earlier that evening, the hooch had been dark and silent. Now I noticed light pouring from numerous cracks and holes in the hooch's walls and around the door. At the top of the door was a two-inch gap that stretched the door's width.

We scanned the area for enemy troops but couldn't see much of anything. I nodded my head in the hooch's direction, and we eased our way over to it. When we got to the door we popped our heads up to the crack and peered inside.

Over in the corner of the hooch was an old woman lying on a bed made out of bamboo poles. I estimated she was in her sixties. She was obviously in pain because she was moaning long and loud. A younger woman, probably in her thirties, was building a large fire in the middle of the room. Two children were also present: a boy about six years old and a girl about ten. They sat there silently, constantly shifting their attention between the old woman's groans and the younger woman's activities.

The younger woman got a wooden bowl and took some herbs out

of a bag that was lying on the floor near the fire. She produced a crude pestle and began grinding up the herbs. She pounded the stuff in the bowl for a few minutes, then took more herbs out of the bag and crushed them up with the rest of the mixture. The old woman continued to moan while all this was going on.

We stood at the door for a good fifteen minutes watching the drama unfold. Now just picture this: two American soldiers peeking through a crack above the door of a tiny hooch in the middle of nowhere in the dead of night. If the kids had looked over at the door they'd have seen two sets of eyeballs staring at them. But the kids were so captivated by what was going on that they never took their eyes off the proceedings.

When the younger woman was finished grinding the herbs into powder, she took the bowl over to the children and held it out in front of the little boy. As she did so the little boy stood up, pulled out his penis, and urinated in the bowl. The younger woman stirred the mixture with the pestle and positioned herself beside the old woman. She gently reached down, put her arm around the old woman's shoulders, and propped her into a sitting position. Then she handed the bowl to the old woman who immediately drank the contents!

As soon as she started drinking we both looked at each other with wide eyes and grimaces. That was one home remedy neither one of us would ever try!

The old woman lay back down and continued to moan, though not quite as loud. We figured that signaled the end of the show, so we crept back to the haystack. We believed that the old woman had arthritis and the cold, damp weather was causing her joints to ache. The younger woman was trying to lessen her discomfort by building a fire to warm the hooch and giving her some sort of medication. I don't know if the home brew was effective, and I have no knowledge of the herbs she was using.

The next morning dawned bright and clear. The rain had mercifully stopped, and the sun was out in full force. A perfect way to start the day, right? Well, when we came out of the haystack that morning we made a somewhat startling discovery. We had been sleeping among scorpions! Several of us had one or two black scorpions about three inches long attached to our bodies. After a moment or two of shock we simply brushed them off our clothing and got ready to move out.

Amazingly, nobody had been stung. The scorpions may have been small, but they were certainly big enough to get our attention if they so desired. I knew there'd be insects in the hay because they don't like being out in bad weather any more than we do. But I never anticipated we'd share our temporary dwelling with such formidable creatures. Thankfully they were tolerant hosts.

We resumed our patrol of the area. We headed for a section of jungle that jutted into the rice paddies about five hundred meters from our overnight lodging. We reached the patch of jungle without incident and proceeded through the intervening bush until we reached another stretch of rice paddies.

As we came upon the edge of the rice paddies we looked out and saw an enemy troop on one of the dikes. Evidently he'd spent the night in one of the farmers' hooches to escape the bad weather or whatever, and now he was making his way back to his unit.

He was approximately 150 to 200 meters distant, walking very casually along the top of a dike that bordered another section of jungle. He was wearing khaki shorts and a pith helmet. He had an AK-47 over his shoulder, holding it by the barrel. He had no idea we were observing him as he strolled along.

Immediately everybody wanted to take him under fire. Our primary job as a recon element was to observe and investigate the enemy without engaging him. But when you're relatively inexperienced in that line of work—which we were at the time—your initial reaction is to put him down. We had been very successful in killing just about everybody we encountered, so we wanted to shoot all the time.

As soon as we saw the enemy troop my M-79 (40mm grenade launcher) man spoke up. He started complaining, "Shit, man. Lemme shoot him. I never get to shoot like the rest of you fuckers with your M-16s. C'mon, man, lemme do it."

After hearing his complaint I said, "Go ahead and get him." I knew he was a good shot, so I figured he'd easily bag the dude.

He eyed his target intently as he slipped an HE (high explosive) round into the chamber. He carefully lined up the weapon, estimated the range and let it fly. The familiar refrain, *thoomp*! followed the round as it left the barrel.

We watched the little gold ball as it arced through the pinkish blue sky toward its destination. The sun's rays reflected off the projectile, causing it to sparkle vividly. In a way it was funny to think that something so pretty was about to ruin somebody's day. Or at least I thought that it would.

The grenade hit the trail about one meter behind him and exploded. Remember now that one meter is equivalent to about three feet. The split second after it exploded he jerked around, obviously startled, and immediately hauled ass into the jungle, which was about ten meters away. He reached the bush before we could get a shot off.

We quickly went to the spot where the round exploded and tried to track the dude, but he was long gone. We were totally amazed by the fact that the grenade didn't appear to faze the enemy soldier even though it landed almost on top of him. That incident clearly demonstrated to me that the 40mm grenade was not a killing round. Shit, in that case it wasn't even a *maiming* round.

THE BRONZE STAR

The Bronze Star Medal. Awarded for heroic or meritorious achievement or service, not involving aerial flight, in connection with operations against an opposing armed force. Bronze *V* device worn to denote valor.

At the risk of sounding modest, I was always mildly surprised when I received a decoration for some action that I had performed. I never did anything with the thought that I was about to do something special and there'd be an award in it for me. Hell, in every case I never thought beyond the moment. There was simply no time to do so. I just did whatever was necessary to save my life and the lives of my people. Each situation dictated my actions. I never expected anything, even after the dust had settled and I had time to reflect upon the incident. I never thought my actions were particularly bold or daring. I viewed my reactions and behavior as part of the job. They came with the territory.

I was still with Recon Platoon in the fall of 1967. I had since been promoted to specialist four. During that time we were given a mission to find a suitable location for an ambush because we'd found several indicators that a large enemy unit was in our AO, including numerous small enemy camps here and there.

We spent the day looking for an area that showed signs of heavy enemy traffic, day or night. The entire platoon as a group started out that morning in search of such a location, but we couldn't find an ideal spot. At about two o'clock in the afternoon we halted and established a patrol base.

One hour later I took my patrol element with me and we headed toward the west. After traveling about one kilometer we came across what I considered to be a reasonable ambush site. A trail came out of the jungle and skirted a large open field for a good distance before turning back into the bush. The worn condition of the path indicated frequent use. I figured if we caught them on this trail and they tried to withdraw, they'd have to go across the open field, which would make them easy targets.

After finding the ambush site we headed back to the patrol base and hung out with the rest of the platoon until the early evening, around six o'clock. At that time my patrol element and I packed up our gear and moved out to establish the ambush.

Turnabout is fair play, I guess, and on the way to the site we were ambushed.

We were less than fifty meters from our destination when my point man was shot through the leg, shattering his femur. I was right behind him in the order of march. Almost simultaneously I heard a scream to my rear as the guy directly behind me was shot in the stomach.

By now everyone had dropped in place to return fire. The enemy was about fifteen to twenty meters to our left front. I started cranking off rounds when I heard and felt a tiny thump next to me. I looked over in the direction of the thump, and there lying on the ground beside me was a grenade!

I can't begin to describe the violent electrical jolt that assaulted my spine when I spotted that frag. Without wasted thought or motion I reached out, grabbed the grenade, and threw it back at them.

As soon as it went off, I jumped up and ran toward the spot where it exploded. It was always my belief that the best way to defeat an ambush was to attack it in the early stages if you had the opportunity. I figured I had the opportunity at that point.

As I ran toward the blast area I suddenly discovered that I was inside the enemy ambush! Out of the corners of my eyes I could see enemy soldiers on both sides of me lying in the bush, firing at my patrol. Obviously they weren't aware that I was there. Apparently the grenade blast acted as a perfect cover. Fortunately, my people saw me rush the ambush so they adjusted their fire away from my position.

I only stood there for a second or two before I swung my weapon to the left and cut loose with several short bursts. I immediately hit and killed two of the enemy lying on the ground. A third enemy soldier scrambled to his feet and started to run. I hit him in the back and put him down as well.

As soon as he went down I turned to my right to engage the other enemy troops. They were gone. I guess they got frightened by all the commotion and headed for tall timber, which was a good thing because they could have easily greased me when I had my back to them.

We obviously had to abandon our ambush plans and quickly evacuate the two casualties to the patrol base. Since the enemy had discovered us it was necessary for Recon Platoon to vacate the AO; we expected to catch hell anytime from the sure-to-come, numerically superior enemy forces. I radioed the patrol base and apprised them of the situation. I also called in the choppers.

My point man lived. The other wounded member of my element died before we reached the patrol base. The choppers arrived shortly after we joined the rest of the platoon, and we were extracted without further enemy contact.

For my actions during the ambush I received the Bronze Star with V device.

UNEXPECTED DEATH

Normally, Recon Platoon's primary function in life was to patrol an area for reconnaissance purposes only, avoiding—if possible—detection and contact. We were chartered to collect information for use by higher headquarters, all (hopefully) without the enemy's awareness of our surveillance. We usually kept the platoon's presence a secret by splitting into a number of patrol elements that swept a particular sector of the AO. A team of five or six guys skulking through the bush was obviously much quieter than a group of thirty-five, and therefore had a far greater chance of not being detected. Each team then reported its findings to the Bummer, who informed headquarters. Headquarters would digest and process the information and determine our next mission.

When the situation called for it, headquarters tasked Recon Platoon to act as a "probe," which meant we would engage the enemy to determine his strength and morale and—if possible—destroy him. This required a reconnaissance in force, meaning all thirty-five guys would approach the target en masse. This action was usually called for when headquarters decided that they really didn't have enough information regarding the size and "mood" of the enemy. In other words, the information we (or somebody else) provided wasn't sufficient for headquarters to determine if Recon Platoon could handle the fight alone or the situation required a larger force. Really, it was a just a matter of economics. If, during the initial stages of the fight, we determined that our platoon could destroy or rout the enemy, we'd proceed to kick ass. That meant that headquarters hadn't wasted a lot of time, resources, and manpower putting in a larger unit that really wasn't required. If, however, we encountered more than we bargained for, we got on the horn and called for help. We'd then fight a delaying action until help arrived.

One day Recon Platoon was performing a routine patrol when we received word that we were close to some enemy activity and we needed to "probe" the target. As we pressed on we noticed the subtle changes in our surroundings that indicated we were approaching an enemy camp.

When it appeared we were very close to our target, the Bummer pulled all six patrol elements of the platoon abreast of each other and we got into a fighting formation. Each element was about fifty meters apart. Once the platoon was on-line we proceeded forward with caution. We were ready to kick ass.

After moving a good distance without running into anything, we stopped. Everyone was a little tired of being on the alert, so while the platoon sat on the ground I sent two of my folks forward to poke around. When they returned several minutes later they said they saw smoke in the distance coming up through the trees off to our right front.

I contacted the rest of the platoon and told them my element was moving forward to investigate the source of the smoke.

We moved out and sure enough we could see a built-up area through the trees where the smoke originated. We couldn't get as close as we would have liked because of enemy activity in the area.

We were in front of the rest of the platoon by about five hundred meters, or roughly a quarter of a mile. I called back and informed the

Bummer of our discovery, and as we waited for them I started preparing for the ensuing battle.

I put my map on the ground and the six of us knelt around it. We began planning for the assault. I turned to my RTO and told him to plot some grid coordinates directly behind the enemy encampment, so in the event they tried to withdraw we could block their exit with artillery fire. He began making the necessary plots.

Next I looked at my point man who was directly in front of me. All of us were kneeling very close to each other, and my face was only about two feet away from his. I said to him, "Now don't forget, when we make initial contact . . . ." I never completed the sentence.

I remember it so vividly, as if it happened only yesterday. I was looking straight at him. Suddenly a small, dark hole about the size of a nickel appeared on his left cheek just under his eye. Simultaneously the air behind his head swirled with a fine red mist. His eyes flew wide open, and for a split second it seemed that he was aware something had just happened to him. His look was one of dismay. But it was only an illusion. He was dead instantly.

I was stunned.

The shot came from directly behind me. The enemy's early warning people had spotted my element and their main body came out to meet us. Their first shot produced the first casualty of the battle to follow.

It was one of the most intense conflicts I'd been involved in up to that point. Their force was much bigger than my element, and they pinned us down right away. The rest of the platoon was already on its way toward us, and they had to kick it into high gear when they heard the fighting. My RTO was relaying our moment-to-moment status to the Bummer, who had already deployed the other patrol elements into attack formation as they came up around our flanks.

A frightening moment for me during the fight was caused by my own people. I naturally had my attention focused on the enemy to my front. One of the teams coming up from behind my element saw people we couldn't see and opened up right away with their machine gun. Man, I almost jumped out of my skin when the first burst of heavy-caliber fire ripped past me. I'm sure it was a good four or five feet over my shoulder, but at the time it seemed like the 7.62mm rounds were zipping right past my ear. A blazing M-60 will definitely put the fear of God in you.

The Bummer reached our position and crawled up next to me. "What's goin' on, Mill?!" He was always very cool under fire.

I gave him the situation. "We got about eight or ten guys directly to my front, but I got a lot of heavy movement to my left. I can hear it moving around the brush. We haven't taken any fire from there yet. I got one dead and two wounded."

I went on to tell him, in a rapid-fire monologue, several other details about our current state of affairs. After he heard what I had to say, he moved away from me and got into a better position to command the battle.

There was little pressure coming from the right front, so two teams exploited the weakness and overran the area. As they swept around they suddenly came under heavy fire and had to halt their advance. They dropped and laid down a heavy base of fire.

The battle raged for almost an hour and was intense throughout. It got to a point where we ran critically low on ammunition. We called in the resupply choppers, but fire from the ground made it too hot for them to land or even get close to us. The chopper crews ended up *throwing* the ammo cans down at us as they flew over.

When it looked like the fighting might get out of hand, we called in a couple of Cobra gunships. When they arrived they put down a tremendous amount of fire, so much that the enemy decided it was time to withdraw. So they broke contact with us and abandoned their village base. They melted into the jungle and got away. We didn't pursue them.

We took control of the small village and captured a small cache of weapons, ammo, and rice, the usual assortment of goodies you find in a guerilla environment. There were several bodies scattered throughout the place, and scores of bloody bandages littered the ground. From the looks of it we'd encountered a platoon-sized force.

Our casualties were one dead, six wounded.

THE SILVER STAR

The Silver Star. Awarded for gallantry in action against an opposing armed force.

It was late 1967. Recon Platoon was on patrol in one of the rugged mountainous regions of the Central Highlands. The particular sector we'd been assigned to sweep was scarred with multiple well-worn foot trails that indicated a constant flow of traffic. Our job was to find out why that area was so popular.

It was humid and heavily overcast that day. The clouds were almost on the treetops, and the sky looked like it would open up at any time and wash us down the towering mountain we were so diligently investigating.

I only wish it had done so.

Recon Platoon came up from the jungle floor like a colony of ants and swarmed over the steepest side of the mountain. We cut across the mountain face midway from the top, covering terrain that was surprisingly easy to negotiate considering the sharp angle. We were descending when we found a promising trail. The Bummer wanted to know its destination. The platoon split and each element got a short distance away from the path, into the covering jungle, and followed it.

Soon we came upon a large, rolling spur, or "finger," that jutted from the mountain's base. The upper portion of the spur was covered with shin-high grass only; no trees grew on it. Down around its base the bushes and trees reappeared as the spur merged into the jungle. The path we were following stretched along one side of the spur, running almost parallel to the top, until finally it went up and over the spur's crest.

We'd seen signs along the way that indicated somebody had recently passed through or was still in the area. Earlier in the day the Bummer, like the good tracker and hunter he was, had noticed that someone had dug up or cut down all the edible vegetation in the area. He could tell from the condition and appearance of the cut that three days ago a stalk of bananas had been removed from a tree. The dryness of the dirt told him that two days had elapsed since someone had dug up a patch of bamboo shoots.

We weren't too far behind them.

But how many of "them" were there, and who were they?

We'd soon find out.

When the mountain bush gave way to the open, grassy surface of the spur we moved onto the trail. Since we were traveling without cover or concealment anyway, it would be easier going and actually safer (as we would soon discover) on the path. Booby traps were much easier to spot on a hard-packed trail than in vegetation. In the jungle, however, you rarely moved on a trail because you couldn't see the enemy hiding in the bush, but he could clearly see you. Suffice it to say, you concealed your movements whenever possible.

As we moved down the trail, it slowly dawned on us that something about the grass didn't look quite right. A closer examination revealed the discrepancy.

Punji sticks.

Both sides of the trail were bordered by multiple echelons of the sharpened bamboo stakes. The first row sat back from the trail about two feet, just far enough to make it nearly invisible. Each succeeding row was spaced approximately one foot apart. It seemed like there were thousands of the little goodies.

Man! All the enemy would have had to do was crank off a couple of rounds in our direction and we'd have automatically jumped off the trail, right onto the sticks. I got chills thinking about it. But now we realized how precarious our situation was. No place to run to— no place to hide. Literally.

We widened the distance between each member of the patrol and continued to move along. Before too long we reached the crest of the spur and halted. We surveyed the scene below us.

Without moving we visually inspected the trail down to the jungle floor until it was obscured by trees and vegetation. Strangely enough, the grass on the top and opposite side of the spur appeared free of punji sticks. That discovery baffled us for a moment but we didn't dwell on it, because somewhere down there we heard water running.

A stream! The perfect opportunity to get cleaned up and refreshed a little bit after about a month and a half in the woods. We'd throw out some security and wash the filth from our bodies. What a welcome break!

Everyone was eager to run on down and jump in, but of course we couldn't do that. We were still in Indian country and had to act accordingly. Since the grass was now free and clear we got off the trail and spread out in a normal rest posture. The Bummer sent the point element down the trail to locate where it crossed the stream and to look around. They were to report back as soon as they'd scoped out the area.

The element moved out. We watched them for about fifty meters until they vanished into the bush. The remainder of the platoon settled back to wait.

Not more than ten seconds later we heard three or four quick shots. Only, the shots weren't those of large caliber weapons such as the AK-47, M-60, or even the M-16. They sounded more like pistol shots.

At first everyone just sort of alerted and looked around like, What the fuck was that? We were used to hearing heavy-weapons fire in an asskick, so we were more puzzled than anything else.

Suddenly we heard an M-16 open up, and we immediately knew that something was going down.

The point element was in high gear as it raced out of the bush toward us. There had been six guys in the element when it had left less than a minute before; only four returned.

The team leader told the Bummer they'd seen the stream and were moving down to it when an enemy soldier popped out of some bushes and shot the lead man in the head from point-blank range. The guy had a Russian automatic pistol which he then turned on the second man in the element, killing him as well. The team leader, who was the number three man in the order of march, greased the guy wielding the pistol.

As he was cutting the man down, two more enemy soldiers emerged from the bushes and took off running. The team leader shot at them but missed both. He and the remaining members of the element then withdrew. They hadn't seen any other enemy troops. Only the three in the bushes.

The Bummer gave the order for everyone to come up on-line, so as to bring everything we had to bear on whatever was in front of us. At the very least we would recover the bodies. Twenty-eight very angry young men stood ready to kick ass.

Unfortunately, we had no idea that we were walking into a nightmare.

We swept down toward the stream and quickly discovered the bodies of our comrades and the enemy soldier. My element was left of the center of mass of the platoon. I constantly repositioned my folks as we moved, trying to keep control and keep us in a good fighting posture in the event we suddenly ran into opposition.

By this time I could see the stream. It ranged from five to ten meters wide at various locations. The trail the platoon was centered on angled away from me to the right. It traced a line to the stream's bank, where it abruptly changed direction by turning upstream and following the water's edge until it finally cut across.

We halted about fifteen meters from the stream. Once we got down level with the stream I immediately spotted numerous gray hooches on the opposite side of the water. The NVA used gray plastic material to construct things such as shelters and storage areas. The platoon held its position as we studied the area; and the closer I looked, the more I realized that the camp belonged to an element far larger than our own, perhaps four or five times our size.

Gray hooches were everywhere—and I mean everywhere—on the gently sloping hillside, starting from the stream's bank and moving up the hill for about fifty or sixty meters. I was kind of awed by the size of the operation. The enemy had cleared some of the underbrush and strung up hammocks all over the place. Personal equipment hung off tree branches and ropes. The overhead tree cover was dense enough that it would be extremely difficult if not impossible to spot anything from the air. The trail that we'd been following went right up through the heart of the place and faded out in a mass of hooches. Light smoke rose from somewhere in the camp.

But as close as we looked, we didn't see a single person. There was no movement whatsoever in the camp. It appeared to be abandoned. However, I wasn't ready to believe that an enemy force of that size would run without firing a shot. I was sure they were still there.

But where?

Finally it came time to make a move. We very cautiously crept forward from our concealed positions, twenty-eight guys on-line spread out forty to fifty meters from end to end. My heart was racing as the blood surged and pounded in my ears. I tried to relax like the Bummer always preached, but my pulse was at the red line.

We crossed the relatively open ground to the stream without seeing any signs of life. We paused for the slightest of moments at the stream's bank while we prepared to cross the lone barrier to the camp. I was still overwhelmed by the sheer size of it all.

Just as we started entering the stream the hillside came alive. In a split second the hidden enemy delivered a devastating volley of fire into us that halted our advance instantly. In my peripheral vision I saw some of our guys knocked violently to the ground. Rounds cracked everywhere: over our heads, at our feet, into trees. Branches splintered and dirt erupted. They killed six guys with their initial burst. One-fifth of the platoon was already dead, and almost half of the survivors received wounds of some degree.

By virtue of the training we received at the hands of the Bummer, we quickly assessed where the majority of the fire was coming from and responded with a huge volley in that direction. It stunned them that we could come back at them like we did after being hit so hard. We may not have hurt them much, but we surprised them with our aggressiveness, and that bought us enough time to get down and take what cover was available.

As soon as we were down, they recovered from their shock and slammed into us again. This time we weren't as exposed as before, and their attack was less devastating; nevertheless, several guys were hit.

We shot at each other for several minutes. Thousands of rounds were exchanged within a short period of time, so that a powder "fog" was created that burned our eyes and throats. No gas had been thrown; the haze that settled between us and them was produced solely by the enormous amount of rounds that both sides had fired.

Suddenly their 82mm mortars went to work from a concealed location somewhere behind their camp. We heard several deep, distinctive *thoomp*s above the din of the fighting, and seconds later rounds came crashing down through the trees all around us. The rounds impacted the ground with terrifying force, splintering trees and throwing hot frag everywhere. More guys perished during the mortar attack.

Our situation—which was critical at best—was about to get worse. We couldn't retreat because that would mean exposing ourselves as we went back up the slope behind us. Besides, their fire was so intense, we simply couldn't move. Mortar rounds continued to rain from the sky. All we could do was fire back to the best of our abilities and hope for a break.

After a few more minutes of static firing the enemy launched an attack. Two large groups of about ten to fifteen troops each assaulted the remainder of the platoon. Their machine guns laid down a heavy base of fire as the enemy elements maneuvered to the right of my position. They attacked what remained of the platoon's center of mass and the right flank. Both enemy elements were stopped at the opposite side of the stream by the few able-bodied riflemen at those positions. They withdrew, only to assault again a minute later in even larger numbers. Once again the platoon halted the human wave.

Suddenly I noticed movement to my left front and discovered a group trying to cross the stream in an attempt to circle around my left flank. I directed my M-60 gunner to take them under fire. He rose up from his position, swung the M-60 around, and cut loose. His fire halted their advance by hitting two of them. As they pulled back he put two more down before they turned and opened up on both of us and the assistant gunner. My gunner took a round in the chest and was killed.

The next thing I knew the Bummer was next to me.

He started yelling above the noise, "I want you to put a final protective fire along the front of the platoon! We've gotta try and break away or we'll be overrun!"

Even as he was telling me to do that, I was already shifting the M-60 into position to fire. At the same time he asked, "Is your radio still working?" I told him it was, and he grabbed the handset. He contacted the M-60 position on the right flank and instructed the gunner to also lay down a final protective fire that interlocked with mine directly in front of the platoon.

Meanwhile the enemy was in a massive assault posture and they were coming across. We couldn't possibly stop them. We could only slow them down. Since the assistant gunner was a fairly new guy I got behind the M-60 and put out a lead curtain not much more than a foot in front of our platoon. The gunner on the right flank did likewise. We dealt death until suddenly the other M-60 was hit with an antitank round and stopped firing.

The enemy started to home in on my position because we had the last "big-talking" weapon. Some enemy troops to my left opened up on me and knocked the front sight off the M-60. Their fire was so intense that I flattened my body and the M-60 on the ground behind the tree root where I was positioned. The rounds ripped so close to my back that they ate up my canteens! Motherfucker! I was petrified as I lay there eating the dirt. I could hardly think straight.

A momentary lull in the shooting allowed me to flip the M-60 back over the tree root and catch a large group of enemy soldiers assaulting my position. They were about midway through the stream when the assistant gunner with his M-16, the Bummer, and I opened up and smoked them.

The almost nonstop firing turned the M-60's barrel red-hot and the gun started to run away, which meant it was firing without me pulling the trigger. To stop a runaway gun you twist the ammo belt, which jams the rounds and prevents them from entering the chamber. I just let it run free because there was no time to stop and take corrective action.

The Bummer moved next to me and poured oil on the barrel to cool it down. You don't use water because it might cause the barrel to crack. The barrel was so hot the oil literally burst into flames on contact.

The assistant gunner wasn't able to link another belt of ammo to the one running through the gun quickly enough, and I ran out of rounds. As I opened the feed tray cover to throw in another belt, an enemy soldier came around the tree and bayoneted the assistant gunner, killing him. I slapped the cover down, slung the M-60 in his direction, and fired several bursts which nearly severed his body in half.

I swung the M-60 back to the front, set it down in position, looked around for a second, dropped down behind the gun again, and engaged another large group that was coming up out of the river toward me.

Since I was now the center of attention, the enemy focused his main efforts on me and relaxed the pressure on the rest of the platoon. Taking advantage of the moment the platoon started to withdraw.

I held my position and continued to fire. We carried anywhere from twelve hundred to fifteen hundred rounds for the M-60; we'd already fired in excess of a thousand rounds. You're supposed to change the barrel every two hundred rounds. Of course there was no time to do so in the middle of all that action. So at that point I'd burnt out the rifling in the barrel. Rounds no longer went straight when they left the weapon; they were just thrown out in the general direction of fire. I watched the tracer rounds rip through the air every which way and adjusted my fire based on their loose groupings.

As I pinned down the troops in front of me, I saw another group cross the stream to my left. I couldn't swing the M-60 around in time, and they cleared the stream as I watched helplessly. I knew then that in less than a minute they'd get to my flank. As this thought crossed my mind, I saw the end of the ammo belt coming on fast.

I had no more rounds. That was it.

I couldn't wait any longer. I jumped up from my position, cranked off the remaining rounds, and literally ran for my life. For some reason I didn't drop the M-60, and it started hanging up on branches and vines as I fled. I heard them coming up on my ass. I was scared beyond belief. Adrenaline fueled my flight through the bush.

As the chase progressed, I tucked the M-60—which was slung across my chest—under my shoulder as best I could to keep it from bouncing and grabbed a grenade. I pulled the pin and flipped the frag over my shoulder on the dead run. I'm sure they weren't expecting it, but the frag slowed them down only slightly. I threw two more grenades; each one allowed me to move a few more precious feet ahead of them.

For the life of me I don't know why they didn't pursue me once I reached the open ground. Perhaps they felt they were moving into an ambush and wanted to scope out the area. Whatever the reason, they quit chasing me as I approached the edge of the jungle.

By that time the platoon was long gone. Tracking them wasn't too difficult. I followed a trail of bloody bandages and trashed personal equipment. It almost looked like someone had dragged a bag of garbage up the hill that leaked all kinds of junk. I eventually caught up to the platoon on higher ground. The Bummer hadn't led them back out the same way we went in. They'd moved up to the open ground and then cut along the edge of the jungle until they'd reached an outcropping of large rocks along the side of the spur. As I got closer I heard moaning. It was about four-thirty or five o'clock that afternoon when I linked up with the remainder of the platoon.

Only ten people made it, myself included. Of the ten who managed to survive the battle by the stream, only six were in any kind of fighting condition. I had fragmentation in my back from the initial mortar attack, but I was still able to kick ass if the situation demanded it. Several guys were in dire straits.

We figured the enemy would attack soon, so we took stock of what we had. It was a good thing that I hadn't dropped the M-60 because the guy who was the assistant ammo bearer with the other M-60 had a spare barrel. Unfortunately, he had only two hundred rounds with him. Well, two hundred was definitely better than none.

We redistributed the M-16 ammo so that everyone had an equal amount, which wasn't much. Below us in the jungle we heard the enemy moving around, getting ready, we assumed, to attack us. If we got into another sustained engagement with them, we'd run out of ammo very quickly.

Things were looking bleak.

Twice they threw a bunch of mortar rounds our way. They had a general idea of where we were, but they didn't know our exact location. The second mortar assault came much closer than the first, but we stayed low in the rocks and nobody got hurt.

After the last mortar round impacted they started shooting into the rocks. We couldn't see them, but we knew their basic position and sparingly threw a few rounds back. After a minute or two of exchanging fire it got quiet. There was no more shooting. The silence was deafening and loaded with menace.

We figured they were going to wait until dark, then pull the old sapper routine by sneaking up on us and blowing our shit away. We all became very tense and stayed wide awake long into the night.

Around eleven o'clock that night the Bummer decided to "go out and have a look around . . . kinda assess the damage. Be watchin' for me when I come back." It didn't make any sense to the rest of us for him to go out there. But the way he said it calmed us down. It made us feel confident and secure. It was a very matter-of-fact statement that had us believing nothing was going to happen to him and he was going to help our cause.

He eased out into the darkness, and we waited. It started getting shitty cold, and a light fog descended among the rocks, making the evening miserable for everyone, especially the wounded guys.

Early in the morning, maybe one or two o'clock, the Bummer returned. To our absolute astonishment he had a wounded guy with him!

The Bummer, already our hero, grew even more legendary in our eyes that morning. He was It; He was The Man. He Who Cometh in the Night.

Our hero forever.

We took care of the wounded guy, and as we dressed his wounds he told us that he'd been taken prisoner when the enemy overran our position. He was tied up and under guard when the Bummer appeared out of nowhere, killed the guards, and snatched him back.

Unbelievable. In my wildest dreams I'd have never thought (at that time) of doing what he did. Common sense said stay with the group. But in the Bummer's mind he wasn't doing anything dramatic; no Rambo, taking the fight to the enemy, or anything of that nature. He was just doing something within his capabilities that needed to be done.

During the night we heard movement, noises, and whistles but nothing happened, so we were positive they'd come after us at first light. The whole time we'd been on the radio to our support in the rear. They couldn't help us. We weren't in artillery range, and since it was dark they told us we'd have to slug it out until the morning when they could get some reinforcements to our location. "Goddamn, man, you guys were just out on a fuckin' reconnaissance," we were told.

Around 4:30 A.M. we received a call from our headquarters telling us that they were going to reposition some artillery to support us. The Bummer got on the radio and gave them grid coordinates for the initial shot. We prayed that they'd get the artillery moved quickly because we feared an attack at any time.

Thirty minutes later a round came screaming through the early dawn and impacted some distance to our left front. The explosion was like sweet music to our ears. It also sent a message to the enemy that we now had some heavy-duty shit on our side. It was such a good feeling to have the big guns as our trump card.

The Bummer made an adjustment and the second round landed almost exactly to our direct front. The entire valley reverberated from the shock wave. Once he had the round spotted to his satisfaction, the Bummer adjusted some rounds down into the valley where the enemy had their camp. About four hundred meters away the jungle was shredded by a continuous stream of exploding projectiles that fell on the area for a good twenty minutes.

While the show was going on we received word that a 120-man infantry company had been choppered into an LZ on the other side of the mountain to our rear and was moving toward our area to assist us. By that time we were feeling much better about our situation and started mentally gearing up for the trip out.

When the infantry company reached us their company commander came up to me and said, "Where's your company commander?"

I replied, "We don't have a company commander. This is Recon Platoon. We only have a platoon sergeant."

He seemed kind of amazed that no officers were in charge. I pointed out where the enemy camp was located. He positioned half of the company around the immediate area, secured it, and then established an LZ. He also dispatched a large force to the site of our battle.

The enemy had long since departed. He probably left as soon as he heard the first artillery round explode, realizing what was in store for him if he hung around.

The six of us who could walk went down to the battlefield. With the exception of the guy the Bummer had rescued, all the others left behind in the asskick were dead. The infantry company helped us recover the nineteen bodies of our fellow soldiers. It was an intensely sad duty we performed that morning.

The medevac choppers came in and evacuated both the dead and the living to the rear. The medic had already patched up the wounds in my back before the choppers arrived. As we were loading the people onto the choppers, I knelt down beside one of the badly wounded guys who was on a stretcher. I put my hand on his shoulder and said, "You take it easy. Just hang in there. You're gonna be OK."

He reached up and grabbed me by the arm. He looked into my eyes and I could see his pain. Finally he said, "Man, we'd never have made it without you. We never would have made it." His voice trailed off and he closed his eyes.

He clutched my arm tightly until they whisked him away.

I will never forget that moment.

I was awarded the Silver Star for my actions while covering the withdrawal of the platoon.

PART THREE

MACV-SOG

LIFE IN THE FAST(ER) LANE

After two years of airborne infantry reconnaissance work I decided I'd like to work for a Special Forces unit. I'd talked to a number of people I'd run into repeatedly during my 'Nam years who were involved with Special Forces, and they convinced me to apply for a job in the exclusive world of the Military Assistance Command, Vietnam (MACV)—Studies and Observation Group (SOG) or MACV-SOG.

MACV was at the top of the pyramid in the force structure of Vietnam. It was the primary headquarters and controlled all the units in country. The Army, Navy, Marines and Air Force were all subordinate to MACV.

MACV-SOG was an intelligence-gathering group working directly under MACV. SOG was an incredibly diverse organization. One of the many operations under SOG was the Ground Studies Group (SOG 35), which had three parts: Special Operations Augmentation (SOA) Command and Control Central (CCC), SOA Command and Control North (CCN), and SOA Command and Control South (CCS). Each "ran" different targets. CCS was located in Banmethuot and ran Cambodian targets. CCC, which operated out of Kontum, was active in Laos. CCN covered Laos and North Vietnam from a camp near the small cities of Hue and Phu Bai.

CCN teams were named after snakes. Asp, Copperhead, Viper. Teams out of CCC were code-named for states, such as Arizona, New Mexico, and California. I don't recall the name group for CCS.

Of the five hundred thousand soldiers we had in 'Nam, about four thousand were Special Forces troops. Of those four thousand guys, approximately four hundred were members of MACV-SOG. That number was deceptive insofar as it included administrative and training personnel as well as combat troops. The actual number of Americans on the ground running SOG 35 missions totalled slightly more than one hundred. CCN, CCC, and CCS had roughly thirty-six Americans apiece.

A primary mission of most Special Forces troops in 'Nam was to teach the indigenous population how to fight, which was excellent public relations for our side. It really was a good plan. The Special Forces people would go out and establish a training base known as an "A" camp. There, about twelve Americans would teach the ways of war to anywhere from two hundred to three hundred Montagnards or South Vietnamese. The instructors simply gathered the surrounding population under their wings and treated them well. They gave them food, first-class training, and weapons. The local inhabitants never had it so good. The feeding and training served to develop a strong alliance between Special Forces and the local people, especially the Montagnards, which greatly enhanced our capabilities. So while many Special Forces missions involved ass-kicking, the majority were geared toward teaching.

Special Forces missions associated with MACV-SOG were basically combat-oriented. The types of missions that SOG 35 people ran were wide-ranging, to say the least. They included everything from setting ambushes to POW snatches to wiretaps. If it involved gathering information or wreaking havoc on the enemy, they did it. Nothing was outside of their range of activities.

That's exactly what I had in mind.

ON MY WAY

Anyway, I got the idea that I'd like to be a member of Special Forces. I'd seen what the regular Army had to offer and decided I'd like to test my abilities in some faster water. I talked to my first sergeant, who had been in Special Forces. He said, "Listen. I'm gonna send you up to Nha Trang. Go up and talk to those guys, and at the same time let's put you in for an extension so you can go to work up there."

With my bags in hand I journeyed to Nha Trang. When I was interviewed they told me, "We need some good people. You've been around, so we'd like to try you out. We're going to send you up to Kontum on a trial basis. But before we can do that we need to upgrade your clearance, which may take a month or two. So instead of having you sit around on your ass for two months we're going to send you to an 'A' camp just outside of Nha Trang."

Several days prior to my departure for the "A" camp I met two guys who would become extremely close friends of mine, Hines and Nealson.

I was in the NCO club at Nha Trang when I spotted these two comedians sitting at a table directly in front of me. I was an E-5 and so were they, but there was a world of difference between us. They'd just arrived from the States and I'd been around for two years. I knew the ins and outs of the country.

I wandered over to their table, sat down, and shot the shit with them. At the time I had no idea that we'd become good buddies. We talked for several hours. I told them all kinds of tales about my reconnaissance work. They ate the stories up. They thought they were spectacular. That was the life they wanted. So when they in-processed they volunteered to go up to Kontum. They were accepted and put on hold to have their clearances upgraded. So now we were all in the same boat.

During the interim they sent the three of us out to Camp A405. We spent about eight weeks there before our clearances returned. Since it was a relatively big, well-known training base for the South Vietnamese, it was the target of frequent enemy attacks. As part of the camp's security measures we would lead the South Vietnamese on ambush patrols in a big valley near the base. Several things happened during our stay.

One night we were out on an ambush and some enemy walked into our position. I was always slightly surprised whenever anyone walked into an ambush because usually you'd set up hundreds of them and never see a soul. After umpteen uneventful occasions you became slightly jaded about the whole thing. But in walked the enemy bigger than shit and we shot it up with them, killing two of about ten soldiers. None of my people were injured.

By now the three of us were really close friends. We'd told our life stories to each other and had developed a very strong bond in a short period of time. We basically had the same wild and crazy personalities and truly enjoyed each other's company. We flat-out had a good time together.

Many's the night we sat swilling beer and liquor in a grimy, dimly-lit Nha Trang watering hole. Most evenings we'd party long and hard with the local whores as we drank ourselves half-blind, swapping outrageous lies regarding our sexual exploits and bravery in the face of death. On occasion we'd nurse a single beer apiece and just sit there together, not feeling the need to speak, alone with our thoughts. During those times I'd start "deep thinking" and contemplate our futures, wondering what was in store for us, wondering if we'd still be around when all was said and done. I tried not to think like that too often because it tended to dampen my spirits and get in the way of my attitude of living for the day, and to hell with tomorrow. I couldn't do anything about the future, so why worry about it, right? Still, there were many times when, try as I might, I couldn't suppress such thoughts.

Besides beer-drinking and bullshitting, another favorite pastime of ours was going to a local cathouse and getting laid. Sometimes we'd make a game of it. Ordinarily we'd be somewhat shit-faced when we stumbled into the place to have our fun. But certain times we'd designate as "Ugly Fuck" night, which meant we competed against each other to see who could find and screw the ugliest whore. And you had to do it stone-cold sober. No alcohol to dull the senses, you see. The loser—the one who screwed the least homely whore, as voted by the three of us (always a two-to-one vote, of course)—paid for the whores and bought booze for the other two for a week. And none of us was afraid of drinking massive quantities of alcohol, especially if someone else was paying for it. So there was plenty of motivation for not throwing the contest and fucking someone less than ugly. Besides, our competitive natures just wouldn't allow any of us to slack off. It was "balls to the wall," so to speak.

We also used to share the same pretty whores. If I was screwing someone whom either Nealson or Hines thought was particularly good-looking, he would saunter over to me while I was "in the act" and say, "Hey, that's a damn fine-lookin' woman you got there! Damn fine, all right. You wouldn't mind if we jumped on for a little bit when you get finished here, huh?"

How can you deny a best buddy's simple request? "Yeah, sure, man, just give me a few more minutes, will ya?" After I'd satisfied my needs they'd take their turns with the lovely lady, and we'd laugh about it afterward over a few beers. A good time was had by all.

What made us more than just good friends was the fact that we would do anything for each other, even if it meant dying. We were very protective of one another; the strong loyalty we shared assured each of us that the others would always be there to cover our backs and pick us up if we fell. I really appreciated the companionship and the secure feeling generated by our tight-knit group.

After almost two months of training in the bush, Nealson and Hines had developed enough expertise to lead their own patrols. One night Nealson and I were out in ambush sites when I heard his element come up on the radio. I heard some shooting way off in the distance. I knew where they were, but it was too far for us to walk to their aid. A few minutes later his patrol reported that one of the Americans had been killed. There were only two Americans in each ambush and about fifteen South Vietnamese.

I was numbed. The dead American was Nealson.

When my patrol came off ambush I volunteered to identify the body. Nobody else wanted to do it.

By this time they had already brought him out of the field and medevaced him to the hospital in Nha Trang. So I went to the hospital and walked into the meat locker where they were holding his remains. The attendant pulled back the sheet and I stared at his face. Someone had put about eight rounds through the side of his head from point-blank range. It was not merely a killing. It was an execution.

When I told the Vietnamese commander what I had seen, he made the determination that the guy next to Nealson on the ambush was most likely a VC. But nobody said or did anything about it. At least that's how it seemed. The next day I just happened to see them questioning him. I never saw that individual again. My guess is that they put a bullet through his brain. That was the way they dealt with an "infection" in their organization.

Hines was extremely upset about Nealson's death. They had been friends for a long time, dating back to their training at Fort Bragg more than three years ago. In an effort to get his mind off Nealson I took him to Nha Trang for a night of drinking and sex. We partied hard until the dawn. But we never forgot.

About two weeks passed and we were told to report to CCC at Kontum. For reasons I can't recall I left for Kontum right away and Hines followed about two weeks later.

When I got there they put me on recon team (RT) Vermont. The team leader, known as "10" (pronounced One-Zero), was going to rotate in a month and the assistant team leader, the "11" (One-One), was an experienced guy who'd been there for about eight months. But I quickly learned that my level of expertise was above theirs. I wasn't necessarily better than they were, but I'd had more experience in the asskick.

I found that soldiers at lower levels of command were more inclined to shoot and want to mix it up with the enemy than soldiers at higher levels. RT Vermont had excellent soldiers who were ass-kickers, but they were slightly hesitant when it came to hosing down the bad guys. I guess it was a matter of attitude. When I was at the lower levels running around with the Bummer and Recon Platoon we constantly took enemy troops under fire. We'd engage them immediately even if we were a small element, just to see how many of them we could shoot. In other words, we were very aggressive.

Folks in RT Vermont were more . . . passive. They'd see the bad guys out in the woods and it was like, Hey. There are some enemy troops. Let's not fuck with them. Let's leave them alone. It wasn't because they couldn't deal with them. They certainly could've ruined the enemy's whole day. It's just that they were more laid-back, more casual.

So when I arrived at Kontum they immediately took me out on an intelligence-gathering mission to test my abilities. We were to recon a particular mountainous area and take pictures.

The team leader seemed like a very competent individual. I liked him. But I realized I was going to have trouble with the number two man. He could see that there was quite a difference between my abilities and his own. He became very jealous and hostile toward me. In the field that's a dangerous situation.

We also had an American as the RTO. All told there were four Americans and four Montagnards on the Vermont team. We were "running heavy" on Americans. Normally we'd have a maximum of two U.S. soldiers per mission.

It wasn't long into the patrol before I determined that the RTO was not what I wanted. I was running tail with one of the Montagnards. The RTO was between me and the team leader, and he made the sometimes-fatal mistake of letting the patrol break into two separate elements. He let the front four guys get about five hundred meters ahead of us. They were long gone.

It just sort of blew me away when I realized what had happened. I wanted to jump dead in his shit. I was furious. There we were in the middle of the woods, and we had lost contact with half the team.

Immediately I got down on the ground and started tracking the lead element. Finally we got together with them, but not before we gave them a thrill. They heard us coming and thought we were the enemy when they saw that nobody was behind them. They got into position to hose us down. Needless to say, we were extra cautious as we approached. Fortunately they recognized us right away and we rejoined them without further delay. That was the first upsetting incident of the mission.

Number two came when we found an abandoned enemy camp. It had been vacated only minutes earlier. I could tell that they'd just moved out because the brush that they used to sleep on was still matted down and was still green.

It was getting dark and I told the One-Zero that we should stay there because it was a secure area. I let him know the enemy just left and probably wouldn't return for a while. The One-One challenged my recommendation. That pissed me off, and we had a short verbal skirmish right there.

The team leader halted the conversation. He saw that I knew what I was doing and could lead the patrol myself. He was aware that I wasn't some "newbie" from Fort Bragg, and that I had twice his amount of experience at running patrols.

We stayed at the camp.

The next day we ran into a four-man squad of enemy troops and smoked them easily. I made the recommendation that instead of withdrawing we should go to a point where we could observe the bodies and hose down whoever came across them. We positioned ourselves and waited, but nobody came along. We left.

After a while the assistant team leader came to the realization that I was starting to run the patrol. I was making the most logical recommendations under the circumstances. But all he wanted to do was argue with me. I cut him off every time he wanted to dispute a recommendation. I didn't want to argue with him. I wanted to successfully complete the mission. I wanted to survive.

When we got back to Kontum after the mission the One-Zero made the recommendation to the commander that I take over the team. That really pissed off the One-One. Right away I got rid of the RTO. He got another job within the unit. The One-One who argued with me all the time was immediately transferred out of the unit. They didn't fuck around with him. They couldn't afford to because they had high-level business going on. There could be no distractions at any time.

The command group saw that I had the experience to be a good team leader. I was now in charge of RT Vermont, and the next mission we ran was in the same mountainous area as before. We were very successful. We gathered some valuable information. I took some very good pictures of enemy soldiers moving along a trail. The pictures were so clear we could easily make out their unit. I used correct procedures for calling in reports and finds. I was making all the right moves.

After every outing we'd have a One-Zero meeting, where all the team leaders would gather together and listen to the people who just did their thing. Each One-Zero would give a blow-by-blow account of his mission. These meetings served to pass along valuable information to team leaders on new things the enemy was doing, and so on. Little tricks to give you the advantage were also discussed. They were very productive sessions.

Thus began my career with MACV-SOG.

THAT SPECIAL TALENT

When you have a talent, a special talent, you are accorded more privileges than someone without that talent. That's a fact of life we're all familiar with. The more special your abilities, the more privileges and benefits you receive, especially if you deal in high-risk ventures. The privileges and benefits might range from greater pay to setting your own schedule to total, unquestioned control of an operation or project. But always there is that special status. That ego thing.

I'll tell you up front that the Special Forces folks in MACV-SOG received privileges and freedom beyond most people's comprehension. That was because most of us had a talent, a very special talent.

We gathered intelligence and killed human beings under extremely hazardous and adverse conditions.

Killing someone is a unique ability all by itself. Not everyone can lay a weapon's sights on a fellow human being and crank off a round. The Army has been keeping data on soldiers' killing abilities ever since World War II. The data supports the conclusion that out of an entire platoon of soldiers, you have perhaps two men who qualify as genuine killers. Men who actually see enemy troops, put the front sight blade on them, and blow them away. These guys are usually the squad leader and the platoon sergeant. Genuine killers are not to be confused with guys who simply spray an area and happen to hit and kill someone. There is nothing wrong with that method, of course. Many situations demand that kind of action. But you'll find that most guys who kill people in that fashion can't perform a calculated kill. A there-he-is-line-him-up-put-him-down kill. It takes a certain something not found in everybody.

But killing becomes a special talent when coupled with the ability to quietly invade an enemy's stronghold and deal with him in his own backyard. Just you and a handful of other people out there relying on your training and skills. No backup. No support other than a chopper to pull you out if you succeed.

His ballpark. His rules.

A character in the movie *Platoon*, while describing why 'Nam wasn't so bad, said, "You get to do what you want. Nobody fucks with you." That was so true with the main ass-kickers in MACV-SOG. As long as you were out there doing your job, killing people or gathering intelligence, nobody fucked with you. They left you totally alone to do whatever you wanted. Any flaws in your character or personality were conveniently overlooked. You were doing something they couldn't do, so you were unique. You were the player. The bandito. The gunfighter.

Contrary to popular belief, not all Special Forces soldiers were "bad to the bone." There were plenty of Billy Badasses running the woods, to be sure. But that was where most of them were, right there in the jungle, in the shit. I'm not saying there weren't serious ass-kickers that stayed in the camps and out of the jungle. But if you were that really bad motherfucker you ran the woods all the time, and everybody knew your name.

It was during my time with RT Vermont I found out that not all Special Forces troops were shooters. I ran across many really good, squared-away individuals who just weren't killers. These guys would go out on missions and gather outstanding intelligence, but the fact that they couldn't bring themselves to shoot the enemy caused them grief. It wore on them. It was a heavy load. When you're exposed to that level of danger it's like going through a mental meat grinder. The pressure would compound their fear to the point where they didn't want to go out anymore. They'd take any job in the camp that prevented them from going out again.

Those guys would stay around because of the status involved. They were somebody because they were at the place where that dangerous job was done. But they didn't want to or couldn't do that job. The staff sections usually had people in them who had been in the woods once or twice. But that was it. They never went back in again.

But you always went back. That's why you could get away with being a cocky bastard and strolling around like you owned the place. In a sense, you did own the place. You were the guy who could do whatever they needed doing. Without you, there was no operation. Colonels called you by your first name, you were well known around the camp, and people liked to be around you. Talk about an ego trip!

As I said before, if you had the skills you got the bennies. Since SOG was like a little military unto itself we had our own aircraft. I used to fly to Bangkok and Taiwan anytime I wanted to go. I also had a "walk on water" card. It looked like an ID card with my picture in the corner, and it was printed in different languages. Basically it stated that I was engaged in a top secret mission and I was not to be fucked with in any way, shape, or form. Detaining me for any reason was forbidden. If I needed a ride it was to be provided immediately, without question.

The perfect accessory for any occasion.

GOOD AND LUCKY

I'll admit I used to do some crazy shit during my free time. Most of what I did was driven by the fact that I had almost unlimited freedom and unlimited resources. I also had rock-solid confidence in my ability to survive anything. After a while you get that way. Sometimes I was reckless, but more often than not I was very calculating in my actions. Of course, luck played a big part in my life, too.

I can recall making several trips from Kontum to Pleiku where I walked much of the distance. I'd get one or two friends and we'd travel the thirty miles to Pleiku to party or visit the finance office there. Many times there wouldn't be a vehicle available, so we'd hitch a ride part of the way and walk the remainder. Our ride might drop us off halfway between the two towns, right in the middle of Indian country.

Many times we ran into American convoys coming from Pleiku going to Kontum. The convoys had twenty to twenty-five vehicles carrying troops armed to the teeth, wearing helmets and flak jackets. They'd have wide eyes and be clutching their rifles with a death grip as they scanned the woods for bad guys. The troops' reactions were always the same when they spotted us walking along the road.

They'd look at us with surprised expressions. Here we were,

walking down the road in the middle of enemy territory. We'd be wearing bandannas around our heads, with a notable absence of flak jackets or helmets. Our tailored trousers would be unbloused, hanging straight down. We'd be heavily armed with strange weapons. We looked sort of like banditos. We'd just smile at them and wave very casually.

I could see them talking among themselves as they passed by. Once I heard a guy say in a high-pitched voice, "Who the fuck are they?" We got a tremendous kick out of their confusion. I knew we'd be the subject of some stories that night. "Hey, man, you won't believe this. Today we saw two strange-looking American dudes in the middle of nowhere between Pleiku and here. The fuckin' VC are in the area, and these assholes are just fuckin' walkin' down this road like nothin's goin' on. Man, is that some crazy shit or what?"

The reaction from the troops at Pleiku was just as funny. They'd ask how we got there, and we'd tell them.

"You did what?!"

"Yeah, man. It's no big deal."

"Man, a bunch of guys just got ambushed on that road about twenty minutes ago!"

Our response would be rather casual. "Oh, so that's what all that was about. Well, we didn't think anything about it." In the back of my mind I was thinking, Hmmmmm. We were lucky. That could have been us. We could've gotten greased today.

But such thoughts never altered my actions. It wasn't so much because I had the attitude that if it was meant to be, so be it. It was just that I felt sure I could handle any situation.

DOING AS YOU DAMN WELL PLEASED

I found out right away that an advantage of being in this line of work was that I had to answer to very few people. When I wasn't running a mission I'd usually be down in the ville. Nobody ever asked me where I'd been. As long as I showed up on time and the mission went down I was good to go. They didn't give a damn as to my whereabouts. They just knew that when I was around I was taking care of business and everything was cool.

Hazel's, Susie's, The Green Door, and Mammasan's were the usual places where I hung out when I wasn't on a mission. I'd get up in the morning and look over my weapons. If there wasn't anything to do that day I'd grab Burko and Hines, and we'd walk on down to Hazel's. What did we do? We hung around with the women and drank beer. We usually didn't get wild or crazy. We just wanted a place to relax and unwind. Mellow was the operative word most of the time.

Other days I did things that ordinary soldiers never dreamed of doing. I'd wander over to the ammunition supply point and get all the ammunition and explosives I wanted. I'd go to the range and shoot all my weapons, throw grenades, detonate Claymores, whatever struck my fancy. I was never denied any type of weapon or ammunition.

Although the boys and I were usually careful about our wild and sometimes dangerous play, there were times when, sad to say, we were totally irresponsible and careless.

One afternoon I heard a loud explosion outside my hooch. I rushed outside and saw a huge hole in the side of a fifty-five-gallon drum that served as a trash can. I stared at the hole and wondered what the hell was going on. About thirty seconds later the team leader for RT New York, a guy by the name of Wilcox, came over to the can. He looked at the hole, then at me, and said, "Oh, shit. It did. It worked!"

I glanced at him. "What do you mean it worked?"

He pointed at his watch, and with a big smile creasing his face he proclaimed, "I put some time-delayed C-4 in there four days ago and set it to go off today. It did, almost to the minute!"

Man! No thought or concern for human life. Anyone could have been standing there and been severely injured or killed. That thought probably never crossed his mind. His only concern was whether or not his little creation would work.

Once Wilcox and Player, the RT Hawaii team leader, accidentally blew up a chopper on the chopper pad. They were on the pad conducting immediate action (IA) drills, used when you run into the enemy. One of the actions you took if the enemy was too big for you to handle was to put a thirty-second time delay on a Claymore mine and leave it in the enemy's path as you withdrew.

Well, one day they really armed a Claymore and then retreated to the other end of the chopper pad. They had forgotten about the mine until it went off. It blew the shit out of a chopper, putting steel pellet holes all over its structure. A Chinook was called in and it airlifted the damaged aircraft out to be repaired. Fortunately nobody was injured. All Wilcox and Player received for their little escapade were mild verbal reprimands.

No sense upsetting the banditos, right?

LICENSE TO KILL—RATS

The rats in the Kontum area were everywhere. I mean everywhere. You'd find thousands of the bastards in every conceivable place. You wouldn't see them during the day. They came out at night. And they came out en masse.

One of our favorite games was rat hunting. A bunch of us would get inside one of the bunkers at night. We'd each have a .45, .32, or .22 pistol and a flashlight. At one end of the bunker we'd take some string and hang a piece of meat or bread with peanut butter on it about one foot off the floor. We'd then position ourselves at the other end of the bunker, put in our ear plugs, turn off our flashlights, and wait.

It didn't take long. Within minutes we'd hear the rats scurrying around as they smelled their way to the food. At a prearranged signal everyone would turn on their flashlights for a couple of seconds and blast away. The flashlights would be turned off and we'd wait a minute or two, then we'd repeat the sequence. Sometimes we'd do this for several hours. The first time I went rat hunting I was startled by the number of rats that would get caught in the flashlights' beams. Ten to fifteen of the beasts would be attacking the bait every time the lights came on.

Can you imagine what all this activity must have looked like from outside of the bunker? One moment the bunker would be silent and pitch-black inside. Suddenly you'd see light coming from the gun ports and bunker entrance, and you'd hear several muffled *boom*s. The light would vanish right away, only to return a minute later, accompanied by more gunshots. What a great way to spend an evening!

We had a fair-sized warehouse where we stored rice. It was always filled to the top with 200-lb. bags of the stuff. After a while we began to suspect that the rice was drawing the enormous number of rats to our area. One day we decided to empty the warehouse and check it out.

We spent a good portion of the day moving the bags outside the building. As we got closer to the floor our suspicions were confirmed. We began finding partially devoured bags of rice all over the place. When we finally uncovered the concrete foundation of the building we just stared in amazement.

Those little bastards had dug under the floor and actually chewed their way through the concrete! There were hundreds of holes marring the warehouse's foundation.

Rats were running over every square inch of the building. The Montagnards saw them and went wild. They ate rats, and there were hundreds for the taking. They weren't regular, skinny garbage rats. These suckers were well-fed and plump. So the Montagnards chased them with reckless abandon. The Montagnards didn't fear grabbing the not-so-little critters. They never worried about getting bitten. Most Americans, myself included, would cringe at the thought of picking up a rat with their bare hands. Not the Montagnards. They'd snatch them up, quickly break their necks, and stick them in their pockets. On the rare occasion when they'd get nipped they'd simply suck their fingers like little kids and carry on with their roundup. No thoughts of rabies or tetanus shots. And they never appeared the worse for wear.

That night we rounded up all kinds of supplies for a little rat-hunting mission. We got Claymore mine blasting caps, .22s with silencers, and crossbows. We then went to the warehouse and had some fun.

The lights were on in the building, but it was shadowy up in the rafters, which presented a little bit of a challenge. We placed the blasting caps up on the rafters where the rats were running. A Claymore blasting cap is a powerful little explosive by itself that would blow off your fingers with ease. We waited until a rat was over a blasting cap and— *blam*!—we'd set it off. We shot at them with the crossbows and pistols, the whole time laughing our asses off. It was a free-for-all. We did that until the wee hours of the morning.

That's what I mean by total freedom to do as you damn well pleased. That's not to say that we'd disobey an order. If the commander came around and told us to straighten up and knock it off, we'd do it. We were smart enough never to cross the line, regardless of how far in front of us it was drawn. But you know, the fact of the matter was that we rarely even *saw* the line.

One more case in point, then I'll get off the subject. Everyone in the camp began cutting up poncho liners to make pants out of them. Kontum was high up in the mountains, so it got cool in the winter.

When the temperature would plummet to about 75 degrees we'd freeze. When you're used to 115–120 degrees, 75 is positively chilly.

So there we were, chopping up good poncho liners to use the material for warm pants. I had the tailor in the camp use my material to make me some bell-bottom pants with a string of buttons down the outside of each leg. About three inches in front of each button was a loop sewn to the pants. If I was on a mission I could fold the front of each pant leg over and put the loops around the buttons, thereby making the pants fit rather tightly, so they couldn't snag on anything. Around the camp or the ville I'd let the pants out in their bell-bottom configuration. Neat, huh?

The very day that I walked out of the tailor shop with the pants on, my colonel ran across me. He looked at me for a moment and said, "What the hell are you doing?"

I looked at him, and in a very matter-of-fact tone I said, "Well sir, see, these pants are loose now, so they're nice and cool. But when I go out into the woods or run into some heavy shit I can fold them over and button them up like this and make them tight."

He just laughed and walked away, shaking his head and rubbing his face, muttering, "My God." He didn't say anything else. He didn't say, "Take that shit off! You're in the fuckin' Army!" He could have said that, but he didn't. In fact, nobody said a word about my pants, other than, "Hey, those are some bad-ass looking pants!"

From these freedoms we developed a professional attitude that nothing was impossible. Mission accomplishment always came first. Play time—and we played hard—was always well earned.

MONTAGNARDS

Montagnard (pronounced in English it sounds something like "Mountain-yard") is a French word meaning "mountaineer" or "highlander." Montagnards, or "Yards" as we called them, are the original inhabitants of Vietnam. Like the American Indian, the Yards are composed of many tribes, each with its own unique personality and traits. And also like the American Indian, the Yards were run off their ancestral land. The Vietnamese, who are of Chinese descent, swept down from China and forced the Yards into the mountains of Vietnam. It was in their mountain retreats that the Yards stoked the fires of contempt for the Vietnamese.

I worked side by side with the Yards during my many years with the Special Forces. I found them to be the most dependable, hard-working, and loyal soldiers I've ever fought with, and I would welcome them into my unit anytime without question.

The tribes in the major areas that I worked were the Rhade, the Halang, the Jarai, the Sedang, and the Bahnar. In many ways it was just like the frontier. The men ran around in loincloths and the women wore skirts with nothing on top. The Bahnar are the most educated of all the tribes. I always had members of the Bahnar tribe on my team because they were capable of speaking all the different Yard dialects. They also spoke Laotian, Cambodian, and Meo. The Bahnar were knowledgeable about languages because they were the traders among the tribes. So regardless of what area you were operating in, you could communicate with the people if a Bahnar tribesman was with you. That was an invaluable asset.

The most warlike tribe was the Sedang. They were the tallest, meanest, and most aggressive. This may or may not be true, but I was told that up until the middle sixties they still had human sacrifices. I wouldn't doubt that after being around these people. They were so tough and hard it was scary.

These people truly lived by the law of nature. Only the strong survive. If a baby has a defect, it dies at birth, or it's not going to live very long. Consequently, most of them were in excellent physical shape, very muscular, and built for endurance. Their knowledge of the woods was unrivaled by any American soldier. Face it, when you're born and raised in the jungle you become intimate with its essence. You learn about the sounds of the animals, how to track prey, what to eat, what to avoid. A Bahnar youngster can construct the little booby-traps you set up for people, because they are the same traps he uses to catch animals. By the time a Sedang child is eight years old he knows all the things they teach you in ranger school about the woods and tracking. All he'd need to do would be learn how to jump from a plane, and he'd be an airborne ranger.

At one time while I was operating with the Sedang, they wanted me to dye my hair black. They felt that if my hair was black we might not get so much shit brought on us because we would all look alike from a distance. I had a really dark tan but my hair was bleached blond from the sun. If the enemy saw us from a distance and we all had black hair and dark skin they might not open up on us. But if they saw that one guy had blond hair they might just want to hose everybody down without thinking about it. So I dyed my hair. I don't know if it did any good, but I stopped doing it after a while because I just didn't like it.

Most of them couldn't write at all. When I'd pay them they'd take their finger and push it down on a stamp pad to ink the tip and then sort of roll it on the pay sheet. Some would take a pen, which they held like a stick, and make an X.

But I'll tell you what. I'd rather have one of them in an asskick than an American, any day. That's not meant as a derogatory comment on American fighting men, but simply a compliment regarding the tremendous fighting abilities of the Yards. They are natural hunters, people born to the hunt. Many times we'd be in a fight and I'd look downhill or across from me and the Yards would be on the move. I very rarely had to tell them anything. I'd see them fix their eyes on the enemy and move like they were stalking game. Once they learned your personality and technique no words were necessary. Eye contact said it all.

One of the most interesting things to see was the way Yards were hired to work for us. We paid top dollar for our recruits. Most would get more than a staff sergeant in the Vietnamese Army. Big money for a guy straight out of the woods. We're talking anywhere from thirty-six to fifty dollars a month, depending on his position on the team. A Yard who was the lead soldier on a patrol—or the "point" of the element—got paid more because that was the most dangerous position.

The hiring procedure went something like this: My commander, knowing how many folks we were short, would put the word out that we needed X number of soldiers. There was always a camp of Yards located around our compound. Once they heard that we were recruiting, they'd go back to their villages and pass the word. From what I've seen, the villages would send their best people to the tryout. The Yards chosen by their communities had to be good because they represented a particular tribe or village. Pride and honor were at stake. They couldn't afford to send old Charlie who might fuck up bad and make the tribe look like a pack of assholes. So you could be guaranteed that the Yards who lined up for inspection were qualified to be there.

Believe me, some of the Yards who showed up on those occasions were . . . primitive. They'd never held a rifle, let alone fired one. They'd stand there wearing a loincloth and nothing else. But, man, you'd see hunter written all over them. They had that look. They were hard as nails. Once one of my Yards got cut in the foot by a piece of frag. Later I took him to the dispensary to have the cut stitched, but the doctor couldn't get the needle through the skin on the bottom of his foot! His feet were tough as leather. The doctor finally resorted to butterfly clips and a tight bandage.

Sometimes the applicants would come with credentials. They'd have letters signed by American commanders—colonels and the like— saying that so-and-so was the best thing he'd ever seen, he was sorry to be losing him, he comes highly recommended, etc., etc. I'd jump on those guys right away.

So the Yards would gather in a big group, and the American team leaders would go through the selection process. I always selected tall people who looked like they could carry somebody if the situation demanded it. I'd move along the ranks, looking for men who had that look. The one that said, I'm an ass-kicker. I'm good. Let me show you.

When I found someone I wanted I'd tell my One-One to pull that guy from the group and have him fall in behind us. Soon I had my quota, and with the entire gang in tow I'd move off to conduct interviews. I'd get my interpreter and ask them if they'd ever been in a unit before, had they ever fired a weapon, and so forth. I asked these questions to determine where I was going to place them in my element. I wasn't going to reject anybody at this stage. I had already selected them; now it was just a matter of matching people to positions.

Once I had an idea of where I was going to put them, I'd run a recon mission in the area to test them out, to see if my assessment of their abilities was correct. The point man had to see things at any distance and detect movement instantly. He also had to be one of the best shooters because nine times out of ten he'd be the one who engaged the enemy first. He also had to have a sixth sense about danger. He had to be able to feel that something was wrong. He had to detect areas that might be traps ready to be sprung.

Running the "tail gunner" position was also critical. The last man in the element had to cover our tracks. He had to put things back the way they were prior to our passing through. When the situation called for it he'd sweep the trail of footprints, replace sticks and stones, reposition vegetation and do a number of other tricks. All these actions were done to slow down or stop the enemy from tracking us. It was an interesting contest because the Yards were experts at making an area look undisturbed, and the North Vietnamese, sometimes aided by turncoat Yards, were excellent trackers. An outstanding tracker could detect a doctored trail, but he wouldn't be able to determine how many people had passed through.

Another interesting observation I made about Yards is that they didn't waste ammo. Americans had a tendency to fire rounds in big bursts all over the place. But Yards really conserved their rounds, making sure that each one counted. That's why I was reasonably sure that some enemy troop went to the ground if I heard a shot fired by my point man or tail gunner.

Yards were basically your bodyguards as well as your killers. My point man was named Hyuk (pronounced with a silent *H* and long *U*). He was good. He was fucking dynamite. Even though he was a Yard, he had once worked as a squad leader in an NVA unit. I don't know if he had ever fought against Americans or why he came over to our side. I never bothered to ask. He was about thirty years old and I was about twenty-five. He always had this very businesslike look on his face. I wasn't afraid to question him about his past, but perhaps it was just as well that I didn't. The only important fact was that he always covered my back and he was always there when I needed him. I had nothing but respect and admiration for him, as I did for all the Yards.

IT DON'T COME EASY

The acronym SLAM concisely represented the essence of a reconnaissance element—Search, Locate, Annihilate, or Monitor. There was certainly no mystery to it; we would search for and (hopefully) locate the enemy. Once we found him we generally did one of two things, depending on the nature of the mission: annihilate him, or monitor—for intelligence purposes—his activities (no contact involved).

If the mission strictly called for gathering information, which was the case the majority of the time, I would almost always use a standard-sized patrol element consisting of two Americans (me and one other American as my RTO) and five Yards. A seven-man patrol usually proved to be just small enough for stealthy movement, yet large enough to survive unexpected engagements with the enemy.

Every once in a while we'd be called upon to SLAM the enemy, as in, "Miller, I want you to prepare for a SLAM mission." When SLAM was used in that context, it meant we were going to execute the A portion of the acronym. On those occasions I'd run a "heavy" patrol of two Americans and eight or nine Yards. The additional three or four Yards provided increased firepower necessary for annihilation operations. The larger patrol would be easier to detect, but that was an unavoidable trade-off for more ass-kicking ability.

One important function of a recon element, which wasn't included in the SLAM acronym, was prisoner capture. Snatching a member of the opposition was always a tremendous boost to our efforts.

So basically recon patrols were either observing, shooting, or capturing the enemy—sometimes all at once. After spending a considerable amount of time doing all three, I developed the theory that there were three basic levels of difficulty when it came to dealing with the enemy.

The lowest or "easiest" level involved shooting him. Now shooting someone isn't always easy, of course, especially when you're doing it in his backyard and he's trying to shoot you. In fact it was downright difficult or impossible at times. But of the three levels it was the easiest one to operate on. Position yourself, shoot the dude, and make your move. It didn't always go as simply as that, but basically that was the drill.

The next higher level of difficulty dealt with sneaking up on the enemy unnoticed and then getting away without him seeing you. During most of our intelligence-gathering missions that's exactly what was required. We had to get close enough to observe and hear him, take pictures, and collect anything that might tip us off as to his intentions. It was just as important to leave the area undetected so he wouldn't know his position was compromised.

There was an intense fear that while we were sneaking up on him we might blow it. But we knew if we paid attention to detail we'd be fine. There were many times when my patrol ran across the enemy sooner than we anticipated because our target was unexpectedly on the move. In those cases we had to drop down quickly where we were and do our thing. That's why it was important to be disciplined during the entire mission instead of merely getting ourselves together as we got closer to the target. Even though many calculated missions went off as scheduled, there were just as many that deviated from the plan. It was almost like a crapshoot every time out.

The most difficult level for us to operate on was the capturing of an enemy soldier. I've mentioned earlier that capturing a healthy enemy troop is not an easy task, especially on his turf. There are exceptions. Sometimes the capture is so easy it startles you. But that's deceptive, because those instances are very rare.

Most calculated captures take a lot of planning, preparation, and, in a few cases, luck. In any case you really have to be on top of the situation to complete a successful snatch.

The chief of SOG once gave us the mission of capturing an enemy soldier. He didn't care what his rank was, but he had to be from a specific area and a specific unit. The chief needed information regarding a new AO that he suspected contained numerous lucrative targets. A prisoner would be the fastest way to obtain the information he sought. So we began preparing for the task.

We knew of a road in the area of interest that this particular unit used for convoy purposes. In this case our plan was simple and time-proven: we'd ambush one of the vehicles running the road and snatch the driver or any survivor of the hit.

We were inserted and moved to the ambush site without incident. Later one evening, just as the sun was sinking below the horizon, we heard trucks coming up the road. We were deep in Indian country and my heart was pounding with excitement and anticipation.

The Yards in my ambush had only one thing on their minds. Their attitude was like, We don't care what you Americans want. If we see enemy we're going to shoot them. I told them repeatedly that we needed at least one guy alive. They knew the purpose of our mission, but it didn't change their thinking. That was their way.

The trucks came rumbling by us. They were spread out a good distance. We let the first two trucks go by unmolested. We had two Claymores set up a fair distance down the road, and when the last truck came by we detonated the Claymores and blew the truck's tires to shreds. As soon as the Claymores went off all hell broke loose. The Yards started shooting like crazy sons of bitches. When they stopped we ran up to the truck. There was nobody in the back of it, just some old ammo crates. When I got to the truck's cab I realized that every motherfucker in my patrol of nine had shot at the cab's door. There were hundreds of bullet holes. The driver was nothing but a mass of pulp. We had fucked up the snatch.

Why? Fear, I guess. You just don't know. You may have stopped a truck that had Rambo in it. But in this business you have to control your fear. We weren't perfect by any stretch of the imagination, and occasionally we'd screw up. Like in this case.

We booby-trapped the truck and split the scene. Well, the enemy didn't take too kindly to what we did, so they got up our asses big-time. They chased us the rest of that night, dropping mortars on us and firing rocket-propelled grenades—B-40s and RPG-7s—in our direction. Moving through the woods at night is extremely difficult, even more so when the enemy is lobbing explosives all around you. We were slipping and tripping constantly. Brush and branches sliced our faces as we ran headlong into them.

All night long we heard the distinctive *thoommpp* of mortar rounds coming out of their tubes. They'd explode in a ground-thumping *wwhhooommmpp* as they hit very near us. Sparks would fly everywhere when a round hit stone. They tried to channel us into a certain direction by forcing us to turn away from the mortar rounds. When I heard explosions in an area I'd wait until they stopped and then I'd move through it. I couldn't let them turn us. We talked to our people back in camp during the chase, but there was nothing they could do for us until daylight.

We finally shook them early in the morning. Some Cobras came in and put the fear of God into them, so they halted their aggression. Choppers came in and extracted us. We spent a total of five days on the ground for that aborted mission.

We still needed a prisoner, so two weeks later they inserted us into an area very near the scene of our failed attempt. Our plan was identical to the last mission's scenario: ambush a road and capture a driver.

The road that we settled on was similar to the other, with one exception. This road had a steep grade that forced the trucks to slow down considerably as they chugged up the long incline. Right away I knew that this was a better ambush site than the previous one. I also decided to ambush the first truck that came along. That way no enemy troops would be up the slope from us when we sprung the trap, which would have given them a definite advantage when they came after us.

We were barely set up when a lone vehicle entered the scene. We hit the Claymores and blew the tires as before. This time nobody shot at the truck. My point and tail men quickly took up positions at opposite ends of the road to give me early warning of advancing enemy troops. Everyone else fanned out on both sides of the vehicle to provide flank security. One Yard and I immediately ran up to the truck to snatch whoever was in it. All this activity happened within a minute of the Claymore detonations.

When we got to the truck's cab and threw the door open we discovered that there wasn't anybody inside. Impossible! We were on that truck in less than thirty seconds. How could the guy have gotten away?

We did an immediate search of the area. I thought, you son of a bitch! You won't get far. I gave a few orders to the Yards, who started beating the brush frantically. We were taking too much time. Any minute I expected the enemy to show in force.

The Yard who went with me to the truck looked back inside the cab again, and this time he saw something we missed during the first search.

A shirttail was hanging down from under the dashboard!

The driver knew what was going on when we hit the truck. He heard me speaking to the Yards and issuing orders. He was so terrified that he had literally wedged his body up under the dashboard and put his legs over the steering column that runs through the dashboard, hoping that we wouldn't see him.

The Yard grabbed his shirt and pulled him down where he could see him. The Yard then said something to one of the other members of the patrol. His tone of voice wasn't pleasant.

Here we had a human being who was petrified and in mortal fear for his life. He was thinking back on all the horrible stories he'd been told by his command about the Americans. He feared that all the tales of torture and mutilation were about to become reality.

Two of my Yards grabbed him, jerked him out of the truck, and held him up to me. Suddenly he was face-to-face with his nightmare. An American.

He had a very docile look on his face. A smart soldier who is captured doesn't have that I'll-kick-your-ass look. He just doesn't want to look aggressive or belligerent. It's too dangerous. The enemy might not appreciate the fact that his prisoner appears to want to challenge him. He might just shoot his POW for the hell of it if he gets the notion to do so. So the captured soldier tries not to upset his captors in any way. He attempts to become as insignificant as possible. It may not save him from torture or death, but at least it doesn't aggravate the situation. Besides, most soldiers are so terrified once they're captured that they couldn't look mean if they tried. Our POW fell into this category.

We put a sandbag over his head and secured his hands behind his back with a large plastic zip-tie. We then took off for tall timber. The snatch took less than two minutes.

It didn't take long for the enemy to discover our handiwork. In no time he was on our trail. But this time we had a bigger lead. By now it was twilight, and to complicate the enemy's pursuit we dropped a mine on our back trail. One of them stepped on it, and that tiny bit of destruction must have convinced the other troops that it was useless to search for us in the dark. They would wait until daylight.

That night we moved as fast as we could. But since we weren't receiving any fire I concluded that our hostile hosts weren't chasing us anymore. I've already mentioned that moving through the woods at night is difficult and risky, so I decided to stop on the side of a ridgeline until daybreak.

During the night they must have discovered that we had one of their people, because at first light they came after us in force. The first thing we heard was a large body of troops crashing through the woods about a hundred meters to the northwest of us. They were making their way to the ridgeline above us. We realized that we'd have to get there first or they'd have us between the ridgeline and the road we'd ambushed. On the other side of the ridgeline was a big valley of deep, dense jungle.

We began moving immediately. We got to the ridgeline and crossed it without seeing any enemy troops. But apparently one of them saw us, because as soon as we crossed over we heard a single gunshot about a hundred meters from our position. The round wasn't directed at us; the soldier just shot it straight into the air. It was a signal to his buddies that he'd spotted us.

The chase was on for real.

We picked up our pace. We'd just crossed a shallow stream when another shot rang out, only much closer this time. I thought, Shit. We're really going to get into it now. I heard a lot of people coming up on us at a fast pace. It was getting deep.

We crossed over a high-speed trail and I motioned for my people to drop. It was obvious that the enemy was moving faster than we were, so we had no choice but to take up a position and face them head-on. I signaled for a hasty ambush. Unfortunately, we didn't have time to set any Claymores. It was going to be primarily an M-16 dance.

Apparently they thought they were ahead of us, because moments later a large number of enemy soldiers came alongside the trail, moving at a pretty good clip, without making too much effort to conceal themselves. I believe they were moving fast because they wanted to get up the trail far enough to prepare a deliberate ambush.

Sorry, guys. We beat you to it.

We opened up on them with a furious burst of fire. Our first volley dropped six of them. The rest scrambled to safety on both sides of the trail. We threw a couple of frags at them and quickly broke contact. So sudden and devastating was our ambush that they didn't fire a single shot.

As it turned out, that was the only engagement we had the remainder of the mission. We moved far and fast. At one point we heard six or seven shots way off in the distance. We had no idea what they were shooting at, and we never found out. At least it wasn't us.

Later that evening our choppers arrived to take us out. Everyone down the line was notified that we were bringing back a prisoner. A POW always generated excitement among our folks. It was a big deal. Everybody understood the significance of a captured enemy soldier. When our extraction choppers landed I could see the excitement as the crews talked quickly among themselves when they spotted our kneeling captive. The pilots were jabbering away on their headsets, no doubt informing our headquarters that the fish was in the net. We loaded our catch and piled into the taxis.

Since we had a prisoner they flew us to Dak To where he would be interrogated by a special team. When we landed they isolated our POW from everyone, enemy and friendlies alike. Nobody was going to talk to our man until the "college boys" (CIA personnel) had a crack at him.

With our mission at an end we flew back to Kontum. When we got to the camp our boss informed us that the boys in the white shirts and khaki pants had already arrived at Dak To to practice their gentle art of persuasion. Apparently they were very convincing, because in a short period of time we had all the information we needed to ruin the enemy's whole day.

The POW was a private in the NVA whose unit was responsible for transporting supplies along a two-hundred-mile stretch of road that came out of North Vietnam through the area where we snatched him. He said he'd been driving that stretch of road regularly for about a year. He revealed the general locations of all the ammo and fuel storage areas, as well as troop areas and equipment parks. Even though he was only a private, our captive turned out to be a virtual storehouse of valuable information.

Since he could point out only the general vicinity of each site, our folks inserted several recon teams from our operation to determine exact locations. They also did high-altitude aerial recons of the road.

The recon teams found all the sites with little difficulty. Although we didn't do it during this mission, one of the more effective tricks we employed was to put "pole beam" in the enemy's munitions storage areas. Pole beam was captured ammunition that we altered for the purpose of destroying the enemy's morale. We doctored everything from AK-47 7.62mm rounds to artillery shells to mortar rounds. A recon team would penetrate an ammunition supply point and plant the rigged ammo among the regular stocks. The enemy wouldn't detect that anything was amiss because our special night deposits were in their original crates and containers. Everything looked the same because it was actual enemy ammo, with a slight twist.

You see, the bogus stuff had a nasty habit of blowing up when the enemy used it. Rounds would explode in rifle chambers. Mortar shells would detonate in their tubes. Grenades would blow up before they were thrown. All these things killed people and had a devastating effect on the morale of the enemy. When they ran across even a couple of altered rounds they immediately lost confidence in the remainder of their ammo. Think about it. Would you want to fire your weapon after you'd seen a couple of buddies blown up by the same ammo you were about to use?

So instead of having some fun with the pole beam, our folks simply bombed the shit out of each and every enemy site. It was a crippling blow to their effort and no doubt upset more than a few bad guys. Make no mistake about it. It really made me and my team feel good that we redeemed ourselves after our botched first snatch attempt.

REAL BANDITOS

Even though I was at ease with and trusted the Yards, I always felt a little unsettled whenever I was out in the Yards' camps. Especially at night. Americans might make up ten percent of the camp's population. Everyone else was a different race and nationality. We were all armed. Campfires blazed everywhere in the darkness. It was the frontier, man. Anything goes. For real. There appeared to be some kind of law and order, but it was really an illusion. If someone really wanted to go wild, for whatever reason, it would boil down to kill or be killed. At that point the man in charge would have no authority. "The commander? Fuck him, I'll blow his ass away, too." So you constantly lived in an armed state where everybody had a gun and was totally prepared to use it 24 hours a day, 365 days a year.

These conditions created an air about you. Other people could see it. They could feel it. When you'd go around support units you'd notice the way the soldiers looked at you. It was almost a look of bewilderment and nervousness that cried, who the hell is that? Where did *he* come from?

The Americans in my unit used to go to the finance office down in Pleiku to get paid. When we'd walk in we'd immediately get that look from everyone. The finance clerks knew who we were. They could see that we were carrying special weapons, we were dirty as shit, and we had that air about us. We were "those guys." They had orders to ensure that "those guys" were promptly taken care of and moved out immediately.

Once, after getting paid, a new man in my unit and I went down to a black bar. I'd never been there before and didn't know it was exclusively black. When we entered the bar everyone looked up at us, like, where the fuck do you white dudes think you are? The entire place suddenly developed one giant belligerent attitude when we white guys strolled in. But just as they looked like they might get rowdy they spotted our weapons. And they saw the way we looked. They must have suddenly realized, Whoa. Wait a minute. These are *real* banditos. Might as well leave them alone and not fuck with them.

The guy I was with said, "I think we're in the wrong place." I told him not to worry about it, and after I said that, we walked over to the bar. I certainly wasn't looking for trouble. All I wanted was a beer.

Even the girls looked at us kind of funny, like, hey, you're in the wrong place. But nobody said anything to us. They all sort of eased back into their seats and went about their business. Occasionally I'd catch people staring at us. But they felt the atmosphere that we generated. We were too relaxed. There's something unsettling about someone who's relaxed in a situation where he should be tense. Being relaxed sends a message to everyone that you're fully confident in your abilities. You can handle whatever comes your way. I'm sure there were weapons in the crowd. Maybe .45s or other pistols. Maybe even an automatic weapon or two. But they saw our automatic weapons, ammo, and frags and *knew* that we would use ours without hesitation on anybody that looked to do us harm. That realization was what kept everybody in their seats and us out of trouble.

IN MY ELEMENT

I can bullshit with the best of them, but I'll tell you straight up one of the major reasons I liked 'Nam so much. When I was a kid I was really thin. I was six feet tall at age sixteen, and I weighed about 120 pounds. Rail thin. My brother was about six-foot four and weighed in at 220 or 230. He used to mop the floor with me all the time. It was his form of fun.

But when I got to 'Nam and they put a gun in my hand—Whoa! It was like a religious experience. I was born again.

I want to make it clear that I never threatened anybody with a gun. Not one time. But I loved it because a gun made you everybody's equal. The littlest guy in the group could kill the biggest guy in the group provided he was good enough with his weapon. Body size and muscle were no longer factors. So I made it my business to become an expert with weapons. To this day I can make an M-16 sing on full automatic. You acquire a feel for the weapon like a race car driver develops a feel for his car.

So I got very, very good with weapons. All weapons. When you're good, as I've mentioned before, you send out vibes unintentionally to people around you. You're a bad motherfucker. You know it and they know it. You don't need to be alarmed at any time under normal circumstances. You've proven yourself time and time again in difficult situations. Each time you succeed your vibes grow stronger.

That's one reason why I liked 'Nam so much. Over there you could be a bad motherfucker. Back in the States you couldn't. Could you run around in the woods kicking ass back in the U.S.A.? Could you legally carry fully automatic weapons down Main Street?

Once you'd been there for a long period of time you became your worst enemy. It was not the enemy in the woods that could cause you the most grief, it was you. I don't mean that you started getting into a head trip kind of thing like, hey, I'm B-A-D. Stay out of my way, motherfucker. I can't be beaten. That wasn't the primary reason— although many people did adopt such an attitude and it eventually led to their downfall.

It's just that after a while you lost respect for other people, for anything they want to do, their lives, whatever. You wanted to be with them and work with them. You tried to keep them alive, sure. But if someone threatened you—holy shit!—would that be a mistake! A threat would require instant reaction. You couldn't take the chance that he was only joking. He might be serious when he said, "I'm going to kill you," or gave you that look.

I've seen the look that goes with the words. When you're in a battle zone and everyone's got a gun, that look means, I'm waiting my turn. I'm waiting for the opportunity to put a round in your head.

If we were in a battle area and you gave me that look, I'd shoot you on the spot. Immediately.

I know it sounds unbelievable. It *is* hard to comprehend that one American would shoot another just because of a threat. Right now you're probably saying to yourself, what a bunch of bullshit. That's just a lot of big, bad Special Forces talk. But if you're a vet who's been there you're probably saying, I understand exactly. You learned not to take any chances when your life was threatened. You also learned not to say anything you weren't prepared to back up.

You also put yourself in the position of judge, jury, and executioner. Some very strange, bizarre thoughts occasionally pop into your mind for no apparent reason.

One night I woke up next to my girlfriend, Judy. I hadn't been boozing it up or anything. I was straight. But as she lay there asleep I looked at her and thought, I should kill her. I should strangle her and break her neck. Then I thought, no, I better not do that. They'll know it was me, and I'll get arrested and thrown in jail.

It was incredibly strange. I was arguing with myself about what I was going to do. No, I'll go ahead and kill her. I have all these special skills. I'll make it look like the enemy did it. But she really isn't a bad person. In fact, she's rather pleasant. Yeah, but what the fuck. She's only a whore. She'll never amount to anything. She'll never contribute anything to the world.

I became panicky because I felt I was going to hurt her. I had to get out of bed and go into the woods for the rest of the night. By morning I was rational again.

To this day I'm not sure why I wanted to kill her. Perhaps it was my conditioning. When you live in an environment where you're taught to be constantly aggressive and hostile, you begin to operate in that mode twenty-four hours a day, regardless of the situation. That's bad business. Usually I was pretty successful at switching gears, but every once in a while the gears would stick and I'd be operating at high speed in a low-speed zone.

TET

I was downtown in the ville at Nieh An with my girlfriend when the Tet Offensive kicked off in 1968. She and I were getting settled in for the evening in the neat little house that her family owned. I was just off taking a little break from the grind. I had all my weapons with me, and I was relaxing with some rather pleasant company.

Later that night I heard the distant *wwhhoommpp*, *wwhhoommpp* of artillery. Not far away from the village I heard an artillery battery unleash a barrage of rounds. I heard muffled explosions near and far. This activity went on all night.

I wondered what the hell was going on. I figured that some heavy shit must be going down. But after a while I didn't think about it anymore. I was with my Judy and we were enjoying ourselves. So I forgot about the little disturbances outside. We just made the world go away.

The next morning I got up early and gathered my gear. As I prepared to leave the house, I remember, my girlfriend told me to be careful.

I stepped out the front door and immediately sensed that something wasn't quite right. The village and surrounding area seemed somehow different. They gave off strange vibrations. The air was rife with tension.

After walking a short distance I ran into some villagers who informed me that my camp was under attack. The camp was about six miles from the ville, but already I could see fast movers stacked up. They were coming in low and fast, raining tons of volatile steel on the NVA as explosions rocked the terrain.

But let me digress for a moment and tell you where I was and how I ended up at that place.

It was late 1967. I'd gotten wounded in my left thigh and was shipped off to a hospital in Japan. While they worked on me they reviewed my records and noticed how long I'd been in 'Nam. They told me I'd done my time there and they were returning me to the States.

That didn't sit well with me. I was really into a personally satisfying way of life in 'Nam, and I wasn't ready to go back to the World. So I pulled a number on them. Back then you could get away with all kinds of shit.

I knew a guy in the personnel section who was kind of a friend of mine. I went down to his place, and after talking to him for a while, I convinced him to cut me a set of orders getting me on the next flight back to 'Nam. The orders were published and I flew back with no hassles.

When I got back to my unit, my commander said, "Glad to see you're back, Mill. I've got a perfect assignment for you that will allow you to tune up for your next mission. While you're recovering from your leg wound and getting back into the swing of things, I'm going to send you up to this place called Nieh An. It's a little outpost. I'll send you up there because you've got a lot of expertise, and there are all kinds of new guys up there and quite a few officers. They're running some kind of advisory thing up there, and they really need someone who knows his shit." I was a sergeant (E-5) at the time. I packed my bags and moved out smartly.

What really blew me away about the place was that it was a relatively "hot" area. It was a heavy rice-producing area, right up against the mountains, and the enemy was always coming down to get the rice. The people in the camp weren't being successful in locating the enemy and mixing it up with him. The reason they weren't successful was because they didn't *want* to mix it up. They had some serious reservations about anything that involved direct conflict with the enemy.

That was my assessment upon arriving at Nieh An.

Now back to the Tet Offensive.

There I was, standing at the end of the ville watching the fast movers do their thing. I thought, shit, I gotta get my ass back to the camp. Brilliant idea, huh?

The first thing I did was run down this hill to a bridge that crossed a stream. The stream wasn't very wide, about five meters or so, but it was deep and mighty swift.

I came to the bridge, or rather, what was left of it. Blown to shit during the night. Gone.

The South Vietnamese had canoes going back and forth, ferrying refugees from the side where the action was to the side where I was standing, the safe ground. They were clearing the AO. They were getting the fuck outta Dodge.

I spotted this Vietnamese dude on a little, beat-up motorcycle and told him I needed a ride to my camp. He looked at me like I was crazy. He refused. I asked again. He refused again. So I asked him how much money he wanted to take me out there.

Under ordinary circumstances it would cost me less than a buck, about thirty-five cents, for a ride to the camp. I got real close to him and said, "I'll give you twenty bucks to take me out."

Bing! His eyes lit up. You could tell he was thinking, Twenty bucks? Might be worth the danger.

I flipped a twenty-dollar military pay certificate, or MPC, on him. He greedily stuffed it in his pocket. MPC was what the military paid us with instead of dollars, which we called "green." MPC was tan in color, and on the front it had a picture of some chick. I don't recall who the hell she was. On the back was a picture of a B-52 strike. Real *Army* money! We also had equivalent coinage, starting with a five-cent piece. We had no penny counterparts. So if you walked into a PX and made a purchase with MPC that resulted in you receiving, say, eight cents in change, you got back a five-cent piece and three sticks of gum. Sticks of gum were used as pennies. Only trouble was, you couldn't save up your sticks of gum and buy anything. They would give them to you, but you couldn't purchase anything with them. Anyway, the Vietnamese would take any MPC they got and exchange it on the black market for Vietnamese currency. The black market would then buy greens from American soldiers at a two-to-one ratio. Two dollars worth of MPC for one green dollar. Even though we were paid in MPC, there were still plenty of American dollars floating around the country. And the dollar was worth far more than the Vietnamese currency. So the soldier doubled his buying power in American facilities, and the black marketeers got currency they could spend.

So I gave the dude twenty dollars MPC. We walked the motorcycle down to the stream bank, put the motorcycle in a canoe, and crossed the river. A couple minutes later we were winding down the road to the "party."

I'm sure the sight of the two of us was comical. Think about it. Here was this tall, white, blond-haired foreign devil with an automatic weapon slung across his shoulder being driven down the road on a little 90cc motorcycle by this tiny, dark Vietnamese civilian in a large hat. Just puttering and sputtering along as the bombs fell a few miles up the road.

The first obstacle we encountered was a five-hundred-pound bomb crater that had cut the road. We simply motored around it and kept on moving.

Pretty soon we came upon the very small village that was midway between the camp and the ville, about three miles distant. As we approached I saw a bamboo pole in the middle of the village. Attached to the top of that pole was an NVA flag.

Uh-oh.

I assessed the situation as we drew closer. The village was small and wide open, making it easier for me to determine what I was going to do next. There was some jungle on the right side of the village, but most of the surrounding area was flat, clear rice paddies. I didn't see anyone in the village. I really had no choice but to go for it.

My driver kept on the gas and on the straight and narrow road. We entered and exited the village without incident.

My heart wouldn't stop racing!

The closer we got to the camp the more bomb craters we saw. The landscape was pockmarked from the air strikes. Huge holes were everywhere. Entire sections of jungle were knocked flat. And yet I still hadn't seen anyone. No bodies, no troops scurrying around, no human flesh, period. I was really puzzled.

Soon we arrived at another small village located right behind the camp. I still didn't see anyone. I had my taxi service drop me off there. I would walk the rest of the way. I didn't want the people in the camp firing me up as I arrived on the motorcycle. They might think I was a rolling bomb on a suicide mission. When in doubt, take 'em out.

No need to alarm the troops any more than they already were, especially at the expense of my own skin.

I warily headed out of the village toward the camp's gate. As I got closer I realized there were dead people in the wire. There were bodies everywhere, mangled, tangled, and twisted.

The Americans in the camp saw my approach. There were about eight of them at this time. The rest of the troops were South Vietnamese.

So the Americans saw me coming. When they recognized me, one of them shouted, "Motherfucker! Where have *you* been?"

I yelled back, "I've, ah, been down in the ville."

He responded, "Holy shit! Son of a bitch, man!"

We started yelling back and forth, and finally I said, "Hey, let me in!"

The guy I'd been talking to said, "I don't know, man. There're a lot of motherfuckers around where you are!" My hair stood on end. I said, "What?!"

He stated, "Yeah, we got hit about twenty minutes ago. We're expecting another attack soon."

I rapidly looked around. Nobody was in sight, but . . . . I yelled, "Quit fuckin' around and let me in!" There was a little sense of urgency in my voice.

I guess they figured they'd screwed with me long enough and let me in. I walked through the long, narrow zigzag wire entrance to the camp. The zigzag approach was designed to prevent anyone from making a straight, unobstructed run to the camp's main gate. If you didn't move slowly along the path, you'd end up tangled in the dense web of wire, where you'd be an easy target.

Once inside, I entered the command bunker and conversed with the guys, including a lieutenant who said, "Man, are we glad you got back, 'cause you know what the hell's goin' on."

Suddenly this major comes running up to me yelling, "Man, get on the fuckin' radio. We need some artillery support *now!*" Almost immediately after he said that I heard the sound of automatic weapons. I went over to the main gate side of the bunker and peered through the window.

I saw NVA emerging from the village I'd just walked through. They were assaulting the side of the camp where only minutes earlier I'd been standing out in the open. I got an icy chill up my spine. How in the hell could I have walked through the enemy and not seen any? How come I wasn't taken under fire or killed outright?

These thoughts quickly evaporated as I jumped for the radio. I told everybody on that corner of the camp to get away from the gun ports and I put some 155mm on our uninvited guests.

It was really impressive. They used airbursts which completely shredded the village after about eight rounds. It was such an awesome display, it kind of took your breath away after each burst. What was left of the enemy force stopped cold and withdrew.

After the NVA retreated, the major said, "Take the lieutenant and get up on top of the main bunker and man the .50. Cover the north-gate sector of the wire." The artillery had not only destroyed the village but had also managed to knock out a sector of our wire. We had a .50 caliber machine gun in a sandbagged position on top of our bunker, and now with the wire gone we had to place some defensive fire in that area.

No sooner did the lieutenant and I get to the position than the enemy started putting their shit on us. They cut loose with 120mm mortars and dropped them everywhere.

I was right behind the .50 when a round landed on the bunker's roof, directly in front of the wall of sandbags surrounding the position. I was sitting on the roof and the lieutenant was down on one knee behind me, looking over my head. He was only about six inches higher above the sandbags than I was. When the round exploded a big piece of frag hit him square in the temple. Blood spurted everywhere as he fell backward onto the roof. In a matter of seconds he was dead.

The rounds continued to fall. All we could do at that point was to man our stations and keep as covered as possible until the pounding subsided.

When it ended we surveyed the damage. They really blew the shit out of the camp. One round landed directly on top of our fresh food conex. No more dill pickles to go with our C rations.

So there we sat, with no fresh food and a gaping hole in our defense via the destroyed wire. We knew that something big was shaping up. We didn't know it was going to be *the* big event of the year, but we were sure the shit was about to hit the fan big-time because of the intensity with which the enemy assaulted us.

Our most immediate problem was the gap in our defenses. We needed to replace the wire if we were going to have any chance of repelling another attack. Unfortunately, we didn't have the necessary resources to perform the repairs. We needed outside assistance in a big way.

As it turned out, an American mechanized infantry unit was in our area. We got on the horn to them and relayed our situation. A mech platoon proceeded in force to our camp. When they arrived, they positioned themselves in a half-moon formation around the missing section of wire to cover that sector of the perimeter. We all breathed a little easier. All we could do then was sit and wait for the enemy to make his next move.

That night a much smaller sister camp of ours came under a vicious attack. It was a triangular-shaped camp like ours, but it was only about thirty meters long. It was manned by two Americans and a handful of South Vietnamese.

The camp was approximately three kilometers away, and all during the night we saw flares and heard the firecracker pops of continuous fighting. We talked to the camp on the radio a couple of times and told them that as soon as daylight came we'd send help over to them. We couldn't do it immediately because we didn't know what was outside our wire. All we could do was watch.

As morning broke we lost communication with them. When we had the opportunity two days later to investigate, we discovered that they'd been overrun.

Nothing happened the first night after the mech infantry joined us. The second night I was up on the .50, just kind of taking it easy. The armored vehicles were all sitting to my front. Suddenly, there was a white flash out in the rice paddy immediately followed by a high-pitched *clang* as red-hot sparks exploded from the front of one of the armored personnel carriers (APCs).

A sapper had crawled right dead up on one of our vehicles and cut loose with an antitank round.

Immediately seven or eight APCs opened up with their .50s. But their tracer rounds indicated they weren't firing out at any distance. They were firing down into the dirt in front of them. They were being overrun!

The action got unreal. The NVA captured one of the APCs and turned the .50 on the camp. They sent a wall of lead our way. The .50 rounds were terrifying as they came in sounding like ultraintense, high-volume bumblebees. As one passed over me I heard a tremendously high-pitched *crack*! Those that hit the bunker below me pulverized the concrete walls and shook the structure. Sandbags around me were hit and literally burst in an explosive spray of sand.

A gunner in an APC located a short distance away from the now-enemy-controlled vehicle realized what was happening and turned his .50 on the intruder, who turned his on him. A frenzied exchange took place. A few seconds later the .50 action from the enemy-controlled vehicle ceased.

The action only intensified over the next few minutes. Fifty-caliber and 7.62mm tracers were pinging and bouncing crazily off everything. A second antitank round found its mark, sending another shower of sparks high into the air. Frantic yells and horrible screams mixed with the heavy stench of expended ammunition. It was chaos of the highest magnitude.

On several occasions the fighting suddenly ceased. Each time, the peace lasted for about three minutes, then the hostilities resumed with greater intensity.

I jumped down from the .50 position after firing hundreds of rounds. Another guy took my place. I got into the bunker and called our supporting artillery unit for 155mm fire. I called the remaining APCs by way of their radios and told them to button up because some serious stuff was on the way.

Once again the artillery stopped them cold. By this time the enemy (and we) had had enough. The remaining NVA broke off the assault and retreated across the rice paddies into the jungle.

The next morning medevac choppers came in to evacuate the wounded and the dead. The scene was incredible. Mangled bodies and twisted, pulverized equipment were everywhere. It was a picture out of a nightmare.

Later that day more armored vehicles showed up from another platoon that belonged to the same organization as the folks already there. They hung around that day and everything seemed pretty cool. But we were still uptight, so we kept calling headquarters to find out what the hell was going on. Finally, somebody told us something big was happening. Between us and the ville they had located a large enemy unit moving through that area, that six-mile stretch. Around noon the mech infantry guys packed their bags and split. They were critically low on ammunition and fuel, so they had to rejoin their company for refueling and rearming. Their departure sent a cold chill up everyone's spine. We were alone and hurting.

Our camp was close to the coast, located in the northern part of South Vietnam. About seven o'clock that evening the battleship *New Jersey* fired a salvo into that six-mile stretch where the enemy had been detected. It fired three, four, then five salvos of twenty-five-hundred-pound projectiles, pounding the living hell out of the area. If we had any doubts as to the seriousness of the situation, they were quickly dispelled as those rounds impacted the earth. When you open up with that much firepower the situation's got to be grave.

The shelling stopped about ten minutes later. As we nervously eyed the horizon we noticed some activity about seven kilometers away. Apparently the mech infantry unit had run into a good-sized force, because during the night we watched thousands of tracers arc up above the tops of the trees, going in every direction. At one point a Spooky showed up. A Spooky is a C-47 aircraft with three 7.62mm miniguns positioned on one side of the plane. Each 7.62mm minigun has six barrels and fires at a rate of six thousand rounds per minute. It's definitely a major ass-kicker.

It made several low passes over the raging battle with all three miniguns blazing, belching fire that lit up the night. The sight of Spooky is enough to send any sane man running for cover, but those NVA were either insane or had the biggest balls in the world, because they started firing up at it. Tracers outlined converging streams of lead from every direction as the NVA actually drove off the C-47. Unbelievable! Everyone in the camp stood there focused on the drama unfolding before us as if we were watching a thoroughly engrossing movie.

Cobras showed up a few minutes later but met with the same fate as the Spooky. Intense fire from the ground forced them to leave in haste. After the Cobras' departure the conflict's intensity appeared to wind down several notches. Sporadic gunfire echoed through the night as the sounds of battle diminished.

About two o'clock in the morning the mech infantry unit came back into our area. It was decimated. The first vehicle that showed up had many dead and wounded in and on it. Only three more vehicles followed the leader. Of the eleven APCs that had left us several hours earlier, only three returned under their own power, with the fourth being towed.

We opened our gates and brought them directly into the compound. Each vehicle was literally covered with people just barely hanging on as the tracks rumbled to a halt. Some wounds were already bandaged somewhat, but most were free-flowing cavities encrusted with filth. It was amazing that the APCs themselves were even functioning, because each one bore the scars of multiple antitank rounds and .50 hits.

Every person in the camp immediately started giving the injured emergency first aid. It was a truly pitiful sight.

The next day bunches of our folks began showing up. Medevac choppers came in to evacuate the casualties. Resupply choppers brought badly needed ammo, medical supplies, and food. Wire and building materials were also flown in so we could repair our defensive perimeter.

Replacements rolled in. Later that afternoon I led a company-sized element up to inspect the battle site.

The mech infantry guys had gotten into it with a heavy-duty enemy battalion on the move. We found about 120 dead enemy troops scattered all over the battlefield. Apparently the mech unit did a good job, but they got their asses severely kicked for their troubles.

We never saw those mech infantry guys again.

That was my perspective on the Tet Offensive, 1968.

STILL MORE SNAKES

Another time I was in Saigon, just relaxing and having a good time. During the course of my merrymaking I picked up this very attractive young lady. We decided to go back to her place.

Her hooch was a very nondescript two-story dwelling along the Saigon River, with the owner of the building living on the top level. She rented the first floor.

We wrestled around on the bed for a few minutes. She got up and went to the bathroom, and when she returned she said to me, "Why don't you take shower? Be more comfortable."

I'd been running around for a couple of days in the sticky, nasty heat and dust of Saigon. I was rather unclean, so the idea of a shower was appealing. I took off my clothes and headed for the "bathroom," which was really just a tiny room that had a shower stall and a hole in the floor for a toilet.

It was dark in that room. There was no light in the room itself, just the light that came from the bedroom. The stall had some kind of white tile on the walls, which made it possible to barely make out my surroundings. I went to step into the shower stall and hesitated. I thought, something is out of order here. I didn't know what it was, but I didn't enter the stall. Maybe it was just the good Lord looking out for me again.

I looked at the shower hose. There was something not quite right about it. It looked strange.

My eyes were adjusting to the dimness of the room by this time, and I stared really hard at the shower hose. Suddenly a chill assaulted my spine. The fucking hose was a snake! It was a krait, a deadly poisonous snake. I almost shit on myself.

I ran back into the bedroom and told the girl about the snake. She kept telling me there wasn't any snake, and I kept insisting there was. Finally, she went into the room to see for herself.

By this time I'd thrown a towel around my waist and retrieved one of my weapons, a 9mm Browning high-powered handgun. I headed outside to talk to the owner about the snake. He was already coming down the outside stairway because he heard all the noise I was making. When he hit the ground floor he saw me standing there, naked except for a towel and holding my weapon.

He got all excited because he thought I was going to shoot someone. We were speaking Vietnamese at this point. I told him I wasn't going to shoot anybody, and I told him there was a big snake in the house. He said, "No, no. No snake in the house." But he could see that I was serious, so he went in to see for himself.

He jumped back quickly when he saw the krait. He hollered for his wife to bring down a bucket of scalding water. I couldn't shoot the snake because the noise would summon the police, who'd think something serious was happening. So boiling water was the solution. It did the job.

After the snake was dead I noticed the absence of my date. She was nowhere to be found. She simply vanished.

I searched for the bitch for several days. I never saw her again.

I can only guess that she was a VC. She probably put the krait in the shower just before I went in there, knowing it would kill me. That's an ideal way to kill someone, too. Silent death. No gunshots or noise of any kind. No direct risk to the assassin. No physical confrontation. Let the snake do the work. Neat.

PUNJI STICKS AND TIGERS

During my years in Vietnam and Laos I was wounded six times. A variety of sources contributed to my injuries. One of my wounds was the result of an encounter with a punji stick.

A punji stick is nothing more than a very long, sturdy piece of bamboo that's been sharpened to a point at one end. Half of the stick is buried in the ground at an angle, so that the pointed end is facing the intruder. If you're going up a hill, and the punji stick is embedded in the side of that hill, in the grass, it's difficult to see as you approach it. This is due to the fact that, because of the way it's angled, you're looking at the stick head-on. You only see the diameter of the stick and none of its length. It's facing right into your line of vision. If you're moving very rapidly there's a good chance you won't see it until it bites you in the ass. And it *will* do you a number.

Most people think that punji sticks were designed as a defense against invading troops. They are used for defensive measures against human beings, but they were developed a long time ago for a different reason.

When people visited villages back then, they occasionally had to stop in the middle of the jungle overnight to sleep. To protect themselves from wild animals they constructed deep barriers of punji sticks around their sleeping area. In the morning they'd clear a path through the circle of sticks and be on their way.

We were up around this place called Dollar Lake, code-named Alpha 6. It was a beautiful little resort spot for the big-time bad boys from the other side. Security was extremely tight in the area, and we were very close to the lake. We were proud of the fact that we'd made good progress, slipping through with relative ease.

We came up from the deep jungle, way below the target, working our way up this big mountain. We swept from side to side, looking for signs of enemy activity. Eventually we started finding abandoned hooches. A little farther on we discovered a high-speed trail that ran for miles along a ridge. It was well-traveled, and we knew it was a lucrative find.

We followed it for a good distance, staying off the trail and down in the dense vegetation. We didn't see anything, but it was a nice day. It was kind of chilly. At that time of year, the mountains and weather in that area reminded me of Colorado. Big pine trees, no roads in the area, and really primitive. Just beautiful.

We soon came to some high ground overlooking Dollar Lake. The lake was surrounded by big evergreen trees. It looked just like a picture you'd find on a postcard that said, "Wish you were here." The trail we were following went down the hill we occupied and ran out into a grassy, open area which covered several hundred meters. The open area ended very abruptly in a dense, forbidding tangle of trees. The trail snaked into the woods, resembling a highway entering a dark mountain tunnel. It looked totally uninviting. We were in severe Indian country, it was getting dark, and the weather was starting to turn sour. We decided to stop there for the night and get some rest. We'd observe what went on, and in the morning we'd sneak down there and take a closer look around.

So we went around to the back side of the hill, figuring that's where we'd sleep. When we got there, we were shocked to find ourselves in the middle of an enemy position.

Apparently the enemy had vacated the hilltop position because it was turning cold and beginning to rain. We were accustomed to 110-degree heat, and the cold front that moved in lowered the temperature into the midsixties. That was very cold to us, and I guess the enemy retreated to more comfortable lodgings, believing no enemy of theirs would be anywhere close.

As we looked out around the area, we could see, even in the diminishing light, thousands of punji sticks emanating from the slope of the hill. I mentioned before that punji sticks are almost invisible when viewed coming up a hill. It's easy to spot them, however, when looking down from the top of that hill. At that point they're angled away from you, and you see the length.

I was puzzled by the presence of these punji sticks. We were deep in enemy-controlled territory. Surely they weren't preparing for regular troops to invade this area. And since we were basically a guerilla operation, they wouldn't be expecting us. So why the sticks?

I would learn later why they were there.

By next morning the weather had cleared up a little, but it was still windy as hell. No possibility of using fast movers that day. In the mountains, wind currents play havoc with aircraft. So we decided to move down as close as we could to the lake.

We moved down the back side of the hill, clearing a two-foot-wide path through the barrier by pulling out hundreds of punji sticks. The barrier was about ten to twelve meters from front to back. As we removed the sticks I wondered why it was so deep.

We ran into a good-sized enemy unit at the edge of the lake. There were seven of us and about thirty-five to forty of them. They immediately took us under fire. To our rear was only tall grass on open ground, which provided no cover.

The chase was on.

It was a real chase. They threw mortars ahead to block our retreat. We beat feet like hell, going right back the same way we had come, because we knew the route. Everything was fine until we got to the barrier.

We didn't hit it square-on, at the point where we'd made our little path. So we put it in low gear and tried to pick our way through it. My heart was in my throat as my element moved excruciatingly slowly through the obstacle.

They got right up on our ass. I hadn't entered the barrier yet, so I dropped down and sprayed rounds at our rear to get the guys who were following our trail through the tall grass. I greased the first two dudes, and the ones behind them immediately spread out on both sides of our trail. I realized we had to get through the shit quick.

By that time the Yards had cleared the barrier. I started through, and soon the enemy was almost on top of me. My Yards were keeping them occupied from the other side of the sticks. I started moving too fast, and the next thing I knew I felt a punji stick stab through my calf and emerge from the other side. God only knows how I got to the other side without being hit or eaten up by more sticks.

The stick was still in my calf when I reached my buddies. One of them pulled it out. Talk about pain! Blood was gushing everywhere. I ripped a shirt sleeve off and hastily bandaged the wound as my guys continued to lay down suppressing fire. No enemy soldier attempted to breach the barrier while we covered it. That allowed us to make our getaway.

I hobbled along as best I could, staying at the rear of the formation as we made our way back. The pain was terrible, and it felt like a hot knife was stabbed into my calf with every step. But as badly as it hurt, I knew that to stop or fall behind meant capture or death. That thought was motivation enough to keep the pace. Believe me, fear is a tremendous motivator.

We took the same route out that we had used going in, which probably wasn't a smart move, but fortunately it worked out OK. We entered the deep jungle and hid out. We remained in hiding the rest of the day. Everything calmed down later that night.

The next morning, just before daylight, we realized they had located us. They were right outside our perimeter. We had our Claymore mines set up, so we were ready for them.

At some predetermined signal they started firing into our position. They weren't exactly sure of where we were, but they had a general idea. After a minute or so of heavy fire they jumped up to make an assault. That was their big mistake. When they started their attack, we blew a single Claymore mine. Just one.

That's all it took.

It stopped them dead (no pun intended) in their tracks.

After we blew the mine we hung tight for a while. It was getting light right about that time. We exchanged a few more rounds with them, but clearly their fighting spirit was blown away by the Claymore. They retreated. Frankly, we were a bit surprised that they gave up so quickly.

Minutes later we went out to inspect our handiwork. What we found was a very ill prepared and poorly organized unit that was not ready to deal with a high-speed, heavily-armed reconnaissance element like ours.

One guy had an AK-47, with a single magazine of about fifteen rounds, and four more rounds in his pocket. Another guy had a MAT-49, an old 9mm French job. He had one magazine of about twenty rounds and another one that had six rounds and didn't even work.

They were all armed like that, with a variety of weapons that were fucked up and semifunctional. This wasn't a regular unit that would be equipped with functional AK-47s and dozens of full magazines. We figured this was a Pathet Lao tracker element that was going to try to keep us in place until the main body arrived.

As we continued to look around we made a big discovery. One of them was wounded and alive! We thought, aha, a POW motherfucker! Information time.

I told one of the Yards to carry him. He was wounded more severely than we would have preferred, but he was conscious and we decided to go for it. We secured the prisoner, threw him over a shoulder, and headed for tall timber.

When you're deep in Indian country, I mean when you're really extended out there with just a small element, it's difficult to capture anyone. The enemy knows you're deep in his turf and realizes you can't have many supporting folks. And usually he's got much more firepower. So he's prepared to fight a lot harder because of these facts. I know lots of people who say, "Fuck no, it ain't difficult. You can capture anyone at any time. Just point a weapon at 'em." I'm here to tell you that ain't necessarily true.

Think about it.

You just don't walk up to a guy who's got a fully automatic weapon in his hands and say, "I'd like you to accompany me back to my base." Nine times out of ten a guy that you bring back has been wounded. Not severely wounded, because you want information from him, and a badly wounded guy might die before you get what he knows. So you only bring in soldiers who look like they're going to live.

The trouble with finding lightly wounded enemy is, hey, man, you're out there to kill them before they kill you. You don't shoot with the intention of just wounding them. You try to terminate their existence on earth. As a result, most guys who are hit have multiple wounds, severe wounds. Sometimes a limb will be severed. An M-16 round is an extremely punishing projectile that will either knock you on your back in a heartbeat, or go through you so fast your body won't even jerk on impact.

So we carried our prisoner with us as we traveled along the side of the mountain. We were on the move all day, stopping only once, briefly, to rest and eat. My leg was still hurting like a son of a bitch. I kept tightly wound strips of cloth around my calf to stop the bleeding. The tight bandages also added to my discomfort. I was taking tetracycline to try to kill any infection.

We took turns carrying our prisoner, and the excess baggage slowed us down considerably. We wanted to put as much distance as possible between us and Alpha 6. We were sure the enemy would not let us stroll out of his territory unmolested, so we moved with a sense of urgency.

We proceeded without incident the entire day and halted for the evening after humping long and hard. We secured our position deep in the forest and called it a day.

Morning found us making tracks in the direction of the frequently used trail we discovered on the way up to Alpha 6. We needed to get to the mountain opposite the one we were on, and that trail was between us and our destination.

We had reached the trail and were about to cross it when our prisoner died. That pissed us off no end. A short time earlier we'd made radio contact with our base, informing them that we had a prisoner. Hey, man, you were hot shit if you brought one back. Not only would we have gotten information from him, but we'd each receive two hundred dollars and a free thirty-day leave anywhere we wanted to go. And here we had lugged the motherfucker for God knows how many miles, and the asshole croaks.

I really don't know why I did it, but I told the Yards to just drop the dude by the side of the trail. I wasn't thinking clearly. Maybe the pain from my wound clouded my judgment, or perhaps I was just so frustrated he'd died. We should have hastily buried him somewhere, because his body would tip off the bad guys that we had been there.

Anyway, we dumped his body in plain sight and took off. We were trying to get extracted now. We contacted our base camp and told them I was hurt and that we'd stirred up the enemy who was undoubtedly coming after us. The camp said they couldn't get any choppers to us because the weather had them socked in. They told us to hang tight, that they might be able to swing it the next day.

Shit! We might not be around the next day.

We hung tight.

The next day arrived and we got the same story. The wind was now blowing like a son of a bitch. We were in the middle of a big-time storm. Rain came down constantly, and the temperature dropped dramatically. We were soaked and chilled to the bone. It went on and on.

We hung tight for five days.

The weather broke early in the morning on the fifth day. By that time my leg was killing me, and it looked extremely bad. I feared it was deeply infected and might have to be amputated if I didn't get it taken care of soon.

We started moving to a place where we could be extracted. As we walked we saw some enemy troops. They didn't see us. There was no exchange of rounds. We just kind of lay on the side of the hill and watched them pass right by us. We thought, that's cool. We won't fuck with them. We weren't in the best of shape.

After they passed, we moved out. We realized how sneaky we were getting when we started seeing game. We'd sneak up on deer and they wouldn't even see us. They'd just stand there, munching away. I was proud of our stealthy movements. Obviously we weren't making too much noise.

We moved at right angles to the enemy, and after much maneuvering we ended up at the same place where we'd crossed the trail and left the body. Only now, there was no body.

In its place were paw prints. Big ones.

I don't know if the animal got the body or not. The dead guy's buddies may have found him and took him away, with the beast merely happening upon the scent in that area. Regardless, the Yards got really excited. It was bad medicine. Any animal that eats human beings is bad medicine.

Several members of my element were excellent trackers. They squatted down by the prints, studying them very seriously. Then one of them pointed at the tracks, looked up at me and said, "Tiger." There was something in his voice, something about what had gone on, that indicated he was really spooked.

That's when I learned the reason why we encountered the punji stick barrier at Alpha 6 and why it was so wide.

We were in tiger country. We were so far in the wilderness that tigers were merely part of the wildlife. We hadn't seen any tigers during our mission. Now that I knew they were around I felt a chill rush up my spine. We could have been attacked during any of our overnight stops in the woods. A tiger could easily have slipped through our perimeter at any time, or even killed one of the sentries.

Tigers are unbelievably quiet and lightning quick. In the dark, we are at their mercy. Knowing this, the Vietnamese had constructed the barrier to keep tigers out of their position. It was very wide because a tiger can leap great distances, and if the barrier isn't deep enough the great cat will jump over it and get in your knickers. Not a pleasant thought, especially when you understand that a tiger can stalk so quietly that you'll never know he's there until he's on top of you. Then, of course, it's too late.

So by this time the Yards were really scared, saying the tiger was a bad omen and we were going to get our asses kicked soon. They were so convinced of it that even I became a little apprehensive. We gathered ourselves and once more set out for our designated extraction point.

I'll be a son of a bitch if we didn't run into a large group of enemy troops later that evening. I thought, oh, shit! Will the Yards' prophecy really come true?

It wasn't a big, sustained contact, but it was a vicious engagement. We expended quite a bit of ammo as we exchanged rounds. I don't know if we killed any of them, but they didn't get any of us. A couple of guys did, however, catch some fragmentation from an RPG-7 tank-killing round. The enemy fired several of those at us. Many people are surprised to hear that they would fire on us with a weapon designed to destroy tanks. My opinion of that is, a weapon is a weapon. The successful troops use everything at their disposal to secure victory. That includes us as well as them. Do you think an artillery round is any more "civilized" than a tank round?

They disengaged as the night closed in. I wondered why. Then I thought about the tiger. Surely the noise from all the weapons would scare off any tiger, right?

But it was quiet now.

We hit the extraction point the next morning after a short hump. I was glad to hear the beat of the blades as our transportation arrived. Less than half a minute later we were winging our way to safer turf, food, medical attention, and a much-needed rest.

We were all in one piece, thank God. There would be no fulfilling of prophecies that day.

OFF COURSE

Every once in a while we'd make a significant discovery due to a screwup. By this I mean that something within our control would not happen as planned, and yet we'd luck out and hit a jackpot. One such incident occurred deep in denied territory.

We were dropped off by chopper in some pretty remote bush late one evening. When we tried to take a bearing to fix our position on our map, we discovered that we'd been dropped off in the wrong place. We were so far off target that we didn't register anywhere on the map sheet we were carrying. We had no idea where we were.

We immediately got on the horn to the forward air controller and reported our situation. He told us, "I'm going to start at the center of where you were supposed to be dropped. I'll fly in an outward spiral and keep flying. When you see me, you tell me."

About an hour later I radioed him and said, "I think I hear an aircraft way off in the distance to my east." He continued to spiral, until a few minutes later I spotted him several miles away from our position. I let him know he was within sight, and eventually he passed over us. We signaled him with a mirror; he noted our location, figured out what neck of the woods we were in, and relayed the information to us. Unfortunately we didn't have the map sheet we needed to give us details of the terrain. But at least we now knew in what direction we needed to travel. More importantly, our support knew where we could be found.

We hadn't covered more than a half-mile when we came across a freshly cut, high-speed trail in the middle of some pretty dense jungle.

The branches of the trees directly above the trail had been laced together to form a living arch. From the air you couldn't see the trail, and you'd never have to replace the camouflage because it wouldn't die and discolor.

It was getting pretty dark right about then, so I decided that we'd wait until morning and set an ambush on the trail to see what we could pick up. We'd do a little fishing and see what we could land.

We slept on the side of a hill that night. The next morning we studied the trail. It ran steadily along the ridgeline; not on the crest of the ridgeline, but rather parallel to the crest, midway between the base and the top. I decided we'd position ourselves on the high ground and ambush down into the trail, firing from an advantageous location.

We approached the trail and began to prepare for our little surprise welcome. The Yards first crossed the trail and dropped their rucksacks off in the positions they were going to occupy for the ambush. After dumping their equipment they proceeded back down to the edge of the trail and moved a short distance up it to place their Claymore mines. I could only see a couple of guys doing this because of the denseness of the surrounding vegetation.

I was with one of my Yards, Hyuk—my point man—as I set up my Claymore in a concealed spot right next to the trail. We were on the right flank of the ambush. After arming the mine I moved to my ambush position, feeding wire out as I walked backward.

When I reached my position I sat down on the ground. Hyuk squatted beside me. I still had my rucksack on, so I leaned back to rest it on the ground and began to slip it off. As I turned my head to the left to remove a strap I happened to glance at Hyuk. His eyes were as big as saucers. Without moving a muscle he whispered hoarsely, "VC, VC."

I very slowly turned my head in the direction he was staring and I saw a dude standing between us and the Claymore. He was very close to the back side of the Claymore. I thought, What the fuck? At first I figured I was seeing things, that it was just one of my people. A split-second later I realized he was one of the bad guys. He had a weapon on his back and was starting to take it off his shoulder because he could see my people down the trail putting their mines up. He was a little confused by what he was seeing.

But obviously he hadn't seen me. Or my Claymore.

I quickly glanced to the side and noticed that there were more guys with him, moving very cautiously along the edge of the trail. They must have seen their man acting confused, because they crept up ever so slowly until they were about even with him.

After assessing the situation for all of five seconds, I reacted. I didn't even fire my weapon. I just quickly plugged the wire into the hand detonator, put a finger in my ear closest to the mine, put my shoulder up to the other ear, and squeezed the shit out of the handle.

I was only about fifteen meters away, sort of flanking the Claymore. He was standing roughly one meter to its rear. His buddies were slightly in front of, and off to the side of, the mine.

The explosion was deafening. The back blast blew his legs to shreds, knocking him flat and killing him. The rear of a Claymore is almost as formidable as the front, provided you're relatively close. Three of the guys who were in front of the mine were hit and dropped. The other three apparently didn't get hit and raced back up the trail the way they came.

As soon as the Claymore detonated, the Yards leapt into action. They moved in my direction, weapons at full port, searching for the trouble. By this time I had rolled onto my stomach and begun firing at the fleeing NVA. My folks opened up in the same area. We didn't hit any of them. Moments later they were gone.

We inspected the damage inflicted by the Claymore. Of the four bodies lying around, only one was still alive. At first I thought we could save him, but a closer look revealed we couldn't do anything for him. He hadn't been standing directly in front of the mine when it went off, but he had been just far enough in front of it that he caught several steel balls in his body. The only one that really did any damage was one that grazed him in the throat and cut his jugular vein. He rapidly bled to death before our eyes.

We started searching their pockets. We got some neat little trophies off them. It turned out they were NVA, not just some jerk-ass unit roaming the woods. It was in one of their pockets that we struck gold.

We found a morning report from one of the major NVA hospitals. It was a really important find, as it listed all the units the hospital was supporting in the area, what their basic health posture was, and so on. It even had some comments that some of the troops were down around the hospital malingering because they didn't want to go back to combat. It mentioned that they had to come up with some kind of plan to get them out of there, and that the units had better send somebody over to pick them up. Also stated was the fact that the hospital didn't have enough food to support all the troops hanging around. They were also pissed off because someone had stolen a .45 cal weapon.

As I said, it was a tremendous find, which gave us great insight into enemy's health, morale, and status of forces. What's more, we now had the location of a major hospital where we could plant spies to keep us informed of current events.

We had earned our pay for the day. We humped to our original insertion point without further incident. If it hadn't been for the screwed-up drop, we might never have found the high-speed trail and our little bonus, which we delivered into waiting hands later that evening.

Job well done. Take a break.

MEO TRIBESMEN

It was really an eye-opening experience working with the ethnic peoples of 'Nam and the surrounding countries. While operating in Laos I had the privilege of working with the original inhabitants of Laos, the Meo tribesmen. Like the Montagnards of Vietnam, the Meo people had been driven from their native lands. Neither the Laotians nor the Vietnamese had any respect for them, and consequently the Meo were extremely anti-Laotian and anti-Vietnamese.

One of the things I admired about these people as a whole was their willingness to do whatever you wanted done without question. They never complained or argued about a task or mission, no matter how insignificant or overwhelming the job may have seemed. They were steadfastly faithful and unwavering in their dedication to your cause. The following story is a radical illustration of these qualities.

I had just taken over an area of operations in Laos. I was in charge of a patrol consisting of one other American and about forty Meo tribesmen. The area we were patrolling was made up of very dense jungle covering uneven, mountainous terrain. The jungle had been deforested at one time and had grown back thicker than before, making the going tough. We were at an altitude of about three thousand to four thousand feet.

We were approximately ten miles from the base camp. We were doing our thing to ensure that the base wouldn't be hit. One night after we'd established our position I called all my leaders in for a meeting. I was running the patrol like I was a company commander and certain Meo soldiers were my platoon leaders. So I gathered them together and put out what we were going to do during the next day's patrol.

After the meeting I offhandedly mentioned to one of my platoon leaders, "Damn, I sure could use an orange soda." I said it very casually, knowing there were none to be had.

My Meo platoon leader looked at me and said, "You want orange soda?"

I just looked at him and smiled. "Yeah, I sure do."

He said to me, "You want one, we get it."

I gave him a puzzled look. I wondered what he meant by his statement. Where was he going to get it? I was certain none of his troops were carrying any soda, and there sure as hell wasn't any grocery store around.

He immediately called over two of his troops. It was about seven o'clock in the evening. Visibility was low and getting worse by the moment. He gave the two guys instructions to get me some orange soda.

I quickly told him I was just joking and asked him not to send his guys anywhere. He said everything was OK, and sent his people off to get me some orange soda. I watched the two troops walk through our perimeter and vanish into the bush. I had long since learned that once tribesmen make up their minds to do something it was nearly impossible to alter their course of action. So I didn't protest further.

That evening we made radio contact with our base camp and all seemed in order. I then went to sleep, forgetting all about the two guys my platoon leader had sent out into the night.

The next morning, while I was eating some breakfast, I watched two people walk through the perimeter. They walked at a slow, steady pace directly over to me as I sat in the leader's area where I had my gear. It didn't dawn on me who they were until they got close enough for me to recognize them. They were the two guys that my platoon leader had sent out in search of the object of my craving.

And son of a bitch if they didn't have orange sodas in their ruck!

These guys had made their way across mountainous jungle terrain in the dead of night to our base camp. They didn't even take a compass with them. They had picked up some orange sodas and brought them all the way back to me.

Unbelievable.

The most amazing thing about the whole affair was their attitude. They weren't uptight or pissed off. They didn't give me a look of contempt or hatred. They simply did what they were told. And after traveling twenty miles round-trip they didn't think anything about saddling up and moving out with us that same day. Can you believe it?

That incident ranks as the all-time greatest display of willing obedience I've ever witnessed.

GRENADES

I'd like to talk a little bit about grenades: specifically, the effects of a grenade exploding in water. Now most people are aware that a grenade is an ass-kicker on dry land. However, contrary to the "nuclear" grenades they throw in the movies, grenades have a relatively limited kill radius. Anyone within ten meters of an exploding grenade will more than likely have his day ruined big-time. Within ten to fifteen meters he'll catch some frag, but it might not stop him from attempting to cause you grief. Outside of fifteen meters it's questionable whether or not he'll get hit at all.

A grenade in water is a different beast altogether. Most of us have seen movies where troops are crossing a waist-deep stream and a grenade or mortar is lobbed into the water in their general vicinity. It blows up, sending a shower of water high into the air as the troops keep advancing. The soldiers show no sign of pain or injury. What the hell, it exploded in the water, right? We all know how water slows down bullets just a few feet below the surface. So the water must have smothered the frag, right? Probably so, but one small detail is overlooked.

The concussion.

One day I got Hines and Burko and a few Yards together, and we all went down to the river that ran close by our compound at Kontum. We were going to fuck around a little and do some fishing at the same time. Only we wouldn't be using poles and bait to catch the scaly inhabitants of the river. We took along some grenades for that purpose.

We got down to the river's edge, and I got ready to throw the first grenade. This particular river was approximately fifty feet wide and about twenty feet deep. It also had a moderate current. I checked up and down the river and lobbed the frag into the water about midstream.

It entered the water with a *ploop* and settled to the bottom. Four seconds later it went off. It made a high-pitched cracking *smack* sound and the surface of the slowly churning river suddenly turned to glass for a split-second. Then a geyser erupted and shot about twenty feet into the air. As the water came raining down, the river returned to its normal state.

Not long after the explosion all sorts of fish came floating to the surface. The grenade's concussion wave had killed them. I sent the Yards out to retrieve them as they were slowly swept along the bank by the current. I chucked a few more frags into the general area and got the same results.

After a while we took our boots and socks off and waded barefoot along the edge of the river. Soon I came upon a place that looked like an ideal spot for a little more "fishing." I found a small rock that protruded above the water, and I stood on it. I yelled at the guys to get out of the river because I was going to throw a frag. Hines found a rock and climbed out of the water. Burko continued to stand in the ankle-deep shallows near the bank. I warned Burko again.

"Hey, man, get the hell outta the water. I'm gonna throw this son of a bitch."

Burko just smiled and waved me off. "Go ahead, throw it. I'm OK."

I cautioned him one more time. "Hey, I'm serious. You need to get up on the bank or something."

"Don't worry. I'll be fine," he stated with a laugh as he crossed his arms in an act of finality.

"OK, suit yourself," I said as I chucked the frag about thirty meters up the middle of the river.

The grenade made its way to the bottom and exploded. The river's surface went glassy for a moment, and just about the time the column of water erupted skyward I heard a high-pitched scream. I quickly jerked around and saw Burko lying in the mud by the river bank. Hines and I went running over to him.

"What happened, man?" Hines and I said in unison.

He writhed in the mud, clutching a foot in each hand. He looked up at us for a second and yelled, "My feet! My feet! It feels like someone cut them off!"

Did we give him any sympathy? Hell no! We laughed ourselves sick. He was lying there in obvious pain and we, like good friends, added insult to injury by laughing at his plight.

"'Go ahead. Throw it. I'm OK'," I mocked in between laughs. Hines kept trying to say something, but he couldn't because he was doubled over with laughter, tears streaming down his face. Burko was moaning and groaning and yelling at us for not helping him. The Yards scratched their heads and must have thought the three of us were crazy.

After several minutes of gut-busting laughter we regained our composure and helped Burko stand up. His feet were a light shade of black and blue. You could definitely tell they had sustained injury. We put his arms over our shoulders and assisted him back to the camp. He couldn't walk right for about two weeks afterward.

We laughed at the time, but we really shouldn't have. A little stupidity mixed with carelessness resulted in an injury. What had happened was serious business. Did it make us more cautious when we screwed around with grenades later on? I don't believe so; however, the incident *did* give us a new perspective on the destructive powers of a grenade when it's thrown into water.

THE WRONG PLACE AT THE WRONG TIME

As the leader of recon team Vermont in the MACV-SOG, SOA CCC organization, I had total control of every mission my team undertook. When I say total control, I mean *total* control. All units working terrain adjacent to our target area and departure/return route were notified that they were to stay clear of our AO, which generally would encompass several square miles. It was like an off-limits corridor in the jungle. No friendly troops could move through the AO; no friendly air strikes could take place until the mission was complete. No friendly support—period—would take place in our AO unless I specifically requested it.

There were reasons for these restrictions. When we were out there doing our thing we wanted to be sure that the only other people moving in our area were enemy soldiers. That way, there would be no hesitation when it came time to take them under fire. A chance encounter would mean instant action instead of first trying to determine whether or not they were friendlies. That small moment of indecision could be the death of us. So the no-friendlies-in-the-area restriction made our job easier: if it moved, shoot it.

Another reason we kept other friendly units out of our AO was that we sometimes dressed in enemy uniforms and carried enemy weapons. This little bit of deception would cause the enemy to hesitate if he spotted us. He wouldn't take us under fire right away because he couldn't be sure of what he was seeing. Of course, if he looked closely enough he'd see a six-foot-three white guy in a group of Yards and realize what was going on. But hopefully his momentary hesitation would allow us to see him before he made up his mind to grease us. We, of course, would have no such hesitation.

Once we were returning from a successful reconnaissance of a target in Laos when we ran into an ambush. We had "crossed the fence" back into 'Nam about nine o'clock that evening. We were moving alongside a well-worn trail when my point man stopped and started melting into the ground. Immediately the rest of the team froze and got down. I got into a crouch and kind of duck-walked slowly up to the point man, until my face was about a foot from the back of his head. He swiveled his face toward mine and whispered, "Ambush."

The hair on the back of my neck stood on end. He no sooner said "ambush" than I noticed a massive amount of movement to my left. At the same time I turned my head in that direction and saw several silhouetted bodies darting between the trees. I distinctly heard a bolt being drawn back.

Without thinking I pivoted my weapon to my left and opened up. All hell broke loose. Everyone in my team followed my lead and fired a tremendous volley into the left side of the trail. As we fired we moved perpendicular to the trail, trying to get into some cover on the right side of the path. We knew that there was a small stream running parallel to the trail about twenty meters away. We scrambled for the stream bank.

I was shocked at the amount of firepower the enemy had. Their return fire dwarfed our initial burst, and we somehow managed to traverse the twenty or so meters to the stream without injury. The stream bank was only two feet high, but it was enough to lie down behind as lead rained over our heads, destroying the surrounding plant life and anything else in its way.

As soon as we rolled into the stream I got on the horn to our headquarters and informed them of our situation. We were too close to the enemy to call in artillery. We'd have to move farther back or sit tight and slug it out. At that moment we couldn't leave the protection of the stream bank because of the volume of fire coming our way. We were pinned down. We really didn't have a choice.

We got our weapons on-line and fired back. It was utter chaos. Tracers lit the night as both sides brought everything they had to bear on each other. It was obvious that their element was far larger than ours. During the engagement my point man and I discovered the location of their machine gun and we concentrated our fire on it. Eventually we knocked it out. But it didn't slow them down much.

The exchange lasted about ten minutes, which seems like an eternity when someone's firing nonstop at you. I was contemplating leaving the relative safety of the stream to withdraw farther to the rear when I clearly heard a voice from the enemy side yell, "Motherfucker, my M-16's jammed!"

It was an American voice!

I immediately told my team to cease fire.

The other side continued to fire at us after we stopped, but then they realized we weren't shooting anymore and they also ceased fire. They must have thought we were dead.

In the intervening silence I yelled, "Who the fuck are you guys?"

I'm sure they were just as startled to hear an American voice as I had been moments earlier. Someone from the other side shouted back, "Motherfucker, who the hell are you?"

I said, "Shit, man, we're a fuckin' friendly patrol!"

"Cocksucker, you fired us up, you sons of bitches!" came the response.

I was getting angry. "What the fuck you doin' in our AO?"

This verbal exchange lasted for about five to ten minutes, during which time nobody moved. Obviously neither side trusted the other. The fact that I spoke English didn't mean we were friendly, and the same held true for them. The other guy and I could have been deserters.

The officer in charge of their platoon threatened to bring artillery in on us, and I did likewise. Nobody wanted to take any chances in the middle of the night, so we decided to hold our ground until the morning.

When morning came and there was plenty of light, I got up from my position and approached them. I carried my weapon with me, muzzle pointing backward and the butt facing forward. Even though I thought they were Americans, I would not approach them weaponless. I never, ever moved without my calling card, regardless of the situation.

As I drew closer I could see by the looks on their faces and their rigid body postures that they were very apprehensive. After all, I was dressed as an enemy soldier. When my Yards got up one by one and followed me, I could tell the tension was really running high. I talked to them the entire time, reassuring them that we were friendlies. And as we got nearer to them they clearly saw who we were and they relaxed somewhat. We finally entered their position after several tense minutes.

They were an infantry platoon, about forty strong. We had walked into their position the previous night just as they were arriving. Fortunately for us we'd entered the site before they had a chance to establish the ambush. If they'd put out any Claymores, my team and I would most likely have been wiped out.

Unfortunately they took some casualties. It was a very sad sight to see three dead soldiers stretched out in the grass. Several more were wounded. It was a terrible feeling, knowing that some gross miscalculation had resulted in the senseless deaths of several young men. Their deaths were accidental, but that fact didn't lessen the pain.

I found the platoon leader and platoon sergeant huddled over a map. The lieutenant was obviously scared shitless. When they looked up at me I could see by their expressions that they were already aware of their mistake. A navigational error had put them about five kilometers off course and well inside our AO where they didn't belong.

What was there to say?

Our choppers picked us up about an hour after I talked with the lieutenant and his platoon sergeant. As we flew away, I saw their medevac choppers on the horizon.

I don't know what happened to the platoon leader and the platoon sergeant. In fact, I never heard about the incident after that day.

Life goes on.

BETWEEN A ROCK AND A HARD PLACE

Hines and I did many things together during our time in Special Forces. We cheated death on numerous occasions and sat around laughing about it afterward. When people go through intensely trying times together they usually develop a very strong bond. We were close and functioned well as a team, so many times we'd work alongside each other during an operation.

Once the two of us were sent to a mission support site, or MSS, on a classified mission. We were the only Americans at the camp, and we were in charge of one hundred Yards. The MSS was situated at a remote location many miles from friendly confines. The nearest friendly force was an artillery battalion some fifteen miles away. After that we'd have to travel a good fifty miles before we'd run into somebody from our side.

Our fifty-meter-square camp sat on a finger located three-quarters of the way up the side of a large mountain. On the opposite side of this mountain lived the enemy, who were well aware of our camp's existence but left us alone. You see, we weren't a direct threat to their operation. They realized we didn't have a big enough force to inflict much damage on them. Although we didn't have a large number of troops, we were heavily armed, so the enemy kept their distance. To ensure that they stayed away from us, we ran continuous patrols throughout the countryside on our side of the mountain.

We'd been at the MSS for approximately four months doing our usual patrolling routine when we got the word that we were going to be involved in a major operation. Hines and I, both E-5s, would take a reconnaissance platoon of 30 Yards and work in concert with a Mobile Strike Force, or "Mike Force," of 150 Yards and 5 Americans, which included an E-7 and an E-6, moving up from the south. Our mission: eliminate the enemy on the other side of the mountain.

It would be no easy task. The mountain's surface was literally covered with enormous boulders, most of which were about the size of a three-bedroom house. Some were far larger than most houses. Trees and brush poked through and around the tremendous stones. Patrolling the area was physically demanding and required extreme concentration because the ground was very uneven and covered by smaller boulders and rocks. Making matters worse was the fact that the enemy had been in the area for a long period of time and had merged into his surroundings. Put another way, he was deeply entrenched among the boulders.

The Mike Force was inserted about ten miles away from the foot of our mountain. The plan was for them to move along the mountain's base on our side, sweep around, and assault through the valley on the enemy's side of the mountain. Hopefully they would catch the enemy unaware and wreak havoc on them. They had a battalion-sized Mike Force in reserve, ready to deploy if needed.

Our part in the operation was one of diversion and harassment. We were to go over the top of the mountain and come down on them. Since our force was relatively small we would draw their attention and keep them busy while the Mike Force came up from the valley.

We climbed to the top of the mountain as the American-led Mike Force made its way around the mountain. When we reached the top we stood fast until we received word from the Mike Force that they'd reached the valley and encountered no opposition. After surveying the enemy's territory from the valley, the Americans in charge of the force altered their plan slightly. They dispatched the 150 Yards to the opposite end of the valley to set up a massive area ambush along a huge ridgeline connected to our mountain. They concluded that my recon element would be able to flush the enemy from their rocky lair and drive them south along the ridgeline headlong into the waiting ambush. It was a rather ambitious plan for the thirty Yards I was traveling with.

After the Mike Force was on its way, they had a chopper come in and pick up the two Americans and fly them to our location. It had been decided by the lieutenant colonel in charge of the operation that my platoon needed more experienced leadership to complete the mission. Therefore, the E-7 and E-6 from the Mike Force were to assume control of my platoon.

I was upset. I felt I was best qualified to lead the platoon, even though I was only an E-5 and they were superior in rank. I'd been in 'Nam almost three years, and they each had less than five months in country.

I didn't like it, but I had no choice. Since the chopper was coming to our location on top of the mountain, we had to clear an LZ for it. Using hatchets and explosives we cut down just enough trees to permit the chopper to land. Soon after the area was cleared, the chopper arrived.

Accompanying the NCOs was the lieutenant colonel in charge. He personally flew with the NCOs to inform me they were taking over. I guess he wanted to ensure that I didn't give them a hard time. I wouldn't have anyway. I was pissed as hell, but I would have cooperated without his intervention. I just wanted to make sure the mission was a success, and I would do my best regardless of the role I played. But I wouldn't like it.

The two NCOs assumed command, and the lieutenant colonel flew off to the MSS. Orders were issued, and we were underway down the mountain.

Evening was setting in, so we stopped and established a patrol base among the towering rocks. Now basically I'm a nosy bastard. While

Hines and I were sitting around bullshitting, we noticed that we could see underneath a huge boulder several paces from us. Naturally I had to investigate.

Hines and I crawled—walked, actually—up under this boulder and came out on the opposite side. The tunnel bored under the stone was easily big enough to drive a car through. When we came out on the other side, we discovered more boulders and more tunnels. So we continued our little odyssey.

I don't know how long we'd been doing this before I realized we were a good distance from the platoon. I came to this conclusion when we rounded the corner of a cliff and found an oil-soaked rag on the ground. Uh-oh. Some enemy soldier had used it to wipe his weapon down. The very next corner we turned revealed an enemy campfire.

It was still burning.

My asshole slammed shut. We got the pucker factor big-time. We quickly backed around the boulder and looked at each other. I automatically reached for my weapon which wasn't there. Hines looked at me and whispered in a panicky voice, "Shit, man, you don't even have your weapon!"

I noted the absence of his weapon. "Well fuck it, man, neither do you!"

He jerked his head downward and threw his hands out to his sides as he realized he was naked, too.

In an incredibly stupid move that could have spelled disaster for us, we'd left our weapons behind. It was not intentional, simply an act of forgetfulness in the face of impending adventure. It was the first time since I'd been in 'Nam that I moved anywhere in the bush without my weapon. I'd never make that mistake again.

We turned around and hauled ass back to our base. We'd used the better part of the evening's light when we crawled through the numerous tunnels and rocks on our way out. Fortunately I have a good memory and sense of direction because the maze seemed more extensive on the way back, plus there was a lot less light. We made it back before total darkness descended.

It was interesting to note that nobody missed us or saw us come through the perimeter. It made me realize how easy it would be for somebody really familiar with the area to sneak inside our position.

Not long after we returned from our sojourn, someone came up on the platoon's radio and said, "Be advised. We just received an intel report that there's a large group of enemy troops moving in your direction, and they're going to kick your ass!"

That got our adrenaline flowing as we got into a fighting posture. A few minutes later the lieutenant colonel at the MSS called and said, "Hey, listen, it'd be a good idea if you called in a defensive concentration of artillery fire to cover you tonight in case the shit hits the fan."

The NCOs running the platoon looked at each other. I could see them thinking, defensive concentration of artillery fire? Shit, this could get bad. What the fuck do we do?

The E-7 thought it over for a minute then turned to me. "Say, listen, Miller," he started off. I knew what would follow. "We know you been around a lot longer, and you can probably call this fire in a lot better'n we can." The bottom line was that neither he nor the E-6 felt they'd had enough experience to do it. The guys who took over the platoon from me because of their "experience" didn't even know how to perform one of the most basic and necessary functions of survival in combat.

Here was the perfect opportunity for me to give them a hard time. I could've said, "Well, not really, Sarge. After all, ya know, you're an E-7 and I'm just an E-5. You're runnin' the platoon because of all your experience. I'm just one of the guys." But of course I realized that the artillery fire was our trump card in this deadly hand, so there was no time to fuck around.

I said, "OK, give me the fuckin' radio." I took the mike and called for a fire mission. This is what happens in a situation like this: Since it is nighttime, the artillery battalion fires one round of white phosphorous (WP) explosive—also known as "Wilson Pickett" or "Willie Peter"—and I spot it. I call back to the artillery battalion and give them adjustments based on where the round landed. They adjust fire and put out another round. I spot it and make further adjustments as necessary. The object of this drill is to get them to drop a round slightly in front of our position. Once the round hits where I want it to, I tell them so. Now the artillery battalion has a fix on exactly what area they need to blow the shit out of if we call for a defensive fire.

So they put the first round out. They told me, "Shot," meaning the round was on the way. Seconds later they called me back and said, "Splash," meaning the round had landed. They knew when it landed based on the shot trajectory and speed of the round.

The only trouble was that I didn't see anything. I waited, and a few seconds later, way, way, way off in the distance I heard a soft, quiet *boom*. It had to have landed miles away because it was WP—at night—and I couldn't see it. But I heard it.

So I called back. "Red Rooster, this is Slashing Tiger. I'd like to make a bold adjustment. Drop one thousand." I'd just told the artillery guys to shorten the distance of the round by one thousand meters to bring it closer to us.

They did so and put out another round. Once again, way off in the distance, I heard a tiny *boom*. I still couldn't see the round.

I couldn't figure out what the hell was going on. That round should have been much closer. I got on the horn again and asked for another bold adjustment of one thousand meters.

Shot. Splash. This time I could see some of the glow from the WP, but it was still very far away. I was baffled. I'd just brought the round in more than a mile from the original shot. I knew that the artillery battery had our basic location. They couldn't or shouldn't have been that far off with the first round. Something was wrong.

I made two more bold adjustments and the last round was much closer but still not close enough. Four shots and I still wasn't targeted. It should never have taken that many rounds. I just started calling for my fifth adjustment when the lieutenant colonel at the MSS who'd been monitoring our net came on line and said, "Slashing Tiger, this is Lethal Weapon. Don't you know where the hell you are?"

I responded that we knew exactly where we were, but it was difficult to make adjustments in mountainous terrain. I called in the fire mission and asked for an adjustment of five hundred meters.

No sooner did I complete the call than the sound of incoming artillery filled my ears, followed by a tremendous explosion as the round landed at the edge of our perimeter. Hot frag saturated the air as the ground shook violently. I got on the radio and yelled, "Check fire! Check fire!"

I was shaken. Fortunately everyone in the platoon was down under cover and in their fighting positions because we expected to get attacked. Therefore the round produced no casualties.

I had not expected the round to land as close as it did. It was an accident. But after a minute the other Americans came up to me and said, "Hot damn! You really know your shit. Put that motherfucker right on target!" They didn't realize I hadn't planned it that way.

What I found out later was that the valley floor undulated like a roller coaster. The rounds were actually falling into the depressions of the rolling terrain, thereby obscuring my vision and deadening the sound. When I saw the next-to-last round impact near the base of the mountain, it looked to be about one thousand meters away from our position. I called for a drop of five hundred meters for safety reasons. I had intended to make one more adjustment after that to bring it more accurately on target.

What I wasn't thinking about was the fact that I was looking down a steep slope and not across horizontal ground. The angle of the mountain face was such that my horizontal adjustment of five hundred meters was enough to bring the round a thousand meters up the face of the slope into our perimeter.

For once I was relieved to see that all my efforts went for naught as nothing happened that night. The following morning we spent our time patrolling the enemy's side of the mountain.

We'd spent most of the day scoping out the terrain to no avail when I turned to one of my guys and said, "I smell shit."

Sure enough, we found a latrine after a careful search of the area. We knew that the latrine would be close to where the enemy lived. That realization heightened our alert posture, and we started moving very cautiously.

Soon we ran across baskets of fresh fruit gathered from the surrounding jungle. But still there were no signs of enemy troops or their dwellings. We continued at a slow and methodical pace, expecting at any minute to turn a corner and run smack into a pack of hostile folks. We operated in a state of high tension that turned out to be unwarranted by the end of the day. We didn't encounter any opposition or find their hideouts. We made camp for the night.

The next day one of the Yards on my left flank started yelling and opened up on something. A second later I saw this guy run across my front and disappear into a hole. I quickly ran to the spot where he'd vanished. I signaled for my folks to surround the area and provide security.

The opening into the rock was approximately eight feet high and wide enough to drive two cars through side by side. I strained to make out any sounds coming from within but heard nothing. I got low and glanced around the side, but it was pitch-black and I saw nothing. I got on the ground and crawled into the opening.

I moved slowly and noiselessly on my stomach, letting my eyes get accustomed to the dark. After a couple of minutes I had maneuvered to the end of the tunnel. Before me was a large room. I couldn't make out much detail because of the darkness, but I knew the room was vast. At the other end was the outline of another tunnel which angled up sharply.

I was just lying there trying to decide what to do next when one of the Americans behind me turned on a flashlight. Before I knew it I was silhouetted in the beam of light.

Suddenly a shot rang out from the darkened room. The round hit well in front of me and deflected away; however, it threw a whole bunch of little rocks that punctured my face, causing it to bleed profusely.

I turned around and screamed, "Turn that motherfucker *off*!" When the guy saw my bloody face in the flashlight beam he hollered to someone behind him. Outside the entrance to the tunnel I heard the RTO immediately inform the MSS I'd been shot in the head.

I quickly withdrew from the tunnel and came out smoking. I was pissed off because of the incredibly stupid incident with the flashlight. I walked over to the RTO who looked at me like he was seeing a ghost. Somebody at the MSS was asking the location of my body and if the platoon had recovered it. I grabbed the hand set from the RTO and said, "Fuck it, man, I'm still alive!" I went on to tell them what happened.

When I finished on the radio the medic looked at my face. There were no serious injuries, so he cleaned it up a bit and put a drop of iodine on each cut. I looked like I had measles.

We went back into the tunnel and flooded the room, expecting a fight. None was forthcoming. Whoever fired the shot at me was gone. So was everyone else.

One thing became apparent to me as we nosed around. The enemy had abandoned the position in haste. We found hammocks, clothes, and cooking utensils. Then we found a massive ammo storage cache off the main room. It was half full of ordnance. One thing I'd learned during my time in 'Nam was that the enemy never left anything behind when they abandoned a location, unless they hadn't been aware we were coming and were pressured into fleeing quickly.

The farther we moved down the face of the mountain, the more vacant enemy positions we discovered. We found several areas where large concentrations of enemy soldiers had been sleeping under gigantic boulders. Enough dirt had been excavated from under the rocks so that entire platoons would be able to rest without fear of detection or artillery. The more we searched, the more it seemed like the entire lower half of the mountain was an underground enemy complex with a roof of thick stones.

It started getting dark, so we set up camp. Outside of the one guy we'd shot at and the one round shot at me, we hadn't encountered any enemy activity during our few days on that side of the mountain.

What we didn't know at the time was that we'd run a large enemy group out of the immediate area. Their unit was far bigger than our platoon-sized element, and either they overestimated our strength or simply chose not to engage us. Whatever the reason, they departed the AO very quickly. Apparently they circled around one end of the platoon and got above us on the mountain ridgeline, just as we planned it. Once they cleared us they probably assumed they were home free and moved out smartly. But when they did that, they ran right into the 150 Yards who were waiting for them.

About a kilometer away we saw flares dot the night sky as tracers streaked the darkness and explosions destroyed the peaceful silence. The sounds of a tremendous battle filled the valley.

When all was said and done the Yards had killed some twenty enemy troops and captured two recoilless rifles, a heavy mortar, and other significant items. We lost five Yards with several more wounded. The majority of the enemy soldiers managed to scatter and escape, but it was nonetheless a successful ambush for our side.

During the next couple of days we continued our sweep of the mountain and the adjacent valley. We encountered stiff opposition on a few occasions but dealt with it through a combination of sheer guts and awesome Cobra gunship firepower.

After we'd cleared the mountainside of all resistance we had bags of CS powder flown to our location. The bags resembled sacks of cement. We put the CS throughout the underground complex and blew up the bags by placing explosives under them. The explosions caused the CS powder to saturate the tunnels and rooms. The dampness under the rocks would hold in the CS for a long time and thus make the complex unusable. Nobody would be moving back into it any time soon.

The lieutenant colonel from the MSS flew in at the conclusion of our mission and extended his congratulations for a job well done. He pulled the E-7 and E-6 out of my platoon and put them back in the Mike Force. They were extracted the next morning after we all enjoyed a relaxing evening of leisurely chow and bullshitting.

As for us, we humped our way back to the MSS after the Mike Force was picked up. Hines and I hung around the MSS for another four months before our services were required elsewhere.

EASY CAPTURE

I've talked somewhat about prisoners of war and the difficulties associated with capturing one. But there were very rare occasions when they just sort of fell into our hands due to quirks of fate.

I was running a patrol in the northern part of South Vietnam in the I Corps region when we came upon an expanse of land that resembled a city park. The large trees in the area were well spaced out and the ground was covered with a short, fine grass. It was a pleasant-looking place and seemed rather peaceful. However, I'd been around long enough to know that appearances were usually deceiving, especially in this part of the country.

Open areas always made me slightly nervous. You were simply too good a target when there was little vegetation to conceal your movements. I far preferred being in some moderately dense jungle where I could blend in with the surroundings.

We quickly moved through the "park" and discovered a winding trail that cut a wide swath through the short grass. Trails always aroused my suspicions, so I decided to follow it. We were about ten meters away from the edge of the surrounding jungle, so we got into the bush to cloak our presence and followed along the trail.

We were moving easily, really taking our time, when up ahead where the trail took a sharp right turn we noticed an enemy troop sitting at the base of a tree. He was just lounging there, looking very casual and relaxed.

We froze. Where there was one there were bound to be more. I decided we'd hold our position and observe the area for a while. We didn't need to rush into anything we couldn't handle.

We must have remained motionless for almost an hour. We didn't dare move for fear that we might have been really close to a large unit. Meanwhile, this guy—who was seventy meters to our front—didn't do much of anything. He remained in the same basic position as the one he was in when we discovered him. All he did was turn his head from side to side occasionally.

After seeing no signs of other enemy soldiers, I decided we'd move closer for a better look at this guy. I was puzzled and wary as hell. We moved deeper into the bush to afford us more concealment and started moving forward. Our movements were very slow and cautious. I still suspected there was a large body of enemy soldiers in the immediate area and we were walking into a trap. Although we were now farther away from the edge of the jungle, we could still see our target. We continued to monitor him for any sudden movement.

We ended up almost directly across the trail from the enemy soldier, no more than twenty-five meters from his position. At first I felt uncomfortable at that distance. We were too damn close. And as I examined the solitary figure from close range I began to realize that something was definitely out of order.

First of all I didn't see his weapon anywhere. In fact, outside of his uniform I didn't see any equipment, period. Then it dawned on me that he wasn't squatting like Orientals do when they rest. He was sitting on his ass with his legs stretched out straight in front of him, and his back was against the tree. His arms rested at his sides with his hands lying on the ground, palms up. What appeared from a distance to be a state of relaxation now seemed like a state of listlessness. He projected a dazed appearance. He looked directly at us at one point, but either didn't see us or didn't care that we were there.

Still suspecting a trap, we sat there for a long time, trying vainly to detect any imminent danger. Nothing happened. Finally I could wait no longer.

I passed the word to my folks that I was going to move in on the dude. I assigned everyone a sector of fire to cover me and both ends of the trail. Once everybody was in position I made my move.

I low-crawled forward through the tangled brush until I was directly at the seam of the jungle and the "park." I would have to traverse about fifteen meters of open space in order to reach the enemy soldier. If any enemy troops had the area under observation I would be dead meat as soon as I stepped out of hiding. I inhaled deeply and took a final look around. Still nothing.

I went for it.

I rolled over on my side, curled up, rocked to my knees, and stood as I aimed my weapon dead on target. As soon as I was erect I quickly covered the intervening distance, keeping my eyes and weapon fixed on the motionless figure by the tree. My entire body was stiff with tension as I double-timed across the grass. Any moment I expected the shit to hit the fan.

When I got right up to him I finally understood what was going on. Suddenly all hostile thoughts fled my mind. All the tension and aggressiveness drained from my body. I just stood there staring at him as I slowly lowered my weapon's muzzle to the ground.

He was sick. He was really sick.

He was so sick it made me feel bad. It almost made me hurt.

I motioned for the rest of the patrol to join me. When they did, I sent two people up each end of the trail to provide security. I then had my medic check him over.

He was dying from hepatitis. His eyes and skin were bright yellow. He had peed and shit all over himself. The disease was in its advanced stages, and there was nothing we could do to save him.

I told the medic to try and pump some fluid into his dehydrated body to ease some of his suffering. He couldn't find a vein, so he had to do some minor surgery to get one. He eventually got a vein and started an IV.

Meanwhile I radioed for an extraction. We made a stretcher out of our shirts and carried him to the LZ about four hundred meters away. Our trip to the extraction point was uneventful, and shortly after our arrival we were winging our way to the rear.

Doctors at the base tried to save his life, but their attempts were futile. Obviously we were trying to keep him alive for more than simply humanitarian reasons. He was a potential source of information. Still, he was a human being, and at that moment I felt genuinely sorry for him.

Before he died, he told us a story about how his fellow soldiers treated him when he got sick. They began to steal his equipment because he was too ill to defend himself. When his illness got worse, they took his food and water. Finally, when he was unable to keep up, they took his weapon and remaining equipment and left him to die by the tree where we found him.

After telling us that story he voluntarily told us what unit he was from and where they were going. He wasn't simply a Joe Blow; he was a staff sergeant who knew the location of the next cache. His confessions came only minutes prior to his death. I guess he wanted us to kick his "buddies'" asses for the way they treated him. We happily obliged.

He was part of a heavy-weapons battalion. We put together a large force and flew out to the battalion's cache. We arrived there long before the heavy-weapons battalion did; they had to hump to it, and we went by air. The cache site harbored massive quantities of rice and water. We also found large deposits of ammo, medical supplies, and other stuff.

We captured as much as we could while destroying the remainder. A big break for us came when we discovered some information that gave—among other things—the location of the next cache.

Back at the base they mounted a massive force consisting of two regular infantry battalions and inserted them at the coordinates we gave them for the next cache. The enemy would undoubtedly have to beat feet to that location once they discovered their chow and other supplies had been destroyed. They would surely be out of food by the time they reached our handiwork and in desperate need of more.

I wasn't on the operation that went to the next cache, but I know that a big asskick ensued. I don't know any details other than that it was a tremendous battle, and we gave better than we got.

And it all happened because one guy's fellow soldiers shit on him. As the line in the song goes, "Who's sorry now?"

A WALK ON THE WILD SIDE

Every once in a while my superiors would loan me to another unit for the purpose of teaching patrolling techniques or leading a mission of particular importance or difficulty.

I had quite a bit of combat experience by the time my bosses started sharing my expertise, and I'll admit that I was a cocky bastard. I figured I was the voice of authority since I'd been in 'Nam much longer and had seen more combat than just about anybody I came across. So when

I spoke I expected people to listen. When they didn't listen, or when they disagreed with me—whether rightly or wrongly—I would get terribly upset. To make matters worse, many soldiers who outranked me resented the fact that a junior guy should be telling them their business. That type of attitude further irritated me.

I was sent to an operation in the Central Highlands of 'Nam that consisted of approximately twenty American and fifty South Vietnamese officers and NCOs. Their camp was rectangular in shape, measuring one hundred meters on each side. The camp's mission was to train the local population, which was like the National Guard of the area. They were commonly referred to as the Regional Forces/Popular Forces (RF/PF).

While I was there two lieutenants kept talking shit to me about how they wanted to kick-off on the enemy's ass. I continued to tell them that, as it was, they didn't do enough around the area to keep the enemy away. I told them the enemy was very close.

Whenever I'd go out with them on patrol, I'd find all kinds of subtle and not-so-subtle indications of enemy activity near the camp. Once I found an enemy soldier's rucksack—complete with diary—in a hole that several guys in the patrol had just walked by. A rucksack! They never even considered that something might be in that hole, so they never looked. When you start finding personal gear you realize the owner can't be too far away. Another time I found the shipping and storage plug to an 82mm mortar, a Russian-made weapon.

I was constantly pointing out these things, but they seemed to turn a deaf ear. I eventually concluded that they simply didn't *want* to find any signs of the enemy. If they'd had proof that the enemy was in their area, they'd have had to do something about it, and I don't believe they were willing to do anything that involved direct contact with the enemy. I'm not implying that they were afraid; I just feel they didn't want to make an effort to engage the enemy.

So one day I got into a big argument with the two lieutenants. They were running their mouths about wanting to kick some ass. I got really pissed off and said, "Hey, if you wanna kick some ass they're right outside the fuckin' wire. Don't talk no shit to me. Get out there and mix it up with them."

Well, they got pissed off at me because I was that arrogant mother-fucker who'd actually seen combat and was rubbing their noses in it. We started hollering and swearing back and forth, until finally I grabbed my M-16, put on a 40mm grenade bandolier filled with four 20-round M-16 magazines, and stormed out of the camp.

The camp was situated on an open piece of terrain with an expanse of rice paddies to our front. Off to our west was a mountain range. Not too far behind the installation was a little ville which sat in a sparsely wooded area. It was typical of the kind that sprung up around American Army camps. Further behind the ville was the edge of some seriously dense jungle. A well-worn trail closely followed the edge of the jungle.

It was a beautiful day when I walked out of the camp. It was sometime past noon, and the sun was brightly shining almost directly overhead. A light breeze caressed the incredibly green rice paddies, which stood in bold relief against the deep blue sky. A few billowy clouds dotted the horizon. Just a picture-perfect day.

I strolled through the ville and got on the trail heading west. For some distance I encountered light concentrations of the inhabitants of the ville. After a short period of time, however, I saw fewer and fewer people, until finally there was nobody to be seen anywhere. At that time I was probably one kilometer from the camp. I continued to stroll along as my frustrations subsided.

Eventually I came across a very shallow stream about fifteen meters wide. All that remained of a once-standing bridge was a single span of steel reaching from one bank to the other. As I walked across the beam I looked down into the water and saw an unexploded Russian B-40 antitank round.

The signs were there that I was getting deep into Indian country, but I foolishly ignored them and kept my pace. I was still kind of pissed off, which clouded my judgment. I was now about two kilometers away from my temporary place of duty and walking straight into trouble.

Ahead of me I saw a guy standing off to the side of the trail. He was about thirty-five years old and he had a young girl with him who looked to be about eighteen or nineteen. Both were standing in a kind of notch in the jungle which was devoid of trees and covered with knee-high grass. Both acted slightly surprised to see me.

I moved to their location. The guy had a short, tight haircut and was wearing a short-sleeved, collarless black pajama top and khaki shorts. Although it was not unusual to see farmers looking like that, he had sort of a military bearing about him. The girl was dressed in traditional peasant garb.

I spoke to them in Vietnamese and asked for some identification. Both produced authentic-looking documents, so I handed them back, said good-bye, and continued walking up the trail.

I came around a slight bend, and about five meters up the trail I spied a very large bush. It sat to the left of, and directly next to, the trail, which disappeared around the bush and reappeared a short distance later to my left front, about fifteen meters from where I was standing. To the left of the bush and the trail was a large rice paddy.

I casually glanced up the trail past the bush and saw two Vietnamese women carrying baskets, who appeared to be handing something to someone in the tall, brown grass bordering the rice paddy. The grass was too thick for me to see who was sitting in it.

The Vietnamese woman farthest away from me turned her head to say something to the other chick, and when she did she saw me standing out in the open on the trail about thirty meters away. She said something very quickly to her partner, and both of them dropped their baskets and disappeared into the jungle. I mean they split like the devil was on their tail.

The events happened in rapid-fire succession. I was already walking before they started running. They took off and I thought, my, that's awfully strange behavior. Just as that thought entered my mind, I pulled up alongside the bush. My next step took me past it. I was still looking straight ahead wondering what the hell was going on with the chicks.

Suddenly I detected movement in my peripheral vision.

It was right next to me.

A North Vietnamese soldier.

He was squatting behind the bush with his AK-47's butt stock on the ground and the barrel pointing straight in the air. He must have been looking at the chicks like I was, wondering what the hell was going on. When I came around the bush he noticed movement in *his* peripheral vision. Simultaneously we looked at each other.

It is almost impossible to convey the feeling I had when I looked at him. When our eyes met it was like two speeding automobiles colliding. It was like a violent, shocking impact. It felt like I'd grabbed hold of a live power line, and a million volts had coursed through my body, freezing my heart.

At that moment I was doing something really stupid. I was holding my weapon in one hand, by the pistol grip. It was at my side with the barrel pointing straight down. Everything that I'd seen should have alerted me to danger and put me in a ready-to-fire posture, but I was still focused on the incident at the camp.

The only thing that saved my ass was the fact that he was not experienced. He jumped up and started yelling in Vietnamese "American! American!"

He never should've taken the time to yell. Instead, he should've put a couple of rounds into me and let the sound of the shots warn the others. By the time he'd gotten the second "American!" out of his mouth I'd brought my weapon all the way from around my side and cranked off several rounds, knocking him flat.

At the same time he hit the ground I realized there was an entire squad sitting there in the grass! All of them were shocked to see me standing on the trail so close to them. I was stunned that I was in the middle of a hostile force, close enough that I could smell them. Time stopped . . . .

. . . And started again as one of them cut loose with a burst of 7.62mm fire. Now, people will tell me that the rounds went over my head and that it was just my imagination, but I swear to this day that a round went right through my hair. Right through my hair! The memory of it makes me think of a straight-line weight on top of my head. Lay the entire length of your index finger on top of your scalp and press down hard. That's what it felt like after I had a chance to think about it.

As soon as the shots were fired I dropped to the ground and rolled to my right off the trail, trying to get into the jungle. There was a small anthill about two feet high in my way, so I snaked behind it and pressed my body to the ground as best I could.

They shot at me from where they were sitting. Since I couldn't return any fire without exposing myself, I pressed even harder against the ground. They ate up the anthill with a steady stream of lead. Rounds ripped into the dirt on both sides of me. Needless to say I was in some deep shit.

I'm not sure why they didn't rush my position and overwhelm me. I was very vulnerable. All they had to do was pin me down with fire and maneuver as a group. But they didn't. And that was a mistake on their part.

I did manage to peek around the base of the anthill just in time to see one of the guys dart from his position in an effort to get at my right flank. He jumped behind a long, tall row of bushes growing in a slight depression about ten meters away to my right front. I wasn't sure exactly where he was until he started shooting. Every time he fired, the branches of the bush he was behind blew aside from the muzzle blast. The height of the blast indicated he was kneeling in an effort to shoot down on me. His initial shots came too close for comfort. In seconds he would have me zeroed in.

I quickly turned on my side and curled into a fetal position to draw my weapon up into a firing posture. Almost simultaneously I fired a couple of three-round bursts about a foot below the spot of the muzzle blasts. No more shots came from that location.

However, the other comedians continued to blast away. So far all this action had transpired in less than thirty seconds. My mind was racing like a runaway locomotive. What the hell was I going to do? I was sure that soon more enemy troops would join the fray and I'd be a dead man. I couldn't take them all by myself.

But a platoon could.

I decided to bluff them.

I immediately started yelling, "Hey, motherfuckers! Somebody move the fucking machine gun up here! I already got two of the sons of bitches! C'mon, let's kick some ass!"

I started talking like I had a whole platoon of guys with me, and son of a bitch if it didn't work! There was a dramatic lull in the action. I can just imagine them suddenly thinking, Shit! There might be a big bunch of American assholes out there! We're only a squad. What the fuck do we do?

The moment they stopped firing, I crawled backward like a crab as fast as I could, keeping my chin practically buried in the dirt as I tilted my head back and stared in their direction. I expected them to wise up and pounce on me at any time, but they didn't. My little game apparently put enough doubt into their minds as to who was out there that they couldn't decide whether to stay or run. Their indecisiveness allowed me to escape.

When I got into the jungle I clocked the world's record time back to the camp. I guarantee you I was the fastest human being on the face of the earth that day.

Several Vietnamese civilians who were in the area of engagement beat me back to the camp and misleadingly informed its occupants that "Some American out there just killed some people." Right away everyone assumed that the American was me and that I'd gone crazy and murdered innocent civilians.

When I returned I told them, "Hey, man. I just ran into a fuckin' enemy squad not too far from here and had it out with them." By this time I was feeling pretty good because I knew I was safe. Everybody else, however, was ready to jump my shit big-time. They wanted to burn me. They didn't believe me when I told them I'd greased enemy soldiers; they were convinced that I'd mowed down a group of farmers. They'd already formed the opinion that I was a weird, murdering motherfucker who didn't respect life. Besides, they reasoned, there wasn't an enemy soldier within ten miles of the camp.

A Vietnamese lieutenant who'd been to American ranger school decided to investigate the situation. He and I had developed a friendly relationship over the months, and he wanted to see for himself if my story was true.

He jumped on a motorcycle from the ville and rode out there, which really surprised the shit out of me. He rode up to the steel beam crossing the stream and traveled the remaining distance on foot. When he returned to the camp he had two AK-47s in his possession. He told the assembled throng that I had indeed killed two *enemy soldiers*. I'm sure everybody was disappointed by the fact that there'd be no court-martial for killing civilians.

Since they couldn't get me for murder, they tried to nail me for being AWOL from the camp. My unit got wind of what was happening and pulled me out of there. In essence they told the temporary camp commander, Fuck you. If you can't appreciate having this guy around, then jam it up your ass!

The day I left, I ran into the permanent camp commander—a major—who was coming back off leave. He'd heard about what had transpired, and he said to me, "Nobody would have fucked with you if I'd been around. I'd ask you to stay, but I know you don't want to. I heard you got two of them. That's two less we gotta worry about. Thanks."

We shook hands and went our separate ways.

PART FOUR

My Death

THE CONGRESSIONAL MEDAL OF HONOR

The Congressional Medal of Honor. Awarded for conspicuous gallantry and intrepidity at the risk of life above and beyond the call of duty.

5 January 1970.

Several days earlier our surveillance folks had intercepted dozens of radio transmissions from an area in Laos where they suspected a large enemy base was located. The number and frequency of the transmissions seemed to indicate that something big was in the works, so quite naturally our headquarters wanted to know all the details. That meant inserting someone into the area to locate the base and gather the necessary intelligence.

The area in question was very close to the tri-border region just north of Cambodia and across the border from Ben Het. My recon team—Vermont—was given the mission, which was pretty much standard fare with a slight variation. On the way to the target they wanted us to search for an intelligence-gathering aircraft that had been shot down the day before. It was estimated to be about three kilometers from where we wanted to go, which would be right in our ballpark. We told them, no sweat. We could handle the additional tasking.

I briefed our colonel the evening of the fourth on exactly how my team was going to run the operation. All aspects of the mission were covered in minute detail. Most of what I briefed was SOP for that type of mission, so the meeting was down and dirty.

RT Vermont loaded onto two UH-1D Hueys—known as "slicks"— at Kontum around six-thirty or seven o'clock on the morning of the fifth. It was overcast and cool, with a ceiling of about fifteen hundred feet. As we lifted off into the gray morning, we were escorted by four Cobra gunships. Our first stop was Dak To.

We arrived about forty-five minutes after pulling out of Kontum. Dak To was the chopper refueling point and standby reaction center for this mission. After the insertion the choppers would return to Dak To and stand by in the event of an emergency or until the mission-complete extraction. Nine choppers would be on the ground there in support of RT Vermont: the two slicks and four Cobras from Kontum, two more Cobras from Dak To, and a "Chase" slick, which carried a Special Forces medic and full medical facilities.

The insertion was usually the most dangerous part of a mission. Face facts—it's not easy to fly into someone's backyard without him knowing about it. Many times the enemy would discover you within the first few minutes you were on the ground. Therefore, the first hour was regarded as the make-or-break point of an operation.

If you dropped in and didn't encounter the enemy within the first hour, the chances were good that the insertion wasn't detected and you could go about your business. If, however, the enemy engaged you right away or soon afterward, you'd obviously lost the element of surprise and needed to be extracted quickly. That's why the Cobras accompanied the slicks. If the shit hit the fan, you needed devastating firepower to annihilate the enemy or make him withdraw so the slicks could pick you up.

The scheme of an insertion into enemy-controlled territory went like this: Seven choppers would leave the launch site, flying in formation, either "on the deck"—just above the treetops—or higher, depending on the enemy's antiaircraft capability. The slicks would fly approximately one hundred meters apart and be flanked by two Cobras, so that all four choppers were in a diamond pattern when viewed from above or below. Two more Cobras would follow at a good distance behind, so they wouldn't be hit or seen right away if an attack was launched against the front four choppers. The Chase would fly further behind and much higher than the two trailing Cobras.

When we reached the insertion point, the Cobras flanking the slicks would break away and start flying circular patterns around the LZ, closely monitoring the radio that I, as the team leader, carried until we were safely on our way. If there was trouble on the ground I would need instant communication with the choppers, so I turned the radio over to the RTO only after I was sure the area was "cold."

The trailing Cobras would fly a holding pattern well behind the insertion point, ready to support if they were needed. Ditto the Chase.

The procedure the slicks followed to put us on the ground was designed to reduce their vulnerability to ground attack. As the slick approached the LZ, the pilot would cut the engine RPMs, causing the slick to descend to the ground in a nose-up attitude. Everyone in the slick would be ready to exit, with our feet on the skids as we sat in the doorway. As the slick got within three or four feet of the ground it would level out. The very moment that it was level we would jump out, because a split second later the slick would nose-dive as the pilot quickly increased the RPMs to maintain his forward momentum. Three seconds after the slick had been level, it would be vanishing above the treetops.

After the team was on the ground, the slicks would move off and fly holding patterns. When they received the green light from me, all the choppers would return to the base, refuel, and stand by.

At Dak To I briefed the "Bright Light" team leader on how we were going to play the game. Bright Light was a reconnaissance team on standby that could be rapidly inserted into an asskick if the situation was desperate enough. My team had been the Bright Light on several occasions. All major operations included a Bright Light team. Bright Light monitored all radios belonging to teams within a certain AO. In our case we would be one of four seven-man teams within a two-hundred-square-mile area. When we arrived at Dak To, three teams were already out. One of them was in contact with the enemy. Two Cobras went to its aid.

RT Arizona had the Bright Light mission that day. I gave the team leader information such as my team's composition—by name—and who was going to be on what chopper, so that in the event one was shot down, he'd already know who was probably dead. My team consisted of three Americans—Green (medic), Hobart (RTO), and me, plus four Yards—Prep (my Zero-One Yard), Hyuk (point man), Gai (interpreter) and Yube (tail gunner).

I also told the Bright Light team leader in what pockets I carried my CEOI and other top-secret information. I told him about everything I was carrying on my body, so if I was killed, he or my people could get my documentation immediately, without having to search for it. The same was true for every member of my team. I was aware of everything they had on them. If the situation allowed it, you tried to recover someone's documents and critical equipment if you couldn't evacuate his body. You never knew when you'd need the recovered items, and by taking them you deprived the enemy of valuable information.

Our code name for the operation was "Cole Slaw."

Thirty minutes after we landed at Dak To we were loading back onto the slicks. By now the weather was getting worse, and the cloud cover was growing thicker. The ceiling was dropping fast, blotting out the horizon and making ordinary flights very hazardous. However, we weren't concerned.

Our high-speed intelligence sources had informed us the day before that a one-mile-wide hole in the cloud cover was drifting down from China. SOG operations had a C-130 that operated at twenty-five thousand feet—all day, all night. During the day it was referred to as "Hillsboro"; at night its code-name became "Moonbeam." It flew an oblong pattern over Vietnam, Cambodia, and Laos, acting as a communication and intelligence center for just about every operation. It was laden with state-of-the-art communication, weather analysis, and surveillance equipment.

Hillsboro gave us the heads-up on the break in the clouds. We established our mission start time based on their calculations as to when it would cross our insertion point. Our plan was to fly above the clouds—thereby avoiding detection—and move down through the hole. The choppers' exposure to enemy surveillance would be minimized. Of course, once the hole drifted away there'd be no coming to get us until the cloud cover dispersed. Such were the risks of the game.

The choppers' turbines began to whine as the pilots throttled them to life. As surprising as it may seem, our mood had been light and easy during the brief stop at Dak To. It was almost always that way prior to a mission, regardless of the difficulty and associated risks. Pilots and ground crews laughed and cut up with us; but as the time approached to do our thing, the overall mood grew solemn. Laughs were replaced by words of encouragement and wishes of good luck; grins gave way to clenched jaws and tight-lipped determination.

Everyone on the team got in a few last-minute jokes and smiles before we climbed into our air taxis. I checked my watch, saw that the time was right, and gave the word to board the slicks. The moment we were all inside, we switched into our business mode. Our insides began to tighten. Smiles vanished and adrenaline flowed. Nervous excitement charged the air.

It was show time.

We got well above the clouds shortly after leaving Dak To. The entire area was really socked in; but sure enough, as we got closer to the insertion point, we saw the huge hole. We watched it move ever so slowly on a course perpendicular to our own, until the leading edge intersected our flight path. As the hole cut directly across our front, the choppers dropped right into it and spiraled down to the deck.

At that point we didn't know our exact location. We knew we were somewhere in our AO based on the pilot's calculations. A quick check of our map indicated we were less than two miles from the primary LZ. The choppers got down on the deck to avoid antiaircraft fire and made a high-speed beeline to our destination.

My adrenaline was pumping furiously, as it always did at that stage of the mission. Feel it: There you are, skimming rapidly above the jungle vegetation as you rush toward the moment when you and six other guys will be swallowed up by a hostile jungle, with no help around the corner. You're fully aware that within the next several minutes you might be killed or—God forbid—maimed. You know only too well that your survival depends mainly on your abilities to move undetected like a phantom and to shoot your weapon with deadly accuracy. You must also rely on the skills of those around you, not to mention a combination of cleverness, audacity, and luck.

Your legs are hanging out, and your feet are on the skid as you sit in the doorway. Your weapon is firmly tucked under your arm and aimed at the ground with one gloved hand as you lean out into the rushing wind, grasping the interior of the slick tightly with the other. A radio is strapped to your back, with the headset clamped between your shoulder and ear so you can monitor the airwaves. The door gunner next to you is swinging his mounted M-60 around, back and forth, staring very intently at the ground for the slightest hint of movement.

You try your damnedest to relax but meet with little success. Your body is rigid with anticipation.

You are primed.

Suddenly the slick's turbine howl decreases sharply and its nose points toward the heavens.

Get ready.

Go!

The chopper was approximately four feet off the ground when it leveled out for that split second. We crashed through the waist-deep grass and vines and immediately fanned out to secure the area. The chopper was almost out of sight when I looked back to ensure everyone was on the ground safely. I caught a fleeting glimpse of the door gunner looking back at us, hand in the air as if he were waving good-bye. The slick vanished beyond the treetops as the beat of its blades faded away.

It was gone just like that. An incredible silence rushed in to fill the void. The LZ was absolutely still, save for tiny bamboo leaves that drifted and spiraled gently back to the ground.

Only a few seconds had elapsed when I heard the other slick approaching at high speed. It did the drill, and moments later the rest of RT Vermont was on the ground. Fifteen seconds later, silence reigned once again.

Meanwhile, the Cobras were doing their grind off at a distance, flying in circles as I gave them our status. I informed them that the LZ was cold and we were moving out. At that point I gave the radio to the RTO, took my ruck off his back and put it on.

Everything became hand and arm signals. Nobody was allowed to talk except the RTO and me. As soon as the RTO was set, I looked at Hyuk and pointed the direction of travel. Hyuk moved out and we fell in behind him.

Right away we noticed that there was a heavy concentration of enemy in the area. Well-worn trails crisscrossed everywhere. You know how the grass looks in a playground that's used all the time? Or better yet, remember the beaten path that cut across an empty lot in your neighborhood? The trails looked just like that: frequently used by many people.

We continued to move in the direction of the downed aircraft, although our movement was hardly in a straight line. To improve our chances of not being detected, we started sweeping around the outskirts of the trail-scarred section of jungle.

By now the clouds were breaking up and sunshine was slicing through the cover. A forward air controller (FAC)—flying well above the clouds—came up on the radio, wanting to know our status. The FAC was flying an Air Force fixed-winged Cessna aircraft, known as an O-2, or "Oscar Deuce." It was a twin-tailed plane with dual propeller engines, one on the front of the fuselage and another at the rear. It could fly faster and stay aloft much longer than a chopper, which could be easily shot down if used to perform the same missions as the O-2.

The FAC's code name was "Covey," and his primary missions involved target spotting and battle coordination. The O-2 carried several seventeen-pound WP rockets, used to mark targets for bombing runs by fast movers, which flew too fast to make out any details on the ground. Covey would launch a WP rocket into the enemy's position, and the fast movers would drop their loads on the white smoke.

Covey also assisted the teams on the ground by spotting advancing or positioned enemy elements as well as key terrain features, and relaying the critical information to the team leaders.

Like the Bright Light team, Covey was assigned a specific AO and would monitor the radios of all teams within his designated sector. As he methodically flew over each team's AO he requested a current status and provided observations about the immediate terrain.

Covey would launch from either Pleiku, Vietnam, or Nakhon Phanom, Thailand, depending on his area of responsibility. Covey was not used on all missions, but his presence was certainly welcomed any time he was on the scene.

I contacted Covey and whispered to him that our situation was "green" and we were proceeding toward our intermediate target.

After twenty minutes of slipping through the bush, I halted the patrol to inform everyone that we were getting close to the estimated crash site. I issued a few instructions and we resumed our patrol.

Much to my surprise we ended up being a lot closer than I thought. We hadn't walked a hundred meters from the place where I'd stopped the patrol when we came across a big open space in the jungle. I stopped the team fifteen meters short of the clearing and took Hobart and Prep with me to the edge of the field for a careful inspection of the area.

The clearing was about forty to fifty meters across and several hundred meters long, completely covered with chest-deep grass. As I scanned our surroundings I noticed, to my left front, that the tops of several trees near the edge of the field had been sheared off. That was an indication that a fast mover had slammed down through the jungle, splintering the treetops as it angled into the ground. The moment I saw the mangled trees I concluded the pilot must have tried to put his aircraft down in the clearing and hit the trees on the approach. I followed what I believed to be the path of the aircraft and—sure enough—down the field to my right and on the far side was something against the edge of the jungle. I was positive it was the fast mover we were looking for, but we were too far away to see it clearly.

I decided that since the grass was so high we'd take a quick stroll in that direction and examine our find. I sent Hobart back with the rest of the team and brought forward my medic, Green. I whispered some instructions to Green and Prep, and the three of us started across the field, bending low as we walked.

About halfway to the plane, the grass began to drop away, and we could clearly see the aircraft.

We froze.

Its crumpled nose was buried in a mound of earth that had been plowed up by the plane as it crashed. Dirt, tree limbs, and uprooted grass were scattered on both sides of a long, deep trench that had been etched into the soil by the crippled fast mover. Remnants of the canopy indicated the pilot hadn't ejected. He must have been dead by the looks of the demolished fuselage.

However, it wasn't the sight of the aircraft that caused us to halt abruptly, but rather what was surrounding it. Thirty-five to forty enemy troops were sitting in the thigh-deep grass around the plane. I saw the plane long before I spotted them; the grass they were sitting in obscured everything but their heads. It was their black hair—matted against the tan grass—that gave them away. They were positioned in a loose circle, guarding their prize. Fortunately for us, all of them were gazing in the direction of the aircraft. Since it had been shot down only the day before, it was still a hot item and drew everyone's attention.

When I finally detected them, we were in grass that was only waist-deep. We'd walked right up on them; they were so fascinated by the plane they didn't even see us. We immediately melted down into the grass. Green looked at me and whispered, "Let's get the fuck out of here." I was in complete agreement, so we crawled back to the rest of the team.

They didn't know what was going on, but they'd observed our actions and were on the alert when we finally reached them. I gave the team a rundown of the situation. I fixed the plane's position and called in a SITREP (situation report) to our headquarters. I gave them the crash site coordinates, and in the same breath told them to forget about trying to retrieve anything from the plane. I provided basic information about the enemy, such as his size, activity, and location. After completing the SITREP, I huddled with the team and laid out our next move.

Our primary target was supposedly located in an area a few kilometers on the other side of the downed plane. We withdrew several hundred meters from the field, backtracking along almost the same lines we had used to approach it. We gave the crash site a wide berth—for obvious reasons—and skirted the field at a distance of about one kilometer.

We'd been inserted at eight o'clock that morning. We'd discovered the plane approximately two hours later. It took us another hour to backtrack and traverse the distance around the field to the other side. At eleven o'clock our path intersected a stream that forked into two branches. One branch cut away into the jungle on our side of the stream; the other went up a small valley on the opposite side.

Little did I know this would be the place.

Moving in the dense brush next to the stream instead of in the water we went upstream until we were about five meters from the Y- junction. At that point we crossed and headed for the valley entrance.

We hadn't moved but maybe twenty-five meters when I heard a shot about five hundred to six hundred meters off in the distance. I immediately took out my compass and shot an azimuth. I glanced at my watch and pulled a notebook from my pocket, into which I scribbled, "1105 hrs. Heard shot. My location—[classified]. Azimuth—225 degrees."

I'd just put my notebook away when our world collapsed.

We were moving in the following order: Hyuk on point, followed by me, Yube, Hobart, Prep, Green, and Gai.

Yube saw something just before I made the notation in my book. He gave a halting hand-and-arm signal to everyone behind him, alerting them to possible danger. Unaware that the rest of the team had stopped, Hyuk and I continued to move forward.

Within the span of several seconds, a large gap formed between us and the main body of the team. By that time Hyuk and I were entering the valley, moving up a slight incline. When the shot was fired and I did my drill, we were on slightly higher ground than everyone else. Hyuk had just reached the base of a very large tree, but hadn't gone around it.

The very second my notebook hit the bottom of my pocket the entire jungle erupted and shuddered.

Strong shock waves assaulted my body and my vision blurred, like a camera being jarred. My initial reaction was to hit the ground, because the first thing you learn about combat is that anything standing gets hit.

Hyuk and I immediately dropped into crouches and quickly glanced at each other. I looked back down the hill toward the rest of the team. All I could see was a cloud of gray explosive powder. Dirt, stones, leaves, and branches were falling back to the ground; I could hear all the shit crashing down through the trees and bushes around me.

As I stared at the gray cloud, a man staggered out toward me. As he got closer, I realized it was Prep.

He was fucked up. Bad.

The explosion had knocked his lower jaw completely off. His weapon and ruck were gone, and his clothing was shredded. I looked back at Hyuk, who looked at me. We were both dumbfounded because we weren't injured in the blast. As I looked at him, the entire jungle around us seemed to come alive with movement. I grabbed Hyuk and pushed him toward Prep, saying, "Take care of that motherfucker!" Those were my exact words, said out of unbelievable rage at what had happened. Hyuk dashed past me to give first aid to Prep, who was about four meters down the slope from me.

Just as Hyuk reached Prep, I detected movement in my peripheral vision and saw part of a squad coming around the big tree Hyuk had just left. I pivoted from my crouched position and opened up on them; Hyuk wheeled, dropped to one knee, and added his fire to mine as rounds ripped through the air. Both of us were in the open, but neither of us was hit. So swift was our attack we knocked the first four or five guys down before they'd cranked off more than a couple of shots. The rest of the squad on the other side of the tree withdrew hastily.

At the same moment the decimated enemy squad split, the hillside to my left rear sprang to life. Suddenly, twenty-five to thirty NVA jumped up and began assaulting the ambush site where the blast had occurred. At first they weren't aware of Hyuk and me on their flank. We dropped empty magazines, jammed in full ones, and tried to stem the onslaught into the kill zone. I had no idea how many of my people— besides Hyuk—were still alive.

Our initial bursts hit several NVA. I'm not sure how many, maybe six or seven. When you hit a large element out in the open, especially from the flank as we did, you can mess them up badly, even with just a few guys doing the shooting.

Not all of the people we hit were killed; some were wounded and fell out of our sight in the vegetation. But the key thing was that we were hitting people. We tried to concentrate on small groups of people as they ran down the slope. Every now and then I'd see one of my tracer rounds impact on someone, knocking him flat. I always loaded my magazines with two tracers near the bottom and two more rounds under them. That way I knew I was near the end of the rounds in that magazine when the tracer rounds flew.

It took a few moments for them to realize we were there. When they did discover our presence, they turned and tried to fire on us. However, they quickly realized that they were shooting through their own people. When they figured out that their position was very awkward they performed a mass withdrawal.

There was still a slight haze in the air when the enemy disengaged. As Hyuk and I quickly headed down into the kill zone to inspect the damage, I saw people lying everywhere.

It looked like the bodies had been put through a meat grinder. Dead enemy troops were mixed in with the prone members of my team.

Prep, who staggered up the slope after the blast, still clung to life by a bare thread. Yube, the one who'd discovered the booby trap, was—unbelievably—still alive. He'd taken the brunt of the blast and had hundreds of holes over his entire body. Amazingly enough, not only was he still alive, but he was the least critically injured of the five who were caught in the explosion.

Hobart, Gai, and Green were all very seriously injured and not capable of moving under their own power. I turned to Hyuk and as calmly as I could said, "Let's get the fuck out of this area. We'll move everyone across the stream and get it between us and them. That way, if they come for us, we'll have some kind of barrier and open ground to help us deal with them."

Less than a minute had elapsed since the enemy withdrew. They wouldn't stay away long; of that I was positive. I was sure that any second they'd regroup and come slamming into us. Fighting down panic, I threw Gai's arm around my neck, grabbed Hobart by his web gear, and literally dragged them across the rocky streambed and through the water to the other side. Hyuk gathered up Yube and placed Green over his shoulder. Once he moved them to our concealed position on the opposite bank, he went back and retrieved Prep.

As Hyuk went back for Prep, I got on the radio and informed our headquarters that we had a "TAC E" or tactical emergency. There were three levels of emergencies: team—when somebody got sick or wounded; tactical—you've been engaged by the enemy, he's superior in size, and there's a good chance he's going to kick your ass; and prairie fire—you're presently engaged, surrounded, and annihilation is imminent.

We weren't presently engaged, so I couldn't in good conscience call a prairie fire emergency, although I really wanted to do so. Back at Dak To the chopper pilots and Bright Light were immediately put on alert. TAC E simply got them in a ready, set, stand by mode. Pilots went out to their birds, and Bright Light team members started putting on their gear and moving out to the slicks, all the while mentally preparing for the fight that was likely to follow. If I'd called a prairie fire they'd have been in the air already. As it was they were on hold until I gave the word or they determined—through monitoring the radio—that the situation had deteriorated to the critical stage. Remember, they couldn't jump too fast because there were three other teams out that might also require assistance; in fact, one other team was presently in contact and several Cobras had been sent to the fight.

I gave them a SITREP. I told them that we'd tripped a mine, five of my guys were severely wounded, and an estimated platoon-sized force was kicking-off on our ass. We were attempting to escape and evade to the best of our abilities.

I wasn't fooling myself. My team wasn't in any condition to move. Everyone was lying on the ground, shivering and gasping for breath. Hyuk and I continued to give first aid, trying everything we could to save people. Two guys had gaping holes in their upper chests. We couldn't give them morphine because it would kill them. It was a grim sight. Blood was everywhere; a bloody trail was visible from the stream bank to our position in the heavy bush.

It was around noon when Prep died. We didn't have time to dwell on his death because the enemy had regrouped and was now spread out and moving back down the hill toward the ambush site. I got with Hyuk and decided we'd move up the slope behind us, thus giving us a better fighting position. Just as we prepared to go up the hill we heard movement above us at the top of the slope. It was a big group, spread out and coming down fast.

We were now in the middle of two large groups, closing in from our front and back. We were between the proverbial rock and the hard place.

I peered through the vegetation at the group moving into the ambush site by the stream. As they approached, two guys hurried down the hill ahead of everyone else and picked up one of their prone comrades. Several more did likewise, carrying and dragging bodies back up the hill.

It wasn't long before our trail of blood was spotted. As the main body flooded the ambush site, the group's leader began shouting orders.

A couple of NVA saw the blood and began shouting "We hit them! We got some of them!" Soon they ran across some of the equipment we were forced to leave. I watched one of them pick up Prep's weapon and thrust it in the air over his head with one hand, yelling about his captured prize. Everyone looked at him and smiles abounded. The weapon was a sign. Soldiers don't drop their weapons unless they're so badly injured they have no thought of fighting back.

Someone found a ruck, shouted his discovery, and drew a crowd. They started picking through it until a platoon sergeant jumped in and told them to knock it off. He began yelling at them, saying that since our gear was there we must still be close, not too far away. He quickly dispersed the group around the ruck and directed each soldier to a position. He moved from one end of the ambush site to the other, shouting orders and positioning troops. It was obvious that the platoon sergeant was tactically squared away and knew his stuff, because his next move was to bring forward a machine gun. He placed it in an ideal location, one that allowed the gunner to cover both ends of the stream and the hillside where we were hiding.

As soon as the machine gun was in place, he sent two people scurrying across the stream. The first one across dropped into a covering position shortly after clearing the water. The trailing soldier hustled past him to the edge of the slope, not fifteen meters from my position. At that point I lost sight of him because he was below the break of a short, sharp rise. I could, however, still see his buddy lying just in front of the stream bank; he had his weapon and attention focused on an area somewhere to my left flank.

From below the rise I heard the lead soldier say, "There's more blood here. A heavy trail—this way."

He was closing in fast. It was only a matter of moments before he discovered my crippled team. I had moved from their location to a position closer to the enemy in an effort to get a better handle on the situation. I had no intention of trying to kick ass or anything of that nature. My only concern was calculating how to get us the hell out of there.

Suddenly I saw the enemy soldier crest the rise and cautiously advance in my direction, his head and eyes sweeping slowly and deliberately from side to side. The entire time he was moving forward, the platoon sergeant conversed with him from the other side of the stream, asking things like, "What do you see now?" and, "How many do you think we hit?" The scout responded after almost every step, "There's blood here . . . Maybe hit three or four . . . There's some more blood over there . . . ."

I remained absolutely rigid. Panic was welling up from deep within me, and I fought hard to keep it down. It was absolutely essential for me to keep my head clear if we were to have any chance at all of surviving. My heart was pounding so hard I was afraid the enemy would hear it. I instinctively took slower and shallower breaths until I almost stopped breathing. I didn't dare turn my head to follow his progress; I watched him out of the corners of my eyes.

He was almost on top of the team. He continued to talk as he walked, until finally he was to my immediate left less than ten meters away. I could barely see him through the bushes next to me. He took one last step, peered around a large clump of bushes and grass to his right, and saw the team lying in the grass about fifteen meters from where he was standing.

Suddenly he yelled something like, "There they are!" and opened up in their general direction.

It startled me when he started shooting. By now half of my attention was focused on the machine gun by the stream. That was the big hammer, and I was trying to decide how I was going to deal with it when—I knew it would be when and not if—we were discovered.

There was no more time to think.

Instincts took over.

Seconds after the enemy troop started firing I leaned back, raised myself up slightly to get a clear shot, and cranked off a single round. It caught him square in the shoulder and slammed him to the ground like a rag doll.

The soldier lying near the stream bed saw me rise up and immediately took me under fire. As he was shooting at me, I was already pivoting in the direction of the machine gun. My primary hope was to somehow luck out and damage the weapon with a burst of rounds. However, it would be tough enough just to hit around it under the circumstances.

But when I turned I found the assistant gunner standing straight up, wondering what was going on. His mental lapse proved costly. I cut loose with a controlled automatic burst in his direction and managed to drop him. The gunner quickly shifted his sights and put some major smoke on me. I hit the ground in a hurry.

After the machine gun opened up, everyone on the hillside followed suit. Since I was the lone target they concentrated their fire on me.

They threw rounds at me the likes of which I'd never experienced before. I was concealed in bushes and tall grass only; I didn't have any type of cover available—such as a tree or rock—to stop the rounds. They ripped through the vegetation all around my prone form, miraculously missing their mark. My one advantage was that I occupied higher ground than my attackers.

The small valley reverberated with the colliding echoes of high-pitched *crack*s for what I know was only a minute or so, but which seemed like an hour. I'd already figured out my next plan of attack, and when there was a momentary lull in the shooting, I popped a CS gas grenade and threw it as far as I could in their direction. At that point I had to be cautious with my use of gas because my wounded team wouldn't be able to put on masks if it drifted into their area.

Gas was one of the best things you could use because it created confusion in the ranks. It was nasty shit that troops on both sides didn't want to deal with. CS gas usually caused the enemy grief and forced him to alter his plans. Unfortunately, it could hinder your own operations as well, so you used it judiciously.

The time was certainly right in this case.

The gas billowed out in a big cloud that engulfed the ambush site. The enemy began withdrawing right away. They apparently were in no mood to be gassed. I then lobbed a WP grenade into the same location. The white phosphorous would mix with the CS gas to create a denser, heavier fog that would hang in and around the area longer.

After the CS and WP grenades finished discharging, I bent over low and scrambled back to the rest of the team. A dirty white haze hung in the air along the stream, looking like a scene out of "The Twilight Zone." I could see shadowy figures running all over the place, trying to get out of that irritating cloud. At least something else besides me was occupying their attention. The situation cooled off considerably, but we needed to move quickly. The gas wouldn't remain forever, and any moment we would face an additional threat: the enemy troops behind us.

Hyuk had been giving first aid the entire time I was doing my thing. By now Yube and Hobart had regained enough strength to move—albeit very slowly—under their own power. I grabbed Green, Hyuk picked up Gai, and we began moving parallel to the stream.

Our flight was time-consuming and extremely taxing, both mentally and physically. I knew we had a long way to go before we were even remotely out of danger. My pulse pounded and my heart rate soared; sweat stung my eyes and blurred my vision. My muscles burned under the burden of extra weight. I was running on sheer adrenaline; I couldn't even guess at what was keeping the wounded guys alive, much less moving.

We'd moved only about a hundred meters before stopping to catch our breath. I'd just picked up the radio to call our headquarters when the bushes twenty meters to our left front erupted in heavy gunfire. I rolled over into a prone firing position and sent rounds screaming into the heart of their attack.

Hyuk, who'd been administering more first aid to Gai and Green, never really had a chance. He swung his weapon around and got off a single, sustained automatic burst as he dove for the ground. Sadly, his actions came a moment too late. He caught a round square in the neck, knocking him flat. His body convulsed for a moment and then went still.

He was dead.

When Hyuk got hit I cranked off several more rounds, then pulled out a frag and hurled it. The resulting explosion neutralized their attack. I don't know how many I hit between the rounds and the frag, but I did manage to see two guys sprint away at high speed. By the time I shot in their direction they were long gone.

Their departure and the subsequent pause in the action only highlighted the desperateness of our situation. It seemed like almost every inch of the valley was full of menace. Low, muffled voices intertwined with the distant sounds of people crashing through the thick vegetation above and behind us. Nobody was pressuring us at the moment, but that would soon change.

It was now approximately one o'clock in the afternoon. I called our headquarters and told them our situation was getting critical. I still reported our predicament as a TAC E; we weren't surrounded—yet. My biggest problem was trying to move the wounded. Two could move by themselves, but the other two required assistance.

After I concluded the SITREP my mind clicked into high gear. I told everyone to conceal himself as best he could while I went forward to see what I could do.

I started moving toward the advancing enemy, surveying the terrain and noting natural obstacles along the way. I was trying to anticipate avenues of approach and areas where they would mass for an assault.

About one minute later I found what I considered to be a good defensive position. It had a couple of good-sized rocks and fallen timber to hide behind and provide cover, and it had a fair view of the areas I believed they'd come through. As I settled into my chosen spot I detected a faint trace of CS. The slight breeze that was blowing through the valley had obviously dissipated most of the gas. There wasn't much in the air where I was sitting, but there was just enough to make my eyes water slightly and make me uncomfortable.

I wasn't in position for more than half a minute when I saw the point man for an element step around a tree twenty meters to my front. Following him were five or six other guys, who spread out a good distance and came on-line, moving forward the entire time. The last man to come around the tree carried a machine gun. He immediately became my number one target. I waited until I had a good, clean shot. They obviously thought the team and I were still some distance ahead of them, because they were moving kind of casually, as if they weren't expecting any contact yet.

Surprise!

In rapid succession I opened up on the machine gunner, put him down, then shifted fire slightly and nailed the next guy. The rest of the group quickly got over their shock and started hosing me down. I ducked low behind the fallen trees as their rounds bored into the dead wood and ricocheted off the rocks. From behind the wooden cover I set my sights on the point man and hit him with a couple of rounds.

Then, from out of nowhere, appeared a grenade.

It didn't hit all that close to my position, but it was near enough that the explosion swatted me to the ground. Hard. I came close to blacking out. Fortunately, much of the blast was absorbed by the trees, or that would have been the end of the line for me.

I cleared my head just in time to see two troops cutting around the rocks near the fallen trees. They were searching for me when I jerked my weapon up from the ground and fired at them. My movement attracted their attention, but they saw me too late to react. Both crumbled to the ground.

Not everyone I hit was killed, and what was left of the element withdrew. I dropped back and rejoined my team.

I returned to the team about 1:30 P.M. I'd been fighting pitched battles off and on since 11:00 A.M. and the two and a half hours of incredible stress were beginning to wear me ragged. My head throbbed wildly. Sweat rolled off me in buckets, drenching my clothing, which clung to my body as if I'd just stepped out of a pool. Every muscle burned and cried out for relief, for a few minutes of inactivity to recuperate. I'd have given almost anything for the time to take a short nap.

But saddest of all was the sight of my team, my friends. The scene was basically composed of two colors, green and red. Blood-drenched bandages attempted to stem the outpouring of life from the four who were scattered in the grass before me. Amazingly enough, all were in various stages of consciousness, though I could tell that at least one of them wouldn't survive. Each of them looked at me with eyes that screamed, *Save us*! No words were spoken; they weren't necessary. There I was, the only guy who wasn't fucked up, and everybody was looking to me, pleading for help—*Save us*! I tried to display a positive and confident bearing, despite the tremendous odds against us and my own doubts. However, I was sure of one thing. I wasn't going to roll over and die. I would go down fighting, as melodramatic as it may sound. I would certainly do no less.

I called in another SITREP. Immediately after my report, Covey, who'd been monitoring my communications from high overhead, came up on the radio and said that he'd located a bomb crater two hundred meters to our east. He stated that we should try moving to it so we could be extracted. I confirmed that we'd make an attempt to reach it.

I told the team to sit tight and that I was going to recon the route to the crater. Covey told me that the area surrounding the crater was fairly open, making an excellent spot for the enemy to assault us. That being the case, there was no sense in trying to move everyone at the same time; if we encountered any opposition my crippled team would actually hinder my actions. I had to be sure the way was absolutely clear before we attempted a group move.

My trip to the bomb crater was uneventful. The terrain, though hilly, was not difficult to traverse, and I reached the edge of the crater in less than ten minutes. Everything appeared to be in order—I hadn't seen a trace of the enemy anywhere along the route. I wanted to take a few minutes to sweep the area around the hole, but I couldn't afford the time.

The sky had cleared up considerably since the start of the mission, and I could see plenty of blue between the clouds. Every now and then I'd catch a glimpse of the Cessna O-2 through the clouds as it circled. While I knelt by the crater I heard antiaircraft fire off in the distance. I was sure they were trying to take out the small spotter plane.

Since I wasn't absolutely sure there were no enemy in the area, I decided not to talk on the radio for fear of possibly giving myself away. Instead, I pulled out a small mirror to signal the FAC. I keyed my radio, which indicated a signal from the ground was forthcoming, and waited for him to hit an open stretch of sky. When I saw Covey I flashed him so he'd know I'd made it to the crater, and to confirm that the bomb hole I was kneeling by was the same one he'd spotted. He keyed his radio twice, which meant OK. I put the mirror away and headed back to try to lead the team to safety.

Suddenly, I was on the ground.

Something was wrong. I wasn't moving—or even standing, for that matter. I was on my side, in tall grass. I didn't know why I was on the ground; I didn't recall even thinking about getting down—or did I? But there I was—*why*?

Slowly, I began to realize that something had happened; something that wasn't my doing. I was trying to think as I lay there. I wasn't unconscious—I think—I remembered movement. Movement in my peripheral vision. My body moving where I didn't direct it. My mind saying, *Bodywhatishappeningwhatdidthatnotthisdirectionmiscalculationmisfire*.

I thought I should sit up. With one arm I pushed my body into a sitting position, with both legs sort of crossed in front of me. I slumped forward. Right away I felt sick to my stomach. I felt something catch in my throat, and I vomited.

Blood.

Lots of blood.

Blood ran down my chin and came out of my nose. A small pool of blood and puke collected in my lap. I stared dumbfounded at the spreading mass of vile liquid.

Panic city!

At that moment I realized I was hurt. I got scared big-time. I thought Oh, shit. Son of a bitch! Motherfucker!

In the blink of an eye I became emotionally upset. The initial Gee, what happened to me? wore off, and panic set in. My mind exploded with a million colliding thoughts. I just sat there. I didn't know what to do. I was going to die.

And then, just when it seemed like my life was over, I heard the Bummer's voice close behind me. Now, everyone will say I was delirious and hallucinating, which was probably the case. But I swear he was right over my shoulder, talking in a clear, calm voice, instructing me what to do next.

I calmed down and felt reassured. More importantly, I started thinking clearly again. I'm convinced the voice saved my life, even if I did imagine it.

I took my field dressing from its case and opened the plastic bag surrounding the cloth bandage. Just before I applied the plastic bag and bandage to the oozing hole in my chest, I suddenly realized I probably had an exit wound in my back. My gasps for air were accompanied by horrible sucking sounds. Every time I drew a breath my lungs quivered violently, like I had a really bad chest cold, only a hundred time worse. I probed around my back and discovered that, indeed, the round had come out; I felt bone fragments and flesh projecting from the wound.

With all the speed of a sloth I got my pocket knife out and managed to cut a small piece out of my poncho to cover up my back wound. I then went about the incredibly awkward procedure of dressing both wounds. I was somehow able to get the bandage around my upper torso, with the plastic bag blocking my chest wound. After loosely securing the bandage, I took the piece of poncho and shoved it up under the wraps around my back. At the time I wasn't sure if I even came close to the hole. Obviously, I managed to cover it. Once the two pieces of plastic were in place I pulled the bandage very, very tight.

I have no idea how much time elapsed from the moment I was shot to the point where I tied off the bandage. Not that it really mattered, because the next thing I knew three guys—with a fourth trailing behind—approached my position. I was sitting where I'd fallen, in thigh-deep grass mixed with short bushes. I watched them as they stepped over a log some distance away, walking straight at me. They didn't appear overly concerned; in fact, they were rather nonchalant.

Looking back on the incident, I'm sure they thought I was dead, or at least totally out of it and an easy capture. I might have made the same assumption—knowing how I was hit—but I'd never approach a fallen enemy soldier like they were doing. You just never knew what might happen; in this case, they would pay dearly for their assumption. As to the reason why they waited so long to come after me—I don't know. Perhaps they thought there might be more Americans around, so they decided to sit tight for a while.

When they finally got up to where they could clearly see me sitting up, they realized that I wasn't dead. Not only that, but shock and fear glazed their eyes when it suddenly hit them that I was swinging my weapon up from the ground. They were so stunned by the totally unexpected turn of events that they barely reacted—and then much too late.

With my weapon down around my waist I fired two or three short bursts at them. Two went down in an instant without firing a shot; the third turned to run but was caught in the back by a couple of rounds and fell in a heap. The fourth enemy troop simply evaporated into the woods.

I don't know where the energy came from, but a few seconds later I was on my feet and moving in a direction perpendicular to the one the fleeing enemy soldier had just taken. I managed to fade into the trees without attracting any further attention. All I had to do was get my bearings and traverse the moderately yielding terrain back to the team.

Surprising myself with the effort, I plowed my way through the bush, expecting at any moment to simply drop dead or stumble headlong into an ambush or a booby-trap. I was making reasonably good time, all things considered. However, I was near the point of mental and physical exhaustion, which caused my actions to became sloppy and careless. Everything I'd been taught about moving silently through the jungle went right out the window. I must have sounded like a bull elephant crashing through the vegetation.

Once again, panic clawed at my emotions. The more noise I made, the more certain I was that the enemy would zero in on me and terminate my existence. After all I'd been through, the image of me spread out dead on the jungle floor played over and over in my mind. My fear was feeding on itself. I picked up the pace and plunged straight ahead, making no attempt to conceal my movements.

Finally, I linked up with the team. By then my body was ready to call it quits; I practically crawled the last fifty to sixty meters. When I lurched into their position and they saw I was seriously injured, the tiny spark of hope in their eyes vanished. Hobart looked at me, slowly shook his head, and said emphatically, "Man, are we fucked now."

I'll admit the situation looked hopeless. But I told Hobart that I'd made the trek to the bomb crater, and the way should hopefully be clear to make our move. Unfortunately, due to everyone's condition—

mine included—I'd have to make several trips to move each person individually.

Can you believe it? I'd been hit bad, and yet I was the most physically fit guy there.

I can hardly begin to describe the genuine effort it took for me to carry, push, and drag everyone to that giant hole in the jungle. The entire episode remains blurred in my mind to this day; I really don't remember too many details. I do recall feeling incredibly tired—I wanted to go to sleep so badly. I remember concentrating on putting one foot in front of the other as one of the Yards hung limp at my side. Once I was on my hands and knees as I pulled someone along by his web gear. Crawl forward a few feet, pull hard, fight the pain. Crawl, pull. Crawl, pull.

In time I somehow managed to assist or flat-out transport each member of RT Vermont to the extraction point. Once we were all in the crater, I established some semblance of security. Hobart and Yube were capable of firing their weapons if push came to shove, so I positioned them where they could provide the most help in our defense.

We waited.

Shortly after taking up residence in the crater, we were assaulted by a sizable force. Rounds began to fly back and forth. Just as the battle was beginning to heat up, a new and unexpected variable entered the equation.

Dramatically, a Huey materialized out of thin air! It simply came out of nowhere and dropped down to within five meters or so of the crater's rim, where it hovered unsteadily. I looked skyward and spotted the door gunner shifting around behind the M-60, scanning the area. I didn't have a clue as to who was in the chopper or what operation they were running. All I knew was it didn't belong to my organization. But man, it was the first sign of friendlies I'd seen all day, and my emotions ran wild.

Too bad I didn't have any time to enjoy the moment.

Mere seconds after the Huey dropped in from out of the blue, the jungle surrounding the crater came alive in a frightening display of firepower. 7.62mm, mortar, and antitank rounds burst out of the light vegetation. All the destructive force was focused on one target: the chopper.

I didn't attempt to return any fire. It would have been useless and a waste of ammo. We were in a whirlwind of devastation, and the best course of action was to hug the ground and ride out the storm. I watched in awe as the drama unfolded.

The noise was deafening. Shit was flying everywhere. Scores of tracers ripped up through the trees, and rockets spewing smoke criss-crossed every which way. If even one of the antitank rounds had hit the chopper it would have been all over; as it was, none found the mark. However, the 7.62mm rounds found their target often. The Huey was being eaten up by the rifle and machine-gun fire. The door gunner was hit and hung limp over the M-60. The chopper's skin was pockmarked from hundreds of rounds. There must have been fifty or more enemy troops assaulting the Huey with but a single thought—bring that son of a bitch down!

All this activity occurred within ten to twenty seconds. How the chopper stayed in the air I'll never know. By all rights it should have been shot down. But stay aloft it did, and badly scarred from the effort, it beat a hasty—if somewhat erratic—retreat. Its departure sent a chill down my spine.

Now the enemy would focus his attention on us.

A lull ensued after the chopper left. No more 7.62mm, mortar, or antitank rounds were fired. There was movement all around us, but no hostilities were directed our way. I couldn't understand why they didn't attack immediately. They knew we were in the crater; surely they could have overwhelmed us with sheer numbers or simply lobbed a few mortars or frags on top of us. As strange as it may seem, I was irritated and concerned as to the reasons for the delay. I knew the asskick was coming. Finally, I concluded that they were toying with us.

Ten minutes later they mounted an assault, although it wasn't quite as strong as I had expected. They laid into us with a heavy barrage of fire as we met the challenge. Hobart, Yube, and I gave as good as we received, and we forced them to back off after a few minutes of frenzied action.

It was time once again to take the offensive. We couldn't afford to just sit back and wait for them to attack us whenever they felt like it. It was now four o'clock. In a few hours it would be dark, and then we'd be almost totally defenseless. Another mounting problem was ammunition, or lack thereof. Already I was into Green's and Gai's basic load, in addition to that which I'd retrieved from Prep and Hyuk. If we had to repel more hit-and-run attacks we'd expend our short supply of rounds in no time, and then it really would be all over.

I told Hobart and Yube to hang tight and that I'd be back in a few minutes. My plan was similar to the one I'd employed before I was wounded: hit them when and where they weren't expecting it.

I dragged myself out of the bomb crater and crawled to the edge of the jungle cover. Fear and nervous energy renewed some of my vitality, and I rapidly covered approximately thirty meters, reaching a spot with good ambush potential. It had cover—a big rock—and plenty of vegetation for concealment. I got down and prepared to do battle. I got out my final frag, my last two CS grenades, and my remaining two magazines, and placed them next to me for quick access. I took up a good firing position based on where I thought they'd be coming from, and then I waited.

Since I wasn't under any pressure yet I had time to assess our situation. I started doing some serious thinking: We've been at this since eleven o'clock; nobody's come to help us yet; I'm badly hurt; each member of the team is either dead or seriously injured; there's maybe one hour of daylight left; there's no indication that we're going to receive any assistance; our ammo is almost gone.

My thoughts were interrupted by the sounds of troops massing to my front. I wanted to cry. I knew that in the next few minutes a whole bunch of people were going to come along, there was going to be a lot of asskick, and everything I could do just wouldn't be enough.

I watched as the large group materialized from its concealed ready line and stalked in my direction. They weren't spread out in proportion to their size because the terrain wouldn't allow it; the fact that they were somewhat channeled was a definite plus for me.

When they were about fifteen meters from my position I took them under fire. Once again I caught them off guard; they weren't expecting any contact forward of the crater. My initial rounds dropped several troops, but the rest quickly overcame their shock and threw a barrage that pinned me down. As I reached for the frag, an explosion shook my cover—they'd hit the rock I was hiding behind with an antitank round. The rocket didn't do much damage to the large rock, and it remained firmly in place.

My attack had caused them to drop in place and return fire, but soon after they used the tank killer they were on their feet and assaulting. I threw the frag, and suddenly they had a change of heart. Several more soldiers went down; the rest kind of scattered. Those still alive after the blast tried to drag themselves away, but I saw my chance and put them down once again, this time for good.

The remainder of the group didn't stay away long. Less than a minute later they mounted another assault, accompanied by intense fire. At that moment I realized my position was no longer defensible and that I was going to be overrun. I popped the two CS grenades and threw them in front of the oncoming wave, creating confusion and halting the charge. They retreated.

As they withdrew I hauled ass back to the crater. I'd just cleared the rim of the hole and gotten into a fighting posture when the enemy came streaming through the gas. I cranked off a couple of rounds while they were still some distance away. Hobart and Yube began shooting as well, and our combined fire slowed, then finally stopped the enemy's advance ten meters short of their target. However, the now-static troops continued to apply tremendous pressure on us.

I'd just shifted my sights to another target when I was hit in the arm. The impact sent me tumbling down toward the center of the bomb hole. When I came to a stop, I was doubled over and sort of kneeling in some grass, clutching my forearm midway between the wrist and the elbow. As I went to get up, I looked at my wounded limb. My entire lower arm was covered with blood, and because of the way I was kneeling my hand was obscured by the grass. My heart stopped. I thought my hand was gone, that my worst nightmare had finally come true. My greatest fear was not dying, but returning home from the war missing a body part.

I half-glanced in Hobart's direction and screamed, "Motherfucker! My hand's been blown off!"

Hobart sat mute for a few seconds, then yelled back, "Son of a bitch! You're the only one who can do anything!" Which was even more true now than before, because Yube and Hobart had been hit again and were for all intents and purposes out of it. They were both stretched out on the crater's sloping grade, conscious but helpless.

We were doomed.

When I pulled erect I discovered my hand was still attached, and a momentary wave of relief and joy overcame me. In retrospect, it seems funny to have experienced such a joyous feeling in the face of certain death. But there was no denying I was incredibly happy that my body still possessed all its original equipment.

The immediate situation flooded back into my consciousness and shattered my hopes. It was almost seven o'clock and darkness was setting in.

Darkness meant our deaths.

I was down to one magazine and a frag from Yube. My left arm was useless and bleeding profusely, in spite of the rag I'd wrapped around it. We were basically no longer capable of defending ourselves. All those wonderful little things you said you'd do, like, "I'll kill myself first," or, "They'll never take me alive"—fuck that. Make no mistake about it—we wanted to live.

I crawled over to the radio and cranked it up one last time. I started to hoarsely sing "Help" by the Beatles. I don't know why I did it. I guess I was half-delirious at that point. I was trying to make light of a bad situation.

I was on the verge of tears because I knew that at any moment we were going to be killed. I was scared to death. All my feelings, all my emotions, were right in my throat, where fear had a tight grip. The switch in my head had flipped from sane to insane, and yet everyone was looking at me for the answers. Unfortunately, I'd given all the answers I had to give—all the first aid, all the tactics, all my fighting skills.

The well had finally gone dry.

I heard movement all around the crater, and as a final act of defiance I took the frag, stuck it between my knees, pulled the pin with my right hand and, without looking, heaved the grenade backward over my shoulder. It barely cleared the crater's rim before it exploded.

Hobart and I exchanged looks of defeat. Tears were running down his face. We didn't say a word to each other, but our eyes spoke volumes. It was the end of our days, forever. We had totally surrendered to our fate.

I heard more movement directly at the rim and thought, Fuck me, here it comes.

This is it.

Yards.

I thought I was seeing things.

I saw a point man, then two or three other guys. One of them was carrying an M-60. Right then and there I knew my eyes weren't playing tricks on me in the diminishing light. They *were* Yards.

The point man motioned to me, asking where the enemy was located. I pointed in the direction from which we'd received the most fire, and the six-man Yard team slipped past me along the edge of the crater.

Seconds later all hell broke loose as the Yards engaged the source of all our grief. The flash from the M-60 lit up the surrounding trees as it sang in its deep voice. No music ever sounded as sweet.

As soon as the battle started, I noticed another team of Yards rush past the crater, and this time they had an American lieutenant with them. He jumped down into the crater alongside me. The first words out of his mouth were, "Motherfucker, this looks like Custer's Last Stand."

I turned and looked at him, but I didn't say anything. I was too far out of it to even attempt conversation. Meanwhile, Yards continued to stream past our position, forming a human barrier between us and the enemy.

What I didn't know at the time was that our headquarters had realized the asskick was much too big for a small seven-man Bright Light team, so they had mobilized a Hatchet Force, which consisted of an entire platoon of Yards with American leaders.

The Hatchet Force swept in and bought us the necessary extraction time, although they definitely didn't have an easy go of it. Rounds flew everywhere for a while before the Hatchet Force was able to beat back the opposition to the point where it was relatively safe to bring in the choppers.

The next thing I knew, slicks were dropping in from the rapidly blackening sky, picking up my folks and disengaging members of the Hatchet Force. I wouldn't let them load me onto a slick until everyone else had been extracted. I was the last man to leave the ground, winging away on the final chopper.

They flew us back to the launch site at Dak To. By the time my slick finally landed, the medics had already stretched out my team on the ground. They told me a medevac was on the way from Pleiku, which was thirty miles below Kontum, so it was going to be a long wait. In the meantime, the medics worked feverishly on the living and bagged the dead.

We waited over an hour, but no medevac arrived. During that time I sat on a bunker, staring alternately out into the darkness and at my people. At one point the doc gave me a quick examination, during which he exclaimed, "Man, I don't know how you made it that fucking long." He didn't want to remove my bandages for fear of causing even more damage.

I didn't realize how mentally and physically drained I was until I had the time to think about it. Emotionally, I was devastated. Tears welled up into my eyes, triggered partly by joy at our rescue, but mostly by sadness. I was really, really down. Some of my folks were dead, while others were in the process of dying. I would miss them deeply, especially the Yards. I'd worked with the Yards for so long that they'd become my family, my constant companions; now they'd never see another sunrise.

My colonel flew up to the launch site to check our condition personally. He walked up to me and put his hand on my shoulder. He started talking to me, trying his best to pep me up. He recalled his time in World War II, about all the ugliness he'd seen and the sadness he'd known. The colonel wasn't trying to say he'd seen some really bad shit, but more or less that, "Hey, you made it. You're out. I've been there. I understand what you're going through."

The medevacs came, and we were loaded for the long flight to the hospital in Pleiku. Attached to my body was a tag identifying me and my unit and summarizing my injuries. It also read, in part: "Location—Classified. Top Secret." Even in my frazzled state of mind I thought that was neat. I could picture everyone looking at me out of the corners of their eyes and whispering to each other that some mysterious, high-speed bad boy had just been admitted. It's funny, the things that go through your mind at certain times.

Medical teams were waiting for us when we landed. We were whisked off of the chopper and into a large room to be prepped for immediate surgery. As I lay flat on my back on the gurney I watched several medics frantically cut the clothing and equipment from Yube's body before wheeling him into the operating room. When he was out of my sight, I turned my face toward the ceiling and closed my eyes. Since I was the least injured—which said a great deal about everyone else's condition—I would be the last one to enter the cutting shop.

Now I could get a little rest.

THE MORNING AFTER

When I opened my eyes I was in a bed. My left arm was bent at the elbow, forming a ninety-degree angle, and encased in a thick plaster cast suspended from a rail. My chest was heavily bandaged, and it seemed that the wrappings restricted my breathing. As I fought my way out of the haze I felt something in my throat that was really bothering me. Finally, my mind cleared up somewhat and I realized that I had a tube running up my nose and an IV plugged into my right arm.

I vaguely recall someone saying something to the effect of, "Oh, I see you're finally with us."

"Get this fuckin' thing out of my nose," I hoarsely cried out to no one in particular. A nurse who was sitting a short distance from my bed immediately got up and began walking over to me, all the while explaining in a soft voice something about draining my lungs or some such thing. I didn't understand what was going on. I was still groggy from the drugs and just wanted the tube removed from my nose.

Before she could stop me I reached up and yanked the son of a bitch completely out. That act expended all my energy reserves. I was dead in the water; motionless. I could do nothing but lie there, and soon the world of reality clouded up again and I began drifting back into a painless world of darkness.

THE FINAL COUNT

A few days later they moved me into a ward. I continued to fade in and out, but as the days sped by I gradually fought my way out of the fog for good.

One day two nurses brought Yube and Hobart by to see me. Both were in wheelchairs. It was the single most emotional moment I experienced during my stay in the hospital. We talked for a long time, but first they wanted to tell me, "Thanks. Thanks for everything." I was so choked up I could barely speak.

When all was said and done, three of seven lived to tell the tale. Yube, Hobart, and I were the lucky ones. Prep and Hyuk had died on the battlefield; Gai and Green expired on the operating table.

After our words were said the nurses wheeled Yube and Hobart away. I would never see or hear from them again.

Farewell, my friends.

RECOGNITION

The day after my emotional reunion with Yube and Hobart, a captain from my unit approached me.

"We're going to put you in for the Distinguished Service Cross," he said in a very sincere tone. The DSC is the second-highest-rated medal, ranked right behind the Congressional Medal of Honor.

I thought, Man, you've got to be bullshitting me. I was blown away. I certainly didn't feel like I'd done anything special; to my way of thinking, I was only doing what was necessary to survive and keep my team alive. But when it comes to awards, it's not what you think— Yes I deserve something/No I don't—but rather what the people around you think.

I was at Pleiku for slightly more than two weeks before they attempted to move me to a hospital in Japan. A couple of days prior to the transfer, the captain from my unit visited me again. This time he informed me that all the paperwork for the DSC had been submitted to the headquarters at Nha Trang, but after reading the narratives they determined that my actions were worthy of the highest award the military could bestow. So they kicked the documentation back to the unit and told them to resubmit the award recommendation for the Congressional Medal of Honor. They were in the process of doing just that, and the captain dropped by to let me know that they hadn't forgotten me. He mentioned that he hoped the news would cheer me up.

Was he kidding? The Congressional Medal of Honor?

I was overwhelmed.

LAND OF THE RISING SUN

When it was determined that I could be moved without further traumatizing or aggravating my injuries, they flew me to a hospital at Camp Zama, Japan. It was one of many hospital facilities established specifically for Vietnam casualties.

The first detail that struck me about my temporary home was that the majority of the patients were not wounded. They were suffering from noncombat-related injuries or illnesses, such as vehicular accidents and diseases. Now I'm certainly not trying to imply that there was anything wrong with them being there; after all, it was a regular hospital, and most of the patients had been injured or had gotten sick while they were doing their jobs. It was just that I was used to seeing combat-related injuries, such as gunshot and mine wounds. I guess because of the environment I operated in, I never thought about all the normal, everyday stuff that happens to people.

I basically hung around with two people during my convalescence. One of my partners in crime was a bizarre guy from Tiger Force of the 101st Airborne Division. The other dude was an equally wild and crazy individual from a quartermaster outfit somewhere around Saigon. Now when I say "hung around," I mean that our beds were next to each other. All three of us were bedridden for quite some time, so our activities—at least initially—were kind of limited.

Our favorite thing was racing slot cars. We had our beds positioned so that all three of us could see the track and control our cars. Since we were confined to our beds, the nurses or mobile fellow patients would put the cars back on the track when they came off. We spent countless hours racing round and round the little black plastic track.

At night the hospital ward became a free-for-all zone. It wasn't run-amok wild or anything like that, but there was definitely a high level of bullshitting going on. The lights may have been out, but I guarantee you that very few people were sleeping. Most people had so much unexpended energy that it was impossible for them to be still. They were restless and on the prowl at night. Anyone who's ever spent a considerable amount of time in a hospital bed will understand how it fucks up your internal clock and thus your sleeping routine.

THOUGHTS THAT KILL

One day a new arrival on the ward was rolled up next to me. He hadn't been operated on yet, and after he'd lain there motionless for a while he looked over at me and said in an incredibly pitiful voice, "I'm having a problem sitting up, and I can't feel my leg. Would you please take a look for me to make sure everything is all right?"

He had a thin, white sheet draped over the lower half of his body. Two full legs were evident under the material, so I realized his numb leg hadn't been partially blown off. Bracing myself for the worst, I told him that I would, and taking a coat hanger I'd straightened out for who knows what reason, I flipped up the sheet just enough for me to glance at his limb.

I silently gagged.

It was gross. Two bullets had struck his leg—one at the hip and another at the knee. The resulting vascular damage cut the flow of blood to his lower leg, and it was painfully obvious to me that his leg was dead from his knee down. It was a dark purplish black; its skin was withered and wrinkled. I knew immediately that they were going to have to amputate it.

Marshaling my intestinal fortitude, I half-smiled and looked him right in the eye. "Yep, it's still there."

That seemed to ease his mind for the moment, although I knew it wouldn't be long before he found out his leg's fate.

Later that day a doctor came to his bedside and broke the news to him. He did it as gently as he could, but the delivery didn't soften the harsh reality of the situation. The twenty-year-old kid appeared to nod slightly as the doctor assured him that the operation was necessary to save his life and that he'd be fine afterward. Understandably, the minute the doctor left, the young guy got extremely scared and fell into a deep depression. He'd been shot by somebody and, on top of that, they were going to cut off one of his legs. He just stared up at the ceiling, tears streaming down his face.

He was all alone.

No family. No friends.

He was scheduled for the cutting table later in the evening, but as it turned out he wasn't operated on until very early the following morning. There were only so many surgeons to go around, you see.

When I woke up the next morning, the bed to my right was empty, and a nurse was making it up. The nurse saw me wake up and look at the vacant bunk. Our eyes met and I didn't even have to verbalize my question. She told me he'd died during the morning, only hours after the operation. The physical trauma of the surgery hadn't killed him; in fact, he was healthy enough to pull through it easily. But, she went on to explain, sometimes the mental trauma of losing a limb is so severe that patients literally will themselves to die.

During my stay I'd see far too many people in the same predicament as that young man.

And worse.

DEVASTATION

I'd seen some severely injured troops during my years of running around in the woods, but none were as horrifyingly mutilated as the soldier who was wheeled down the ward's center aisle one afternoon.

I was reading a magazine when two nurses barreled through the double swinging doors, escorting his bed at a quick pace. It was evident from the number of IVs and tubes radiating from his body that the newest patient on the floor was in dire straits. They rolled his bed into an empty slot halfway up the ward from me, then paused around him to ensure all the tubes and such were secure and functioning. As soon as they finished their visual examination the nurses departed, somber looks masking both of their faces.

Our collective curiosity was only natural, so those of us who could get out of bed—I was able to by this time—did so and took a very slow stroll past the guy's bed. All evening long he had a stream of curious and concerned onlookers flowing in his direction.

It was a shockingly grim sight.

Although no one told us how it happened, it was pretty simple to piece together the puzzle.

With his right foot, he'd stepped on a mine which blew off his leg at mid-thigh. His left leg had been severed just below the knee. The blast came up between his legs and ripped away all of his ass and most of his inner thighs. Dark streaks were carved into his body from his abdomen to the top of his forehead by fragmentation. One hand was missing. Chunks of flesh were gouged from his face, and he was blind.

It was enough to turn a strong man weak. And make no mistake about it—he was in pain.

Real, deep, genuine pain.

He constantly moaned. There was no stopping him. All the drugs the hospital had to offer were ineffective against his unrelenting misery, and his moans were an ever-present reminder of his torment. There was no escaping them.

My first reactions upon seeing him were, How did he manage to live, and Why did somebody save him? The latter may sound cruel, but what life was there for him if he pulled through? In this case, I believe it would have been better for all concerned if he'd died on the battlefield.

He lived for about ten days. During that time all the bullshitting on the ward ceased, and he became the main topic of conversation. His presence had a sobering effect on us. It became an unwritten rule— as long as he was alive we would show respect. He'd earned at least that from us. If anyone started to act up or get rowdy, he'd be glared at until he got the drift: knock it off. Even though many of us were hurting, we tried to take up as little of the nurses' time as possible, so they might spend it on him. Our pains seemed small in comparison.

At first we thought he'd make it, but as the days passed all the signs pointed to his death. The doctors, who normally checked his progress twice a day, began making trips to his bedside every hour. We knew his condition was deteriorating when we saw a priest visit him twice within two days. We saw the end coming.

Four days before he expired I was talking with the guy from the 101st Airborne when a woman entered the ward. She had on a hat and a long wool coat—a mom's coat. She looked like anybody's mom in that coat. I thought how she looked out of place; she didn't look like a nurse, and she appeared too old to be in the military.

She hesitated for a moment, then walked down the main aisle and turned in beside That Guy's bed. When she saw him she knew right away that it was her son. Her hands flew up to her mouth, and I could see her trembling all the way from my bed.

Everyone tried to make themselves busy to afford her as much privacy as possible, instead of sitting there and watching her every move. After some time I grabbed a nurse and quietly grilled her for some information. The woman was in fact his mother, and his parents had scraped together just enough cash to send only her.

The nurses and doctors were very pleasant and accommodating. They brought her a big chair and allowed her to sleep right there next to his bed. The nurses brought her food and drink throughout the days, and she rarely left his side. She talked to him in spurts, softly whispering in his ear at times. He lay there motionless the entire time, except on one occasion.

I happened to look in their direction as she was hunched over close talking to him. I couldn't hear what she was saying, but suddenly he turned his head toward her voice. He didn't utter a word; at least I didn't hear him speak, if he did say anything. Somewhere in the recesses of his shattered mind he must have realized that it was his mom speaking to him. His mother jumped slightly at the unexpected movement, a look of surprise and hope spreading across her face.

But that was it. He didn't move again.

Something woke me up around two o'clock the morning that he died. It was completely dark on the ward, with the exception of the light at the nurses' station and the light next to his bed. When my eyes got accustomed to the blackness I noticed that just about every patient was awake and staring intently as the drama unfolded. Unfortunately, we all knew that there would be no happy ending.

A priest scurried in, presumably to administer the last rites. Doctors and nurses shuttled in and out of the light, doing their best to save him or make his passing as painless as possible. They worked at a measured pace, but the air of death rushed in, and soon it was over. The moment of his death was almost visible, like the air around his bed suddenly changed into something tangible, something touchable.

I never even knew his name.

A WEEKLY THING

Everybody on my ward always had a perfect haircut. Getting a weekly haircut was a very pleasant experience because it was the first time in our careers that we'd had our hair sheared by women—pretty Japanese women with incredibly soft hands.

It became a once-a-week ritual that was never missed, mainly because in addition to a really squared-away haircut, you got a fantastically soothing facial, neck, and shoulder massage. Just being around a woman—having her hands caress your skin and massage your muscles—was enough to keep you coming back for more.

My attendance record was perfect.

TURNING POINT

As my physical condition rapidly improved, my pucker factor rose dramatically. During my last couple of weeks in the hospital I made it a point to tell my doctors—every chance I got—that I really, *really* wanted to go back to Vietnam.

They always shook their heads and chuckled, like, Boy, there must be something wrong with this individual. "Yeah, some guys are really dedicated, ya know, but, ah, it's time that you sorta went back to the World. That'd be the best thing for you. You've done more than your share. Go home."

They couldn't begin to know, but 'Nam was where my heart longed to be. The doctors thought they were doing me a favor by sending me "home." They were going to square me away by sending me back to the States and saving me from combat, knowing very well that somebody would have to take my place.

I went through the drill of trying to get them to legitimately reassign me to my old unit, but to no avail. Time was running out for me. If I didn't make something happen soon I'd find myself back in the U.S.A.

But I got lucky once again.

One night I was partying it up outside of Camp Zama when I ran into an E-7 who worked in the orders section of Camp Zama's personnel administration center. I immediately started in on him, saying how much I wanted to return to 'Nam and what a bummer it was that they wouldn't let me go back. He asked me if I was a Special Forces guy. When I replied that I was, he responded, "Yeah, I can understand that! I always wanted to go Special Forces myself, but, you know how it goes. I hurt my knee a long time ago, and I can't jump or anything, but man, I always wanted to do shit like that."

We got to drinking into the night, and finally he said, "I'll tell ya what. I'm gonna head back to the office now, and you meet me here tomorrow night." He stumbled off into the darkness.

I linked up with him the following evening. He led me to a shadowy corner of the bar, where we sat on two rickety chairs around a stained and sticky table. When we were seated, he leaned way over next to me and whispered, "I'll be able to pull it off. I've got an officer friend of mine who's gonna go ahead and sign the orders. I'll also square ya away on gettin' ya out of the hospital." I gave him all the information he needed, and we parted company.

The next day I stopped by his office and he had my orders waiting. "Here ya go," he beamed as he handed me my ticket back to 'Nam. "I'm really glad ta help ya out. It feels good ta know that I've done my fair share for the cause." He went on to tell me that he'd coordinated with the hospital for my release. He told them that my orders had come down and it was urgent for me to return to my old unit. The hospital could do nothing but comply since I had almost fully recovered and, after all, I *did* have my orders.

I was delighted. I thanked him profusely, telling him what a wonderful patriot he was and how I wouldn't forget him. Clutching the papers with a death grip, I shook his hand, said good-bye, and proceeded without delay to initiate my discharge from the hospital.

My signing out of the hospital went without a hitch. They never questioned the legitimacy of the orders, although I did get some suspicious looks, like, Going back, eh? Mighty coincidental, don't you think? How did you get so lucky? Oh, well. We tried to do you a favor.

By this time I'd secured some jungle fatigues from a bunch of Air Force types whom I'd run into around the local ville. I finally looked and felt halfway normal once I put on the uniform. Prior to acquiring the fatigues, I had been forced to wear clothing donated to me by patients and local folks, since all I had before their generosity was hospital garb. Patient gowns didn't go over big in the ville, so out of necessity I borrowed enough pieces of clothing to allow me to party it up outside the hospital confines. However, beggars can't be choosers, and my attire was, well . . . not stylish. In fact, I looked like a jerk. My pants were about four inches too short, and my shirt was a size or two too small. But what the hell, they provided me freedom for pleasure, right?

As fast as I could, I got down to the Military Airlift Command (MAC) terminal. I walked right up to the counter, presented my orders and ID card, and told the guy that I wanted to get on the next thing smokin' to 'Nam.

As luck would have it, a commercial troop plane—a Flying Tiger— was arriving in a few hours on a brief refueling stop before proceeding to 'Nam. There were several empty seats, so I was all set. Before I knew it, I was winging my way "home."

GETTING THERE IS HALF THE FUN

Boy, did I have fun on the way back. There I was, dressed in jungle fatigues bearing no rank, name, or insignia, while everyone else had on brand-new khakis, fresh from the U.S. of A. I thought I'd get them in the proper frame of mind, so I told horror stories during the entire flight. I even showed them my injuries, much to their dismay. When we got over the coast, I pointed out that the flashes of light they were witnessing were the result of artillery shells exploding. I momentarily thought back to the first time I'd seen the white dots of light. "They must have located the motherfuckers. The shit's gettin' deep. All right!" I pronounced with glee. I had everybody's undivided attention until the plane touched down in Bien-hoa.

As the "fresh meat" filed off the plane, they were greeted by NCOs who took control and directed them into a big formation. As soon as I hit the ground I split off from the group and started walking toward a cluster of hooches. I paused for a moment, turned around, and shouted back at the formation, "Take it easy now! You behave yourselves. Don't worry about it. You'll be OK. You guys got one year, so what? I just got through spendin' all this time here and I'm back again. You'll have a good time, believe me! See ya later!" The NCOs running the formation all glanced at me, like, Who the fuck is this asshole?

I crossed the tarmac to the Special Forces "B" detachment, which was the next line of support for the forward-deployed "A" teams. I knew some guys there, so I told them the whole story and that I needed to get to my old unit. But first I wanted to visit my old girlfriend for a few days before I reported in—and why not? I had a set of phony orders. Nobody knew I existed. I was in limbo. My old unit sure wasn't expecting me, and the hospital had washed its hands of my case. I was free to do whatever the hell entered my mind.

I borrowed a hundred bucks and jumped into a Vietnamese motor-cycle taxi for the twenty-mile journey to my girlfriend's home. She was excited, to say the least. I'd known her for several years, and I cared deeply for her. When I stopped seeing her—because of my hospital stay—she'd figured that this time I'd been fucked up beyond the point of no return. So when I showed up that day she was beside herself with joy, and I felt likewise.

I stayed with her for about a week. Although I was having the time of my life and didn't want to leave, I started feeling guilty about abusing my clever scheme. I began thinking about all the guys running around the woods kicking ass, while I was shirking my duty. I indulged myself one more night with my girlfriend, then headed back to Bien-hoa.

HOME IS WHERE YOUR HEART IS

When I got to the "B" detachment I contacted my unit and told some friends of mine that I'd be up there soon. I then got together with the appropriate personnel and found out that a C-123 was headed up to Kontum later on that day. I gave them a copy of my orders and was placed on the manifest.

My heart was beating fast with excitement as we approached Kontum. I was ecstatic at the thought of seeing my old friends and being back in the environment where I felt totally at ease—where I belonged.

They were waiting for me. Parked next to the tarmac was the only vehicle that existed in the company—a jeep we had named "Cheap Thrills." Standing around it were two of my Yards and a couple of RT leaders. When I saw them I got a little choked up. As I rushed forward, all I could do was throw my arms out wide and yell, "Mother-fuckers! Here I am!"

They coolly hesitated until I was close to the vehicle, then they lurched forward and swarmed around me. Backslaps, hugs, and smiles abounded. It was like a homecoming.

"Son of a bitch, man, we didn't believe it was you!" one of the RT leaders exclaimed. "We thought it was somebody bullshitting us by saying that you were coming up today. We never figured to see you again." The Yards were like little kids full of unbridled enthusiasm. They hugged me tightly, saying, "We really miss you, One-Zero. We really glad to see you."

The ride from the airstrip to the camp was pure magic for me. We passed through sections of jungle, open fields, and the village/town of Kontum. Though it was slightly overcast I kept thinking, What a beautiful day! Everything seemed right with the world. Strong emotions coursed through my body. The feelings were strong; they hit me all at once—I knew this place. I lived, worked, and played here. The smell of the jungle. The sights and sounds of Kontum. Weapons everywhere.

"Cheap Thrills" bouncing along a dirt road I'd traveled hundreds of times. Yards.

I was back where I belonged.

I was home.

I HAVE RETURNED

The colonel was crossing the compound when our jeep slid to a halt in front of the company. He did a double-take when I stepped out. He stood there for several seconds with his mouth hanging open, then finally called out, "Where the fuck did *you* come from? I thought we got rid of you!"

I just smiled and gave him the classic line, "You can't get rid of me that easily."

He walked over to me and shook my hand. "How the hell did you get here *this* time?" he asked in amazement.

"Well, sir," I started off, hesitating. "I guess I'll give it to ya right up front. I don't belong to anybody. I'm sort of a free agent."

He knew something was up and that I'd pulled some sneaky shit to get back. He simply laughed.

"It's good to see you again, but right now I don't believe you're ready for the woods. You need to recover fully, to convalesce, before I put you back out into the shit. I'm going to send you to a small, isolated camp operated by a friend of mine, where you can drop out of sight, relax, and stay out of trouble for a while."

I spent a total of about two months at that camp. When the colonel concluded that my situation was straightened out and I had fully recovered, he pulled me back to Kontum.

Everything was just like before; I had a regular routine once again. I ran missions. I raised hell with my Yards and fellow RT leaders. My girlfriend came up to be with me, and we moved back into a small house I owned in "downtown" Kontum. Yes, indeed—life was sweet.

A TASTE OF OUR OWN MEDICINE

I was at Kontum for about one month when, after all these years, the enemy—in the area that we worked—finally made the connection as to where we were based. Having discovered our base of operations, they naturally decided to employ some of our own tactics against us.

So one night we were hit by a sapper, or commando, unit.

Hey, I'll admit it—they were good. Their plan was well timed and precise, and they penetrated the compound before we knew what was going on.

I was lying in my bed around ten-thirty or eleven that evening when I heard a series of maybe four or five loud, high-pitched explosions. I sat straight up in bed, wondering what the fuck was going on. All of a sudden I detected the scent of CS gas.

I leapt out of the rack, ran to the door of my hooch, and flung it open.

Son of a bitch!

The tactical operations center (TOC) was a mass of flames! People were running every which way, their forms silhouetted against the huge fire that enveloped the brains of our operation. Shots rang out all over the compound.

It was total chaos!

The other guys in the hooch were scrambling and grabbing for their equipment as I dashed back to retrieve my weapon. I scooped up my web gear and threw it on, and all of us rushed headlong out the door.

We made a beeline for the TOC. Confusion reigned supreme. All around us people were shouting and shooting. We dodged our way through the traffic and reached the TOC unopposed.

The TOC was a large, permanent building shaped like an L that had one floor aboveground and several below. All our intelligence-gathering and -processing equipment resided in that building, including a photo-developing and -analyzing lab, map rooms, high-speed communication equipment, security safes, and the like. Completely encompassing the TOC was a tall chain-link fence and several security bunkers. The TOC was so vital to our operation that even though it was located inside the compound's perimeter, it had its own defense system.

When we got inside the building, we found several officers running up and down the hallway and darting in and out of offices. I asked a captain what had happened and he replied that a sapper had fired an antitank round at the TOC. The rocket barely cleared the chain-link fence and struck several major power lines running into the structure. When the lines were cut they shorted out against the building and started the fire.

The fire hadn't destroyed much of the structure yet, although it was evident that quick thinking and fast action was necessary to save the untouched parts. At that moment the blaze was confined to the colonel's living quarters and office area. The wall adjacent to the colonel's office was hot and smoking. The officers were using fire extinguishers, but they were having no effect; the fire was too intense. It was getting out of hand.

The solution came to me in a flash.

"We can square it away right now," I proclaimed.

"How can you do that?" asked one of the majors.

"Hey, Burko," I yelled. "Go get about twenty pounds of C-4. Bring it here, and we'll slap it all over the wall and blow the old man's hooch down, away from the TOC."

The officers immediately rejected the idea. They were worried about the large amount of explosive material being in close proximity to the fire. I tried to tell them that we'd arm and detonate it so fast that the possibility of someone being injured was slight. Besides, I reasoned, if we didn't do something soon the entire TOC would be lost.

But they didn't want to listen to us. After all, weren't we just a bunch of radical motherfuckers who always wanted to destroy stuff? Since they probably saw us as a pack of wild Indians running around unchecked, they figured my plan to use explosives was simply an extension of doing whatever we damn well pleased. Well, they weren't going to let us "get away with anything." "You can't do that. You're in the TOC now, and what we say goes," scolded the S-3 officer.

Can you believe it? There we were in the middle of a burning building and some guy was afraid of us doing damage to the place! What an idiot!

Sure enough, what he said went; they wouldn't let us implement our plan—which I'm confident would have worked—and the TOC quickly burned to the ground. Not a single piece of equipment, photograph, or map survived. The entire building—above and below ground—was reduced to a large pile of hot, glowing ashes.

So much for higher intelligence.

When the situation settled down, we pieced together what had happened. Eight or nine enemy commandos had crawled up through a small drainage ditch that extended outside the compound's perimeter. The ditch served as the garbage receptacle for the Yards' mess hall. The garbage was swept along by a steady stream of water.

We'd placed a couple of rows of wire inside the ditch to secure it on the outside of the perimeter, but apparently the wire wasn't enough. The enemy had crawled up through the center of the wire and the garbage until they'd gotten just inside the compound's bunker line. They then cut the wire in several places and emerged from the ditch.

On some signal the two fortified perimeter bunkers adjacent to the drainage ditch were hit with antitank rounds. The commandos inside the fence then flipped satchel charges into two more bunkers that were close by. They then proceeded to their primary target—the TOC—and fired several antitank rounds at it. The chain-link fence forced them to aim high and subsequently miss their mark, save for the fluke hit on the power line. But as it turned out, that was all they needed.

During the ensuing chaos somebody managed to lightly wound and capture one of the commandos. He took the enemy troop over to the medical hooch to have his injury treated, but in the confusion the medical personnel dressed the commando's wound and let him go. They didn't realize he was an enemy soldier; they thought he was a Yard.

So much for tight security.

ON THEIR TRAIL

At about three-thirty that morning, the colonel came over to me and said, "I want you to take your team, get outside of the wire, catch up to those guys, and fuck them up. I'm also sending RT Arizona with you."

All I was wearing at the time was a pair of light blue corduroy Levi's and flip-flops. I quickly replaced the sandals with jungle boots and threw on a T-shirt and field jacket. I put on my web gear, grabbed my weapon, and rounded up my team. I explained the situation and our basic plan of attack. Fortunately, I always kept maps of the area in my gear, so we wouldn't be traveling blind on this occasion. I did the necessary coordination with perimeter security, and soon we slipped through the front gate. We followed the perimeter wire to the back of the camp until we came to the drainage ditch. There we picked up the enemy's trail. Everyone switched into an ass-kicking mode as both teams forged ahead through the dense vegetation.

We'd penetrated the edge of the jungle only a short distance when we came across the position from which the enemy had launched a mortar attack on the camp. In all the excitement I wasn't even aware they'd been dropping mortar rounds on us. Their escape route was much clearer at this point. We pressed onward.

Their trail lead us up the face of one of the big mountains surrounding Kontum. The enemy had beat feet in a no-bullshit manner—they traveled in a straight line up the steep, rugged slope with no wasted side-to-side traversing. They were headed for tall timber at the top of the mountain, and they were taking the shortest—albeit roughest—route.

The Yards were doing an excellent job of tracking and never lost the trail for a moment. By now the sun was coming up on the horizon behind us, which made the Yards' job much easier and allowed the teams to move much more rapidly.

CAPTURE

We'd almost reached the summit when my point man alerted. He froze in place and stared intently off in the distance directly to our front. I remained motionless for several seconds, then quickly walked up next to him.

There was an enemy soldier about thirty meters ahead of us. He had his AK-47 slung across his back and was squatting on the ground. He was brushing over the dirt and grass with a large, freshly cut tree branch, apparently trying to hide the signs of his group's passing.

Signaling the point man that we were going forward, I quickly raised my weapon and advanced toward the enemy soldier with long, rapid strides. The point man was on my right, matching me stride for stride. The squatting man looked up and realized that he was at an extreme disadvantage; the thought of resistance never entered his mind. Terror filled his eyes, and without hesitating he threw his hands straight up in the air. He was understandably petrified.

We took his weapon, blindfolded him, and began the descent to Kontum. Once we arrived at the compound, the Vietnamese interrogated him and found out where he came from. Using the coordinates provided by our prisoner, the colonel sent two RTs by chopper to our captive's base camp for a little surprise visit.

RIGHT DOWN TO THE T

The enemy's camp was deserted when the teams got there. The most significant and startling find was an accurately detailed mock-up of our compound—laid out on a sand table—which included the ditch they'd used to penetrate our defenses. The model was so detailed that it even had the little piles of garbage and junk that collected around the outside of our hooches. It seemed that they'd been studying us for quite some time before making their move, and we didn't even know it. Not bad.

The sapper unit returned while the teams were searching the camp. A firefight followed, with both sides taking casualties before the enemy broke contact and withdrew. The RTs gave chase but couldn't catch them. Both teams hastily returned to the enemy's base camp, captured everything of value, and destroyed the rest. Finally they torched the camp, moved out smartly to the extraction point, and were brought home.

THE PRESIDENT REQUESTS YOUR PRESENCE

I'd been at Kontum for almost a year since I'd left the hospital when my unit received a message from the president of the United States of America, requesting my presence at a ceremony in Washington, D.C. The reason: I was to receive the Congressional Medal of Honor from President Nixon.

One week prior to my flight I went down to Nha Trang to pick up a new class A uniform. I'd been in 'Nam so long I didn't have any dress greens that fit correctly, and since I had to have my picture taken for the folks back at the Department of the Army, everyone concerned decided it would be best if I started from scratch. So I got the new suit with all the appropriate ribbons and insignia, and did the picture routine.

That took all of one day, so I spent the rest of my time with my girlfriend. We had a pleasant time together, but she was worried that she'd never see me again. I assured her that would not be the case— I'd return as soon as possible.

The day of my departure I linked up with a captain who acted as my escort. We flew first class, and I enjoyed every moment of the flight. All the stewardesses knew why I was there—I mean, not too many people were flying out of Vietnam in the first-class section. They were really super nice. I wasn't used to the comfortable surroundings and all the attention I received from the crew. What impressed me most, however, was a very simple thing. One stewardess asked me what I wanted to eat and I replied, "You probably don't have what I want."

She just smiled and said, "Well, we're pretty squared away here in first class. I'll bet we've got what you're looking for."

I returned her smile and said, "I'd like a hot pastrami sandwich on rye." I wanted one badly, but I was sure I was out of luck.

To my surprise she answered, "You got it." And minutes later, I did. Fantastic!

BACK IN THE WORLD

My mother, stepfather, and brother met me at the airport in Washington, D.C. Aside from my immediate family, I was met by a captain who would be my protocol officer during my stay. With him was a rather large individual with a bent nose who was introduced to me as an assistant who was there for my "protection." I was sure he was CIA or FBI. I don't recall his name, but based on his physical appearance I'd say he could've answered to "Rocko" or "Muggsy" quite easily.

I had the time of my life during my five-day visit to D.C. The captain took me everywhere that was anywhere in the city. Every single minute of my day was programmed to extract the maximum amount of enjoyment. Truthfully, it was exhausting, but I wouldn't have wanted it any other way.

We went to posh restaurants for every meal. A photographer assigned to our little group took my picture at all the famous places, like JFK's grave. Let me tell you—it was fast-paced sight-seeing by day and romping nightclubs after the sun set. When it was time to recharge the ol' batteries for the next day, my chauffeur dropped me off at D.C.'s top-rated hotel. Man! I couldn't have asked for more.

A few days prior to the award ceremony, I received a call at the hotel from Burko. He was out of the Army and living in the Baltimore area. He got word that I was in town and tracked me down to say hi. I was overjoyed at hearing his voice and invited him to join me straightaway.

When he showed up he was driving an emerald-green Harley-Davidson. He had long hair and a big Fu Manchu mustache. He looked totally outrageous, which was in keeping with his personality. We went up to my room, ordered sandwiches and beer from room service, and sat around reliving the glory days. He missed the Army life somewhat, but he was out now and he could never go back. Too many bad memories. All of our close friends were dead. What was left?

He stayed for several hours before leaving. I was a bit sad to see him go, but he promised to keep in touch.

I never saw him again.

Six fellow soldiers also received the Congressional Medal of Honor on that warm, clear day in June, 1971. However, only one man stood beside me. Tragically, the other five were awarded posthumously. Such sorrow reflects the magnitude of the actions of those individuals who are considered for the CMH. A female lieutenant colonel once asked me if I knew why they gave me the medal. She asked the question in such a way that I took it as meaning *she* knew the reason—did I? Her question pissed me off. I thought, What the hell do you know? How could you, who have never seen combat, possibly know? I replied very sarcastically, "No. Suppose you tell me." I was preparing to give it to her with both barrels at the conclusion of her comment.

However, she said something profound that hit the nail right square on the head. She said, "They gave you the medal because they realize that something has happened to you that they can't understand."

You were absolutely right, ma'am. My apologies.

When President Nixon put the medal around my neck I felt an incredible rush of joy and sorrow intermixed. As President Nixon shook my hand, he said, "I've given a few of these out, but I'll tell you what—there's just something about the medal and the people who receive it that touches me every time. There's something different about you."

After the formal ceremony, I was talking with the president when he asked me, "Well, Staff Sergeant Miller, what would you like to do?"

I didn't have to give it much thought. I knew that I could write my own ticket anywhere, but I only had one place in mind. I looked him right in the eyes and stated, "I'd like to go back to my unit in Vietnam."

He looked over at General Westmoreland with a make-it-happen look. General Westmoreland asked me if that was what I really wanted, and I replied affirmative. He said, "No problem."

So be it.

METAMORPHOSIS

Something happened to me while I was in Washington, D.C.—something that I was not aware of. I was no longer the same person who had breezed into the nation's capital in June of 1971; I'd suddenly changed—changed in the eyes of everyone around me.

The funny part about the whole situation was that I had nothing to do with the "new" me. Physically and mentally I was no different. I didn't develop a new personality or alter the one I'd nurtured in 'Nam. I didn't strut, talk shit, or act like I was master of the universe. At no point in time did I try to use the medal's influence to set myself apart from my peers. I never considered myself better than anyone else just because my superiors saw fit to present me with the military's highest decoration. I saw myself as someone who was fortunate enough to live through a harrowing moment in his life—a guy who wanted nothing more than to continue living the life he'd grown accustomed to.

But it was not to be.

The moment President Nixon clasped the medal around my neck, I became much more than a decorated soldier; I became an object of admiration, envy, and jealousy. I was now a shining symbol of all that was right with the military, a person to be emulated. Along with the medal came the awesome responsibility of living up to everyone's expectations. It was like being a superstar college basketball player who became the number one pick in the NBA draft. I'd now live my life in a glass house, my every move scrutinized and compared to the lofty standards set by the medal.

But what most people don't realize is that CMH recipients are also human beings, with all the failings of mortal men. I was certainly not a model soldier before receiving the CMH, nor did I become one afterward. They gave me the CMH based solely on a single action, not on my personality or on the combination of prior actions. Even though CMH recipients do share a common bond of tremendous courage and genuine concern for their men, their personalities and the ways they live their lives vary, just like any other group of people on earth. And believe me, none of us are perfect.

THE TIMES THEY ARE A-CHANGIN'

When I got back to Kontum from D.C., I continued to run missions, only now I was being called on less and less to do the job. At first I couldn't understand why. It was generally conceded that I was their best man, so why didn't they want me to head up as many missions as possible? I always enjoyed the challenge of each trip into the woods, and I began to get a little annoyed at my inactivity.

After I had spent several months basically sitting around and not doing much of anything, my superiors suggested to me that I should consider working on the staff in the headquarters. I was stunned and genuinely confused. Something was wrong. What was going on? Why wasn't I out in the woods where I belonged, where I was at my best?

I learned much later that there was an unwritten rule governing CMH recipients—they will not be killed on active duty and especially not in the same area where they earned the award. That would be very embarrassing for the Army. Medal winners were few and far between, and those who survived their ordeals were to be protected and displayed. I'm sure that my commander sweated bullets the few times I went out after my return to 'Nam. If I were killed, he'd swing— it was that simple. In light of that fact, I'm surprised he let me go out at all.

They pressured me enough that I accepted a staff assignment in the S-2 intelligence section. That lasted all of two months. I couldn't handle it. I craved action and excitement, and I sure wasn't getting either behind a desk. I made my demand—play me or trade me. The colonel saw that I was determined and wasn't about to be put off, so in a compromise move he sent me to a place where I could train local inhabitants and run the woods without much risk of enemy contact. I would be surrounded by friendlies and thus protected.

THE FINAL ACT

Early in 1972 I started to see the handwriting on the wall, and I began to get scared. Really scared. The war was winding down, and I could see my way of life coming to an end.

I didn't want it to end. Ever.

You must understand that my formative years were spent in Vietnam. I'd barely turned twenty when I planted my feet on Vietnamese soil. Six years later I'd been assimilated into the culture of Southeast Asia. I'd lived, worked, and played with the people of the land, and I'd learned to love their honest and simple way of life. My first real experiences with women—both frivolous and meaningful—occurred there. I'd felt more alive than ever before. I did more living in one year in Vietnam than in all my previous years in the U.S.A. combined.

My world was coming to an end, and I was frightened at the prospect of life after the war. Before you get the wrong idea, let me make my position clear: I was and still am extremely proud to be an American, for I feel America is the greatest nation on earth, and I really mean that. I never at any point questioned the war or my government. I simply did what they wanted me to do, and I did it to the best of my abilities.

In addition to my leaving Vietnam, I had one other major concern about our pulling out of the conflict. Not only would I have to leave the land I'd grown to love, but I'd return to a peacetime Army. I would go from a staff sergeant who could, at any time, call for and get—without question or hesitation—an airstrike or artillery barrage, to . . . a staff sergeant. I'd go from someone who wielded great power to just another G.I. Joe.

In 'Nam I was somebody who commanded great respect because of my unique abilities. Back in the World, my unique abilities weren't needed, and I'd be just another face in the crowd. No missions to run, no challenges to conquer. When you've basked in power and excitement at the levels I have, it's devastating to imagine life without either.

Apparently my inner feelings were clearly visible to those around me. When I reflect on that time, it's easy to understand why everyone knew my intentions. First of all, I was always very vocal about not wanting the war to end. When I finally accepted the reality of our impending withdrawal, I began quietly making plans to get out of the

Army and stay in-country. Had I been just Joe Blow, nobody would have thought twice about such a decision.

But, you see, I was That Guy. The CMH recipient. Can't very well have one of America's heroes appearing to forsake his country, now, can we? Besides, how can we get any mileage out of an American hero who's not living in America? We need to keep him in uniform somehow for display purposes, right?

I can, to some degree, understand the Army's motivation. Since the war was not very popular with most folks back home, the Army needed to present as positive an image as possible to combat all the negative press. What better way to do that than to have guys around who'd received symbols of gallantry in an "ugly" war? But since it didn't appear that I was going to go home willingly, the Army had to figure out a way to send me back with a minimum of ruckus or hassle. They finally determined that they'd have to sneak up on me and catch me off guard. I'm sure they felt what they were about to do was in the best interests of the U.S. Army and the United States of America.

They were right. Pulling off something underhanded was the only way they'd get me out. If I had thought for one moment that they were attempting to move me out of country, I'd have talked to anybody and pulled every trick in the book to stay. That's why to this day I'm only slightly bitter about what happened next.

LAST GASP

One day late in November 1972 my boss came up to me and said that he wanted me to report to the aid station for a physical exam. I didn't think anything about it because it had been well over a year since I'd been released from the hospital at Camp Zama. As a matter of fact, it seemed like a very normal and logical request. So I did as I was told.

The physician poked, prodded, and twisted my body for about an hour. At the conclusion of his exam he stated, "Listen, I can't complete your examination because we don't have the necessary EKG machines here. I'm going to send you to a hospital where you'll have the necessary readings performed." I still wasn't suspicious that anything was up. So far everything seemed in order.

When I arrived at the hospital, I checked in with the front desk, and they summoned someone to escort me to the proper clinic. A very large individual dressed in white greeted me with the words, "Right this way, please."

The next thing I knew I was in the psychiatric ward.

Immediately my antenna went up and I got really bad vibes. I started getting pissed off and then I got a little paranoid. I asked in a very surly tone, "What the hell is going on—why the fuck am I on the nut ward?"

The very large individual assured me that nothing was wrong, that I'd have to wait until tomorrow for my EKG, and the psychiatric ward had the only available bunks for the night. I told him thanks, but I was leaving and would be back in the morning.

He told me I wasn't going anywhere.

I stayed the night.

The next morning a doctor came in and informed me that the Special Forces people up at the camp had made a statement that I was going around saluting telephone poles. The doctor was there to determine if I was mentally stable or not.

He presented me a battery of situations and asked questions that didn't appear to have any relevance to determining whether or not I was crazy. The only discussion I clearly remember went something like this:

Doctor: You're walking down the street and you discover a letter-sized envelope lying on the ground. There appears to be a letter inside. The envelope is addressed and has a stamp on it. What do you do with it?

Me: I'd probably put it in a mailbox.

Doctor: Wouldn't you be curious as to what the letter said?

Me: Sure, but I'd still probably just put it in the mailbox.

Doctor: If nobody saw you pick it up, would you open it?

Me: No, probably not. I'd mail it.

After that exchange the doctor scribbled something in a book and gave me another situation. Now you tell me how that question was going to provide him any insight into my mental stability, regardless of how I answered it.

The doctor wouldn't let me leave the hospital that evening, saying that he had a final battery of questions he would ask me the following morning. I'd have to stay one more night. I was unbelievably furious at this point, but the very large individual dressed in white was there to ensure the situation didn't get out of hand.

I don't know what happened after I went to sleep that night. The only explanation I can come up with is that they drugged me at some point, for when I came to the following morning I found myself—still in pajamas—strapped to a stretcher and being shuttled to a waiting aircraft.

What the fuck?!

Unbelievable! I was back in the States.

Just like that.

To say I was in a hostile mood while I was on the plane would be a severe understatement. I saw red. I was boiling mad. I couldn't believe that I was being railroaded. I was released from the stretcher once we were in the air. There was nothing I could do at that point except sit and fume.

We landed at Fort Bragg about four o'clock in the afternoon. I was taken off the plane and escorted into Womack Army Hospital where they admitted me to the psychiatric ward. The long flight had blunted my rage to a large degree, so I went along quietly, waiting for the opportunity to heat up my anger once again. A nurse informed me that my doctor would see me in the morning.

Bright and early the next day I was joined by a colonel who turned out to be the head shrink of the hospital. When he'd heard I was coming he decided he'd personally handle my case, which I didn't find unusual. Hey, man, I had the Medal of Honor; it was only natural that he'd want to be my doctor.

We talked for about two hours. Our conversation was vastly different from the inane banter I'd engaged in with the other shrink. This colonel asked me what I considered to be intelligent and meaningful questions.

"Why'd you stay in Vietnam so long?" he asked.

I replied, "I was getting job satisfaction. I got a sense of importance from what I was doing. I had worth there; I was valuable. I loved the culture, the atmosphere."

"How do you feel about killing?"

"Sometimes it's necessary. Primarily, though, I'd do it to make sure nobody did it to me. I don't go out of my way to kill people. In fact, I'd avoid a fight if I thought I could get away with doing so."

So it went. Afterward he said to me, "I can't find anything wrong with you. But I'll tell you one thing. I've seen this happen before. It's a common trick used in special operations to get people out of an area."

We talked a little while longer. He concluded with, "I'm sorry this happened, but rest assured there's nothing wrong with you. Good luck in your pursuits."

They released me that day.

AFTERLIFE

I was assigned to a Special Forces unit there at Fort Bragg following my discharge. But I'll be candid—I was worthless to the Army for the first couple of years after that. My prevailing thoughts were, "You sorry motherfuckers. After all I've done."

It seemed like the entire world knew I'd come out of Womack's Nut Ward, and as a result I was accused of everything from shoplifting to armed robbery to murder. Nobody took my word for anything. Any derogatory stories that could be told about me were given maximum dissemination. When you have the Medal of Honor, all actions—good, bad, true, or false—are magnified, and an undue amount of significance is attached to each. My every move—real or imagined—became front-page news. Maybe I'm exaggerating, but not much.

I would have made a quick and spiteful departure from the Army right away, but the last time I reenlisted while I was in 'Nam I took the full hitch—six years. I still had five to go. Even though I was feeling much ill will toward the Army, I wasn't prepared to do anything rash that would get me kicked out. I didn't want derogatory information on my permanent record.

As time passed, the anger subsided and I slowly, painfully tried to get back in step with the Army. But a major obstacle to my being assimilated into a normal peacetime routine was the fact that all my unique abilities were no longer required. Compounding the problem was the fact that the Army, as well as the majority of the American public, was very much down on 'Nam vets. If the truth be known, the Army went out of its way to find guys like me—ass-kicking 'Nam vets who ran the woods and lived on the edge—and systematically weeded them out of the service.

Why?

Because we were misfits.

We didn't fit the mold. We just didn't fit in. We were renegades used to operating independently, with few people pulling our strings. We disregarded the established rules and created our own. I take that back—there were no rules for us. We did whatever the situation demanded, developed our own courses of action, never questioning the morality of what we did to survive and complete the mission. Maybe that's why we were successful out there in the deep bush. But that attitude surely was out of place in a peacetime environment, and the thought of keeping guys around who were disdainful of authority and might not toe the line was a little too much for the Army to deal with. So the hard-core guys were sent packing. Fortunately for me I had the medal, which gave me too much visibility to be fucked with completely, so I was spared the ax, though not the hassles.

A noncombat lifestyle was everything I'd feared. It was very boring. It was unbelievably slow-paced. And worst of all, my free-wheeling, do-as-I-damn-well-please lifestyle had come to an end.

It took a long time for me to throttle back from the 'Nam years. In 'Nam, I didn't have to wait for anything—I got everything instantaneously. Order an airstrike and *wham*! Fast movers appeared immediately. Crank up the radio and ask for artillery and *bam*! On its way. I operated in a high-speed environment that was stripped of normal rules, bureaucratic red tape, indecision, and bullshit. Those conditions simply didn't exist, couldn't exist, in that realm. A sense of urgency was attached to all actions—and with good reason.

But now I was faced with a world of forms in triplicate, senseless decisions, procrastination, delays, five levels of approval, and rules out the ass.

Frustration reigned supreme.

I felt like I'd been put on a leash. The Army had taken a high-performance engine and drastically untuned it. Not only had my activities been severely curtailed, but the special status that I once enjoyed quickly evaporated. I was no longer that unique individual who did the dangerous job most others were reluctant to do. Since cunning, sharpshooting, and bravery were not required in my new environment, I had nothing to set me apart from the crowd. I quickly found that the Medal of Honor was more a novelty than anything else to most noncombat soldiers, and really had no place in a peacetime Army. My extensive combat skills and ass-kicking abilities were no longer needed, appreciated, or even wanted. I ceased being unique. I became just a face in a sea of green, separated from the spotlight. That was perhaps the hardest adjustment I had to make—adapting to the role of Mr. Average Guy.

It was a maddening nightmare for me.

So, why did I stay? Why didn't I just say "Fuck the Army" after I'd finished the five years remaining on my reenlistment?

What kept me going?

Soldiers.

After a couple of years I began to realize that I was in a position to strongly influence the young soldiers coming up through Special Forces. After my return to the States I eventually hooked up with another reconnaissance unit at Fort Bragg. It was strictly a training operation, and I assumed the responsibility of teaching our future ass-kickers the basics of running the woods.

At first I was just going through the motions. I couldn't put my heart and soul into mere training, even though I knew I was doing something important, something worthwhile. But playing the training game was just that, a game to me. I'd been deeply involved in the real thing, so to me training soldiers was akin to practicing for a sports team. If all a sports team ever did was practice—with no chance of ever playing a game against an opponent to test themselves—it would be really hard to stay motivated. There would be nothing to strive for, no goals to attain. There would be nothing at stake, so where would the excitement come from?

That's how I felt initially. I'd walk through the woods with my students, explaining surveillance techniques, how to move about properly, how to set an ambush. For the most part the young soldiers were eager to learn, but I was reluctant to open up and give them all the knowledge I'd garnered through years of trial by fire. It was my way of getting back at the Army. Why give them what I knew after the way I'd been treated?

But ever so slowly my tremendous reserve of self-pity dried up, and it suddenly dawned on me that it wasn't really my superiors I was shortchanging; it was the young troops who looked to me for the knowledge that would make them successful or that just might save their lives someday. I thought about how I'd feel if I withheld critical information that resulted in someone's death because he didn't know what to do.

It left a sour taste in my mouth.

As I saw it, my choices were two: get out of the Army as I'd planned, thus turning my back on my responsibility to prepare young men for survival in future wars; or stay in and give it my damnedest.

I really wanted to leave, but I told myself that I had the best qualifications, the best credentials for the job of developing the next generation of warriors.

All of a sudden, I felt obligated.

Almost overnight I decided to apply myself to the task at hand. Although I still harbored a great deal of animosity toward the system, I would no longer let that interfere with how I conducted myself around my students. They weren't responsible for the shabby treatment I'd received. I would not direct my hostility at them.

I launched into the training full tilt. I would tell each new group of students, "Look, I don't know exactly what it is I have that allowed me to do the things I did and survive. But whatever it is, hopefully some of it will rub off as we walk around the woods."

Once, a student asked me what the secret was to being a good combat leader, a man who commands the loyalty and respect of his subordinates. That was a question I'd been formulating the answer to for many years, almost from Day One when I set foot on Vietnamese soil. My answer to him and the class was a simple one which I would repeat many times throughout the years.

"If you want a soldier's respect and loyalty, especially in a combat environment, you must demonstrate two things. First, you must show that you know more than the soldier you are leading. Your subordinate must be aware that you have knowledge he does not possess, and that you are trying to teach him.

"The second thing you must demonstrate is a genuine concern for his safety and well-being. The concern must be real, because a young soldier can spot a faker a mile away. If your concern for him is genuine—and he knows it—then you can rest assured that he will follow you into the jaws of death."

And so I began in earnest my awkward assimilation into the training environment and the peacetime Army. And after all the trials and tribulations, the blood, sweat, and tears, I'm still in the Army today, twenty-five years and untold heartaches later.

Maybe I'll make it a career.

GLOSSARY

AK-47: A selective fire, Russian-designed and -manufactured assault rifle used by the North Vietnamese. Fires a 7.62mm round at a muzzle velocity of 2,330 feet per second. Noted for its simple and rugged construction, it is much heavier than an M-16 (11.3 lbs. vs. 8.42 lbs.) and harder to control (harder kick because of the heavier round) when firing on full automatic. A somewhat crude but effective weapon.

B-40: Forerunner of the RPG-7.

CEOI: Communications and Electronics Operating Instructions. This was a document (booklet) we used to authenticate radio transmissions. It contained transmission codes and procedures necessary for ensuring that communications were being transmitted and received by authorized personnel.

CIA: Central Intelligence Agency.

Claymore mine: An unbelievably devastating antipersonnel weapon. Seven hundred steel balls (almost twice the size of BBs) are sandwiched between layers of a plastic explosive in a slightly U-shaped flat mine. The mine is placed on the ground, anchored by two sets of V-shaped legs that are jammed into the earth. The convex side faces the enemy. The mine can be detonated by rigging a trip wire or using a hand-held "clacker" that sends an electrical charge through a wire connected to a small blasting cap inserted into the mine. When it explodes, the steel balls are thrown out at high velocity in a fan-shaped pattern. I guarantee it will decimate any human being within its range. It is a highly regarded and effective weapon that we carried everywhere.

Cobra: Commonly referred to as a gunship. It was the U.S. Army's primary attack helicopter (AH). The AH-1G Cobra was equipped with a variety of formidable armaments, including rockets, 40mm grenades, and 7.62mm miniguns (Gatling-style machine guns). Cobras were very effective against ground troops, and more than once came to the aid of U.S. soldiers in tight spots. Their presence was greatly appreciated by us and especially devastating to the morale of enemy troops.

Conex: A large metal container used for storing supplies. A conex is big enough to walk into (stooped over) and usually has two lockable doors.

CS: Nonlethal tear gas.

C rations: Combat field meals packed in metal cans.

C-4: A plastic explosive (which is also called plastique). You could light the plastique and it would burn like Sterno. We occasionally used it to heat water or C rations. Required a blasting cap to detonate it.

DLOG: Directorate of Logistics.

Frag: Short for fragmentation grenade. Can also mean shell fragments (shrapnel) from a high-explosive shell.

Gunship: See Cobra.

Hooch: A slang term for a small dwelling, especially a thatched hut. We used "hooch" to describe just about anything we used as living quarters, from the poncho tents we constructed out in the bush to the canvas-and-wood sandbagged structures in base camp.

Indian country: Slang term for enemy territory.

LZ: Landing zone. Basically, any area that a chopper uses to insert or extract troops, supplies, casualties, etc.

Mission support site: Usually a small, permanent base camp in a remote or classified area, used for surveillance or as a support base for missions into a particular area.

M-16: The standard personal firearm (rifle) of American troops. In my opinion, the M-16 is superior to the AK-47 as a killing instrument. Although the M-16 fires a smaller caliber round than the AK-47 (5.56mm vs. 7.62mm), its muzzle velocity is far greater (3,280 feet per second vs. 2,330 feet per second). The increased muzzle velocity creates a tumbling effect on the smaller round; the round will tumble and ricochet off bone once it penetrates flesh, causing enormous damage as it rips crazily through the body. I've seen an M-16 round create an entrance hole no bigger than a dime, yet leave a hole the size of a softball upon exit. I've seen it blow off limbs at the joints. I've used both the AK-47 and the M-16, and I far prefer the latter. On the Medal of Honor day, I was shot through the chest with an AK-47 round. Had it been an the M-16 round, I can almost guarantee you that I'd have been killed instantly.

M-60: A general-purpose machine gun used by American and Vietnamese troops. Fires a 7.62mm round with a muzzle velocity of 2,820 feet per second. The M-60 was usually the "heavy" (largest caliber and most ass-kicking) weapon in a platoon. Its importance in a firefight can't be overstated because of its large-caliber round and high rate of fire (two hundred rounds per minute vs. one hundred rounds per minute for the AK-47, which fires the same caliber [though a less powerful] round). In fact, it was generally the first weapon that either side would try to neutralize in an engagement. It was used everywhere, being carried by foot soldiers, placed in defensive bunkers, and mounted on helicopters and armored personnel carriers.

NVA: North Vietnamese Army. NVA was used by Americans to refer to a North Vietnamese soldier or soldiers, as in "He was NVA" or "They were NVA."

RPG-7: A shoulder-fired, Communist antitank rocket launcher that fires an 85mm rocket-propelled grenade (HEAT—high explosive antitank—warhead). Although the weapon was designed for use against armored vehicles, it was often used against human targets.

RTO: Radio-Telephone Operator.

Slick: A utility/troop-carrying helicopter without armament. Technically, a UH-1D Huey with an M-60 mounted in the door opening couldn't be called a slick. However, to Special Forces soldiers, anything with less armament than a Cobra was usually called a slick.

SOP: Standard operating procedure. Means performing or reacting according to established rules. To follow an existing manner of doing business.

Tet: The lunar New Year as celebrated in Vietnam. As referred to here, it means the huge offensive mounted by the Communists during the 1968 Tet celebrations.

Tracer: A bullet that leaves a smoky or luminous trail. The bullet is constructed with a chemical substance (normally phosphorus) attached to its base, which burns when the bullet is expelled from its casing. The burning phosphorus traces the bullet's path through the air, allowing the shooter to see where the bullet is impacting. Usually, during combat, every fifth round in a magazine is a tracer round.

VC: Vietcong; a South Vietnamese guerilla. Vietcong is a contraction of *Việt Nam công-sam*, or Vietnam Communists. The VC belonged to or supported the National Liberation Front of the former nation of South Vietnam. Also referred to by Americans as "Victor Charlie" (phonetic alphabet) or just "Charlie." VC were almost impossible to tell apart from the local population—such is the nature of guerilla operations—which made for many difficult situations. VC were usually not as well equipped as NVA.